WHERE THE SPIRIT LEADS:
American Denominations Today

Introduction and Afterword by
Martin E. Marty, Editor

John Knox Press
ATLANTA

The essays in this book appeared originally in the *Christian Century* series
"The Churches: Where from Here?"

Library of Congress Cataloging in Publication Data

Main entry under title:

Where the spirit leads.

1. Christian sects—United States. 2. Judaism
—United States. 3. Christianity—Canada.
I. Marty, Martin E., 1928-
BR516.5.W45   280´.0973   80-82197
ISBN 0-8042-0868-9

Published by John Knox Press
Atlanta, Georgia
Printed in the United States of America

ACKNOWLEDGMENTS

The persons who contributed to the making of this book are many. We owe a special debt of gratitude to the seventeen authors who so graciously gave of their time and energy in setting down their assessments of the various denominations for these chapters, which originally appeared as articles in a series titled "The Churches: Where from Here?" in The Christian Century. Many of the authors subsequently gave additional effort to the task of revising and updating their essays.

Thanks are also due to members of the staff of The Christian Century. Editor James M. Wall had major responsibility for the selection of authors. Managing editor Dean Peerman supervised the production, from start to finish, with his usual attention to accuracy and precision. Associate editor Jean Caffey Lyles had primary responsibility for manuscript editing and revision. Associate editor Linda Marie Delloff served as liaison, initiating and coordinating arrangements between the Century offices and John Knox Press. Associate editor Jill Drum Floerke read all the manuscripts and made many helpful comments, suggestions and corrections. Editors Peerman, Lyles and Delloff proofread the final galleys. The task of manuscript typing was competently and patiently accomplished by Elaine Kreis, Sydell Reeves and Kathleen Wind.

Martin E. Marty.

CONTENTS

INTRODUCTION

Denominations:
Surviving the '70s

America has been undergoing some sort of
religious revival, but one that has not led to
prosperity for most of the denominations.

MARTIN E. MARTY

In 1944 the then "undenominational" Christian Century published several articles under the heading "What's Disturbing the Churches?" Nineteen years later, in 1963, the now "ecumenical" weekly took another turn and had numerous writers ask, "What's Ahead for the Churches?" By that time, according to Editor Kyle Haselden, the earlier question was no longer apropos. The editors of 17 years ago were bothered that little if anything seemed to be disturbing the churches, which were still riding relatively high after their boom in the 1950s. The question was, how would churches face the idealistic challenges of the era of President John F. Kennedy, Pope John XXIII and Martin Luther King, Jr.? Most authors in the series asked whether the churches would risk many of their resources to deal with political, ecumenical and social issues.

Those who enjoy the cycles or pendular swings in history may be charmed to note that in 1980 the churches are bothered again. Some of them did use resources for the struggles of the 1960s, but they were also weakened by those struggles; many were bewildered by both spiritual and secular changes in that decade. As we reread the essays of the last series, it impresses us to note how low the institutional expecta-

---

Dr. Marty is an associate editor of The Christian Century and Fairfax M. Cone distinguished service professor at the University of Chicago divinity school. His most recent major book is A Nation of Behavers.

tions of most mainline church writers were. But at that time they were less preoccupied than people now seem to have to be with institutional survival as such.

Many American denominations have lived during the past ten years somewhere between Rainer Maria Rilke's "To Survive Is All" and the graffito "If we don't survive, we also won't do anything else." Not that any of the medium-sized church bodies in America is at the point of near-extinction; yet statistically only the Southern Baptist Convention and the Church of Jesus Christ of Latter-day Saints have much to brag about among the larger groups. Catholicism holds its own so far as membership ticker tapes are concerned, but no one doubts the extent of the crisis reflected in disastrously declining mass attendance and vocations to priesthood and religious orders, to say nothing of the crises of faith and meaning that go with these other declines.

All the churches have survived, and most of them will continue to do so, languishing somewhere between 1 and 3 million. They have little prospect of seeing their graph lines go up radically in a time of decline in the rate of population growth and in the face of numbers of other contrary societal forces. The more conservative churches are still growing, riding the boom in both authoritarian and experiential religion that the mainliners have not quite known how to exploit. The evangelical-fundamentalist-Pentecostal subcultures have expanded significantly since 1962, and their meaning-systems have been drastically transformed while these churches embrace the world of advertising and celebrities, sex manuals and affluence, theological adjustment and new styles of witness. But there is something of a revolving-door character to their parade of accessions, as people convert from group to group. The market potential for conservative religion, larger than anyone predicted, is finite and quite possibly on the verge of being reached. In any case, thoughtful people in these churches where the language of survival has been less urgent—and such thoughtful people are legion—are asking questions of meaning which show that they too are "bothered" and have to look at "what's ahead."

Modern Inventions

Obscured behind these queries about the relative prospects of various religious factions and styles in America is the tantalizing one: Why bother with denominations at all, as late in Christian and American history as 1980? The denomination seems to be a very curious agency, one that hardly merits much attention and concern. Nowhere in the Bible will you find a trace of anyone's anticipation of this form—unless negatively in Paul's questions about Christ being divided, with some followers belonging to Cephas and some to Apollos and some to Paul. Nowhere in 15 or 18 centuries of Christian history will you find serious theological proposals for defense of such forms. They are modern inventions, usually justified on political, economic (laissez-faire, free-enterprise competition) or, among the most conservative, Darwinian evolutionary ("survival of the fittest") grounds.

Though the word "denomination" began to appear in England before the American experience came to full term, it was the separation of church and state, the disestablishment of the churches, and the voluntary principle in church life which created the void on the spiritual landscape that denominations were invented to fill. No great theological genius devised the form; perhaps Thomas Jefferson did more than anyone else to necessitate it, as he sketched out the grounds for the American Revolution. The itinerant revivalists of the First and Second Great Awakenings in America played their part as they called into question the churches of the established order and asked each citizen to decide for himself or herself to "get religion" and what form to get.

The denomination has served America well. It drained conflict into harmless channels. Replacing the holy wars of the Old World have been religious patterns that left few dead bodies, though competitive denominational missionaries in many a new suburb have come down with ulcers, heart disease, endocrine disturbances, alcoholism and, as they say, "other specifically Christian diseases" in their scrambles. Without question, the competitive business model, whether or not it has been religiously justifiable, has worked.

Denominationalists added greatly to the vitality of U.S. and Canadian religion, for they helped minimize the anticlericalism that goes with establishment, permitted few believers to relax, and were able to offer something for everyone. Indeed, they still do. There are few ecological niches and crannies in the environment that some new denomination cannot be designed to fill. No space exists between denominations in our sociological forms. Start a movement, be anti-institutional, work for "emerging viable structures of ministry," try to unite all the churches, and you soon find yourself designated a denomination in the *Yearbook of American and Canadian Churches*. That process gives no sign of diminishing or being ended in the immediate future.

Identity and Issues

Denominational life is rich in paradoxes and contradictions. Denominations were formed to help assure the integrity of each group's creed and way of life, yet on most vital issues one learns little about what people believe and how they act by learning to which church they belong. This has long been true of the creedally vague mainline denominations, but it is surprisingly noticeable among the professedly more defined conservative ones. Who knows to which denomination Dwight Moody, Billy Sunday and other evangelists belonged?

Attend a National Association of Evangelicals convention and watch the delegates talk about what concerns them most. Almost never do they concentrate on the sacramental issues that help constitute them as Baptist or non-Baptist, or on historic Calvinist-Arminian lines that once separated them. Attend a lay gathering of conservatives and you will walk away thinking that their denominations are named the Followers of Corrie Ten Boom, Pat Boone, Francis Schaeffer, Marabel Morgan, Anita Bryant, Robert Schuller or Ralph Martin.

Denominations were supposed to provide the battlelines between Christian groups. But today it is seldom that one denomination pitches battle against another. All the real spiritual bloodshed occurs *within* the communions, as Catholics, Southern Presbyterians, Missouri Lutherans, even Southern Baptists and most certainly Episcopalians have demonstrated in recent years. You cannot tell the players without their programs and can almost never tell them by their denominational names when scraps over Pentecostalism, scriptural interpretation or even church order surface and engross people.

Local Expressions of Faith

A third paradox: denominations themselves generated much of the ecumenical ethos that led many to predict that the denominational form would wither as the ecumenical spirit prospered. Yet while the ecumenical movement is in trouble, the ecumenical spirit never had it so good—Christians in general are quite at ease with each other on many levels. Nonetheless, denominationalism outlasts all the theologies designed to replace it. The relative declines in status and power of world, national, regional, state and local councils of churches occurred for many reasons, not the least of them being a "new denominationalism" that found people scurrying back to and huddling in their denominational homes in a time when senses of identity were hard to come by.

The nonblack world was told that there was supposed to be something called "black religion," but to the knowing analyst of the black churches it was dangerous to confuse AME, AMEZ, and CME brands of black Methodism, to say nothing of the competitive styles of black Baptist groups.

A fourth paradox: while the denominations survive as some means or other of helping people link up with traditions and find spiritual families, they are grossly undersupported. While per-capita giving increases in most churches each year, the gains do not keep up with horrendous inflation. This factor leads hard-pressed congregations to keep funds close to home, and the bureaucratized church bodies have had to cut staff and programs as a consequence. At the same time, people have chosen to favor regional and even more local expressions of faith. This choice has inspired them either casually to drag their feet or willfully to withstand some of the appeals from "headquarters." So denominations are curiously caught between the ideology and spirit of ecumenism and the practice and spirit of localism.

Beyond the Language of Survival

To list all the besetting circumstances around the denominations is to describe institutions that seem to have little future. Few denominational leaders are either celebrities' or well-known spiritual guides in their own church bodies; the media have created spokespersons entirely outside the line of appointed and elected officialdom who tend to speak for the churches. People from one denomination do not care much about what goes on in another, and as a result, news of church bodies rarely receives coverage. Paradenominational agencies keep springing up to distract people from the church bodies. "Invisible religion," the do-it-yourself, customer-oriented personal faith that spreads so rapidly today, leads people to ignore the denominations even when they no longer protest against structures.

Alternative kinds of pension plans and health-care programs liberate many professionals from their mystical reliance on their own denominations.

In short, we have seen one final paradox: that America has been undergoing some sort of religious revival—let's leave it at "some sort" today, shall we?—but one that has not led to prosperity for most of the denominations, even though they are the most entrenched means of organizing religious response beyond the local zone. Seventeen years ago almost all the series authors expressed at least halfhearted confidence that each denomination would survive. Then each could move to ask questions about relations between them and, even more, how they would use their resources to face theological and ethical issues.

By now, churches have all heard the message that they will prosper to the degree that they choose to distance themselves from others, arrogate truth claims to themselves, and become aggressive and competitive and triumphalist. Conversely, they are told that they will suffer if they wish to make an ethical impact on the larger society, be friendly to one another, be open-minded and open-ended. Now it may be that the climate will soon change and that just as the latecomers would tool up for the inverted style, people will begin to look for something different. Dean Kelley properly pointed out early in the 1970s that conservative churches are growing—but not all of them grow, nor do those that grow all do so for the same reasons and at the same pace. Meanwhile, mainline churches struggle to hold their own and often suffer loss, but not all congregations within these bodies experience such loss, and from their experience some of the denominations might take clues for their own future course. Finding the balance between institutional self-preservation or self-assertiveness on one hand and the act of living with open hands and hearts in service of others or to interpret a surrounding world: this seems to be a challenge that will continue to face churches both left and right in the years ahead.

'Tribal' Life: What's Ahead

We who edit The Christian Century are committed to both ecumenical and local ventures, but we also confess to being "institutional church freaks," observers of and participants in denominational life. As such, we hope that those who do use their treasures and traditions for the sake of others will prosper in new if chastened ways. We will remain friendly critics, puzzled at their survival capacities and hopeful about their intentions. Somehow they tend to serve as "tribes," forms of more-than-familial life that keep people from being overwhelmed by the blur of generalized religion yet challenge them to look at more than their own backyards and neighborhoods.

Now it is time for us to join readers in listening to people who can give close-up views of the churches' life and prospects today, to ask both "What's disturbing them?" and "What's ahead?"

1

The Episcopal Church: Conflict and Cohesion

The issue is whether Catholic, evangelical and liberal elements in the Episcopal Church can each stand for their own convictions while affirming the legitimacy of the convictions of the others.

EARL H. BRILL

The Episcopal Church has come through some rather turbulent times in recent years. It has experienced angry debates over national church policies, vigorous dissent from decisions of the General Convention and, finally, outright schism resulting from the conviction of some church members that the Episcopal Church has strayed from the apostolic faith.

One major cause of that turmoil was, of course, the decision of the 1976 General Convention to permit the ordination of women to the priesthood. For Anglo-Catholic traditionalists, that action was not only wrong; it was impossible, making the official Episcopal Church apostate from Catholic faith and practice. The most militant of these traditionalists have broken with the Episcopal Church and have gone on to form a new denomination, the Anglican Catholic Church.

Most dissenters, however, have remained loyal, though feeling various degrees of malaise, ranging from "I don't much like it, but I'll go along" to "I can't recognize the validity of women priests." Though this latter position seems to be held by only a small minority of Episcopal loyalists, Presiding Bishop John M. Allin has made that view his

Dr. Brill is director of studies at the College of Preachers, Washington, D.C.

own, with the result that his relationship to the women priests is precarious at best.

The ordination of women is not the only issue that separates dissident traditionalists from the mainstream of church life. For the past several years the Episcopal Church has been moving away from many inherited positions on questions of moral theology. The 1973 General Convention made a major revision of the rules regarding the remarriage of divorced persons and, in the process, explicitly repudiated the medieval doctrine of the indissolubility of marriage on which the previous rules had been based. The 1976 General Convention adopted a moderate, balanced position on abortion, which offended a militant contingent of traditionalists who wanted the church to declare that abortion is murder. Questions of sexual morality and homosexuality have generated suspicion and hostility among those who see the church departing from traditional moral teachings. These concerns are not confined to the Anglo-Catholic wing of the church. Indeed, each issue seems to produce its own constituency, making it difficult to generalize about "liberals" or "conservatives."

The deeper issue underlying all of these controversies is whether the dissonant—and sometimes discordant—elements in the Episcopal Church can stay together by standing for their own convictions while at the same time affirming the legitimacy of the convictions of the other groups. Though something of an oversimplification, the description of the Episcopal Church as Catholic, evangelical and liberal helps to sort out these diverse tendencies. The Catholic movement has tried to uphold continuity with the pre-Reformation church by emphasizing liturgy, sacraments, orthodoxy in doctrine and a Catholic understanding of priesthood and episcopacy. Evangelicals focus on the gospel as the center of Christian loyalty and the Bible as the locus of authority. They affirm the legacy of the Reformation and concern themselves with conversion, personal salvation and evangelism. Liberals foster a respect for intellect and a commitment to follow the leading of free reason. They support high standards in education and are sympathetic to modern biblical criticism, scientific thought and theological innovation.

Today these movements seem to be subject to two opposing currents. Centrifugal forces are pushing them apart, emphasizing their differences from each other and leading them toward possible disintegration. At the same time, centripetal forces are moving them into closer dialogue and interaction, to the extent that many Episcopalians, both clergy and laity, would find it hard to describe themselves without using categories from all three orientations.

Anglo-Catholic Fragmentation

It is ironic that Anglo-Catholics predominate in the schismatic movement, for if one were to identify the most persistent theme in the life of the Episcopal Church in the past 25 years, it would be the ascendancy of the Catholic movement within the church. There was a time when celebrating Holy Communion every week, wearing eucharistic vestments and making the sign of the cross were all regarded as such exotic practices that parishes would be torn apart at their introduction. Today such things are regarded as quite normal, even in many parishes that regard themselves as "low church."

Catholic ideas have come to permeate the thinking of the church. Kenneth Kirk's assertion that episcopacy is of the *esse* of the church and the concomitant view that non-Episcopally ordained clergy are simply not valid ministers have become so widely adopted that most Episcopalians assume that their church has always held those views.

The irony consists in the fact that just as the Catholic movement prevailed, it fragmented. The split follows the same lines as are visible in the Roman Catholic Church since Vatican II. Some Roman Catholics have adopted modern views of Scripture, theology, liturgy and church authority, while others have refused to budge from traditional positions. The same could be said for Anglo-Catholic Episcopalians.

The ordination of women priests illustrates the fragmentation of the Catholic movement. While most of the opposition to women priests has come from traditionalist Anglo-Catholics, other Anglo-Catholics have been prominent supporters of the movement to ordain women. Theological arguments in favor of ordaining women came from such Anglo-Catholic theologians as Richard A. Norris, Jr., and J. Robert Wright. Anglo-Catholic bishops—G. Francis Burrill of Chicago (retired), Harvey D. Butterfield of Vermont (retired), C. Kilmer Myers of California (retired) and Robert C. Rusack of Los Angeles—voted for the ordination of women. Indeed, a significant number of the women priests themselves would want to be called Anglo-Catholics.

The same is true of the movement to revise the Book of Common Prayer. The early impetus for liturgical reform came primarily from Anglo-Catholics at a time when most other Episcopalians had little interest in rites and ceremonies. And while traditionalist Anglo-Catholics were writing pamphlets to show that the new rites were theologically defective, other Anglo-Catholics were acclaiming those same services as triumphs of Catholic thinking. The Standing Liturgical Commission, the official body that produced the new prayer book, was itself heavily populated with Anglo-Catholics.

On the whole then, the Catholic movement seems firmly in the saddle, though many who worked and prayed for this kind of triumph seem unable to recognize or affirm their victory. Anglo-Catholicism has transformed the Episcopal Church, but has itself been transformed in the process.

Evangelicals and Charismatics

The evangelical impulse in the Episcopal Church has in recent years been manifested most prominently in the charismatic movement. Though it first attracted attention because of the exotic phenomenon of "speaking in tongues," the movement has grown in size and importance as its emphasis has shifted to spiritual renewal through the baptism of the Spirit.

Local clergy feel both attracted to and threatened by this predominantly lay-led movement. On the positive side, it has contributed to a reawakening of the spiritual life of the church—even in circles that would not regard themselves as charismatic. On the negative side, it frequently exhibits all the rigidity and intolerance of traditional revival movements: combating "unsaved" clergy, insisting on its own version of religious experience as the only authentic one, splitting congregations into warring factions.

Like the Catholic movement, the charismatic movement is diverse and complex. Not all charismatics share the movement's literalist tendencies or its claim to represent the only authentic version of Christianity. Nor, indeed, do all charismatics come out of the evangelical sector of the church. Many would describe themselves as charismatic Anglo-Catholics.

Some charismatics sit loose to their membership in the Episcopal Church, finding more in common with charismatic Christians from other denominations. Their intense commitment to the power of personal religious experience maintains an uneasy balance with liturgy and the sacraments. Then too, some charismatics recognize the fact that most Episcopalians do not—and perhaps never will—share their orientation to the Christian faith. After all, the Episcopal Church has traditionally drawn much of its adult membership from among former members of evangelical churches who were repelled by the excesses of revivalism and who appreciated the reverent dignity of Episcopal worship and the intellectual freedom of Episcopal life. If charismatics are to find a permanent place for themselves in the Episcopal Church, they will have to make more room in their thinking for sacraments, liturgy and human reason.

Many evangelicals have been somewhat embarrassed by the charismatic movement, though they admire its fervor and frequently seek to emulate its techniques. Evangelicals have come to realize that their concern for personal conversion and witness still has an important place in the life of the church. Most evangelicals have been supportive of women's ordination and prayer-book revision. As in the case of the charismatics, some evangelicals are moving in the direction of biblical literalism and antisacramental positions. Dissatisfaction with the alleged modernism of the church's seminaries has led a group of doctrinaire evangelicals to establish their own school of theology in which "sound" doctrine can be taught and the Bible given the central place in the curriculum. It is too soon to tell how widespread these developments will prove to be, but they do reflect similar tendencies in the wider American Protestant community.

Liberals and Radicals

One major aspect of the Episcopal Church's English heritage has been a commitment to the use of reason in the search for religious truth. Thus biblical criticism was accepted in the Episcopal Church with little evident struggle. Modernist theological positions have been entertained without heresy trials (though a few did take place—to the embarrassment of most church members).

Along with this liberal (for want of a better word) orientation has gone a tradition of social analysis and critique, though not always by theological liberals. Anglo-Catholics have contributed their share of social and political criticism, often working from a medieval conception of church and society.

The most trenchant critique of American society and economic life in recent years has been coming from Bishop Robert DeWitt's Church and Society network and his publication the *Witness*, which has spoken with real effectiveness on some major social issues: the place of women, racism in the church, world hunger. William Stringfellow is perhaps the most respected radical critic because his social analysis is always grounded in the biblical perspective. Other radicals' tendency to rely on neo-Marxist categories guarantees that they will not be taken very seriously by most church members.

The liberal perspective is most significant when it takes the form of an ethos that permeates all of the various groups within the church. Liberal Anglo-Catholics entertain new ideas and practices, while others do not. Charismatics imbued with the liberal spirit regard noncharismatics with a tolerance unknown by their more hot-eyed colleagues. On the whole, I believe that the liberal attitude is a major distinguishing characteristic of the Episcopal Church—one which it particularly needs to maintain today.

Decline of the WASP Establishment

The level of conflict in the Episcopal Church has been intensified by a long-term development in the larger society that affects the way in which the church arrives at decisions. I refer to the gradual breakdown of the old "eastern establishment" which once dominated the informal network of power and influence in the Episcopal Church.

Most outsiders still regard the Episcopal Church as the ecclesiastical embodiment of the WASP establishment. Many Episcopalians still take great pride in the number of wealthy, prominent, upper-class people who are members of their church. There is still some correlation between the Episcopal Church and the Social Register. Episcopal churches are still preferred for the most fashionable weddings in some cities. Many older parishes still subsist on endowments left to them by the great families that once dominated their life. But those are mere survivals. In important ways, the establishment has declined in influence within the church just as it has in the larger society.

There was a time when diocesan conventions were run by wealthy lawyers, bankers and stockbrokers. They held the important diocesan offices and served as deputies to the General Convention. In many dioceses, election was a mere formality as the same deputies served at convention after convention. Among the clergy a similar situation prevailed. Clergy from upper-class families constituted an informal gentlemen's club within the larger body. They held the "cardinal rector" positions and dominated the House of Bishops.

These men, whether high church or low church, conservative or liberal, were all part of the same old-boy network. They grew up together, went to the same exclusive boarding schools, vacationed at the same elite watering spots. They managed ecclesiastical affairs within the bounds of a certain genteel propriety. Controversies could be settled over brandy and cigars in the privacy of the leading men's clubs, without making lurid headlines in the secular press.

Today the upper class, while not absent from Episcopal ranks, is no longer in control. The leadership contingent is being constantly refreshed by the infusion of new blood. Diocesan conventions see a significant turnover of lay parish delegates each year; at the last General Convention, nearly half the deputies were serving for the first time.

This change has had a major effect on the way in which decisions get made. Church leaders now argue out their differences in public. Everybody gets into the act. In the recent movement to revise the Book of Common Prayer, an elaborate process was designed to enable congregations all over the country to experiment with the new services and to communicate their responses to diocesan and national liturgical committees. On the one hand, this venture into populism probably helped to ensure the ultimate passage of the new prayer book at the 1979 General Convention. On the other hand, it encouraged dissenters to organize efforts to reshape or defeat the revision process. The best known of these efforts was the Society for the Preservation of the Book of Common Prayer, which raised an impressive amount of money, sent frequent mailings to convention deputies, organized protests on the local level, and mounted a massive lobbying effort at three General Conventions.

Black and Anglican

No treatment of the Episcopal Church would be adequate without some mention of its small but significant black membership. Most black Episcopalians belong to all-black congregations served by black priests, though a critical shortage of black clergy requires that some be served by whites. During the 1960s an attempt was made to open up positions for black clergy in predominantly white churches, but little was achieved. Today black clergy express some ambivalence about that project. They still want equal consideration for vacant positions, but more and more of them express the conviction that their first responsibility is to make sure that black congregations are adequately served.

Though cities such as New York, Chicago and Philadelphia contain large and affluent black parishes, most black congregations are both small and poor. Many of those in small cities and towns, both north and south, are unable to support a full-time minister. Without such leadership, they are not very likely to grow.

The unofficial Union of Black Episcopalians serves to keep its members in touch with one another—a genuine achievement in light of the diversity of that group. It includes the conservative and conventional as well as the radical and militant. It includes a significant number of foreign-born, mostly from the West Indies, and even these differ from one another. Most black clergy and their congregations tend to follow the Anglo-Catholic tradition, though their deep loyalty to the Episcopal Church is evidenced by the fact that none of them showed any interest in the schismatic movement.

Many younger black clergy have been deeply touched by the resurgence of black self-awareness and have tried to incorporate elements of the black religious heritage into their parish worship, often against the opposition of their more traditional parishioners. One black priest recently reported that some of his parishioners complain about his "Bapto-Catholic" innovations. Other black members are gratified to learn that becoming Episcopalian need not rob them of a rich legacy of preaching, worship and music that has meant much to them and their people in the past.

Parishes and Priests

National church issues may be more interesting and newsworthy, but in the Episcopal Church—as in most other American churches—the real action is in the local congregation. Here the Episcopal Church is showing significant signs of vitality, despite a loss of membership that has given both liberals and conservatives something for which to blame the other. With the wholesale dismantling of national staff and a lack of vigorous national leadership, dioceses and parishes have been pretty much left to their own devices.

On the whole, the parishes seem to be doing rather well. The extensive liturgical experimentation of the past 15 years has revitalized parish worship, while retaining the order and dignity that Episcopalians have always prized. A new concern for spiritual growth has deepened the religious life of many congregations. In some parishes an attempt has been made to develop faith communities with a common discipline of prayer, study and social engagement. Christian education programs are being developed locally, without reliance on mass-produced national curricula. Meditation groups, study groups, prayer groups, retreats and conferences abound.

Faith Alive, an evangelical organization, runs weekend conferences devoted to personal spiritual renewal, offering for many an attractive alternative to the charismatic movement. Cursillo and Marriage Encounter, both borrowed from Roman Catholicism, have won a wide following. PEWSaction and other lay-led efforts at evangelism coexist in a friendly fashion, enjoy an overlapping membership, cosponsor major events, and share a common voice in *New Life,* an irenic, renewal-oriented magazine published by Philip Deemer.

The current state of ordained ministry is one of the most pressing issues confronting the Episcopal Church. In the past, most Episcopalians shared a very high view of ordained ministry. The parish priest, whether high church or low church, was an authority figure long after the pastor had ceased to be such in most Protestant churches.

That is no longer true today, when laypeople are beginning to feel their oats. Apparently the church has been doing something right, be-

cause a seriously committed, theologically sophisticated, articulate laity is beginning to emerge. Laypeople are demanding that the clergy
provide them with adequate spiritual and educational leadership. One
result of this new mood is that the authoritarian style of leadership is
being replaced by a more collaborative style. Another result is a new
concern for the meaning of lay ministry as well as for the meaning of
ordination.

The situation of the clergy is complicated by an oversupply in the
ranks of the ordained. Of course, the ordination of women complicates
this picture, but the problem has been around for more than ten years.
Since 1955 the total number of Episcopal congregations has declined,
while the number of clergy has increased by nearly 5,000—or 62 per
cent. In the absence of any national authority to control ordinations, the
problem continues to worsen, despite the number of pious voices urging that "something should be done."

One reason for the oversupply is the awe with which most people in
the church still regard the ordained ministry. Since ordination is so precious, it cannot, apparently, be withheld from any earnest seeker who
seems reasonably well qualified. This evidence suggests that, despite
the current enthusiasm about lay ministry, Episcopalians have not yet
assimilated the idea. Even marginal candidates for ordination are eased
along a complicated but undemanding selection system with no one
willing to take responsibility for asking, "Is this ordination necessary?" A few dioceses have declared a moratorium on ordinations, but
there is nothing to stop an aspirant from simply moving to a more com-
pliant diocese.

A second factor contributing to the oversupply is a deep suspicion
of the church's seminaries in the more conservative dioceses. Some
bishops regard the seminaries as centers of heresy, secularism and
loose living. They prefer to raise their own clergy in diocesan night
schools, far from the corrupting influence of big cities and higher education. Their candidates are usually men of middle years, already so-
cialized by the business world and the conventional pieties of church
life, guaranteed to raise no fundamental questions, challenge no established authority and rock no ecclesiastical boats. Nearly one-third of
the new ordinands in the Episcopal Church are products of these nonseminary programs.

There are, of course, nonseminary programs of high quality which are legitimate and imaginative responses to local clergy shortages. The clergy oversupply is most evident in metropolitan areas where urbane, sophisticated seminary graduates tend to cluster. Rural areas and minority ministries still have a shortage of clergy. Programs such as the Dakota Leadership Program and the Leadership Academy for New Directions (LAND) are working to ensure a supply of trained and competent clergy and lay leaders for the church in these nonmetropolitan areas.

Despite the lack of jobs and the difficulty of moving into better positions, clergy morale, oddly enough, seems to be getting better. The past few years have seen a reaffirmation of the value of parish work and a resurgence of confidence in the possibility of making a useful contribution to people's lives through the Christian ministry. Personal and professional development is being taken seriously. Continuing education is being included in more clergy agendas, as well as in diocesan and parochial plans and budgets. Clergy associations, originally a response to unsatisfactory parish situations and diocesan policies, are developing into agencies for self-renewal and peer support.

Starving Institutions

Church contributions are increasing, but so are costs, with the result that more and more money stays in the parish. Less is available for diocesan or other extraparochial ministries—still less for national programs or overseas mission. Church institutions other than the parish can anticipate lean years, however effective they may be.

Theological seminaries offer the best illustrations of this paradox. Despite the complaints of the nostalgic and the philistine egghead-hunters, the Episcopal seminaries are in good condition today. Nearly all of them have undergone significant changes in leadership, style and educational program. Mergers and cluster arrangements have facilitated a more effective use of limited resources. A new crop of deans has taken charge—able and dedicated scholars such as Harvey Guthrie of the newly merged Episcopal Divinity School in Cambridge, O. C. Edwards of Seabury-Western in Evanston, Frederick Borsch of the Church Divinity School of the Pacific in Berkeley, Gordon Charlton of the Episcopal Seminary of the Southwest in Austin, and James

Fenhagen of the General Theological Seminary in New York. Though outsiders still talk about the seminaries in terms of what they were 30 years ago, they are more alike today than any of them resembles itself of a generation ago. In that sense, the seminaries provide a major impetus for the centripetal forces that are likely to hold the church together in the future.

Despite their excellence, however, the seminaries suffer from the lack of any regular support from the church at large. Unlike the seminaries of most other churches, they enjoy no subsidies from the national church or regional bodies. They are forced to go around the church with their begging bowls, hoping that they will be able to raise enough money to get through one more year. And every year it gets a little harder.

Leadership

The new egalitarian character of church life does not encourage the growth of giant-sized church leaders. There are no present-day equivalents of Henry Knox Sherrill, Angus Dun or James Pike.

Presiding Bishop Allin has seemed preoccupied with keeping the most militant dissenters within the ecclesiastical fold. He has so identified himself with the opponents of women's ordination that he has jeopardized his standing in the eyes of the main body of church members. It is embarrassing to have the presiding bishop on hand for a service at which an ordained woman functions in a priestly role. It is difficult for the women priests—and their supporters—to acknowledge him as "their" presiding bishop. If Bishop Allin is to exercise a major role in pulling together the various sectors of the church, he will have to find his way to a more central position, one that can at least be affirmed by the majority of his clergy and lay leaders.

A new generation of church leaders is beginning to emerge. John T. Walker, Washington's first black bishop, is asserting national influence through a coalition of urban bishops launched at the Minneapolis General Convention in 1976. That group is evolving into a larger urban coalition, which includes clergy and laypeople. They intend to get the Episcopal Church committed once again to mission and evangelism in our larger cities.

William C. Frey of Colorado, who was host to the 1979 General

Convention in Denver, may yet emerge as a major influence in moderate-conservative circles. He is a man of conviction and good sense who enjoys the confidence of charismatics, Anglo-Catholics and renewal groups.

Urban T. (Terry) Holmes, dean of the School of Theology at the University of the South (Sewanee), is becoming as much of an intellectual leader as the Episcopal Church is likely to tolerate. His books are widely read by the clergy, and he is a popular leader of clergy conferences. H. Boone Porter, the new editor of the *Living Church*, is an exemplary Anglo-Catholic modernist who will no doubt be a major voice in Episcopal circles in years to come. Meanwhile, the church's own scholarly quarterly, the *Anglican Theological Review*, is taking on new life under editor W. Taylor Stevenson, as is the *Historical Magazine of the Protestant Episcopal Church* under John Woolverton.

Looking to the Future

The General Convention of 1979 left observers with the feeling that the forces of cohesion have begun to assert themselves. The atmosphere was warm and conciliatory. Moves were made in both conservative and liberal directions. The same House of Deputies that refused to support the District of Columbia voting-rights amendment because it was "political," also voted to support ERA because it was a "human rights" issue. The convention restored funds for urban ministry to an already tight budget, voted to launch a peace-education program and approved the agreed statements on Eucharist and ministry prepared by the Anglican–Roman Catholic International Commission (ARCIC).

The most controversial issue to come before the convention, the ordination of homosexual persons, illustrates the mood of the church at this moment in history. The convention decided that "it is not appropriate for this Church to ordain a practicing homosexual, or any person who is engaged in heterosexual relations outside of marriage." That pleased conservative members. But the resolution was not a new canon law but merely a recommendation to bishops and other diocesan agencies which pass on the qualifications of those to be ordained. Thus traditional standards were upheld, but no effort was made to put legalistic teeth into the proposal.

The fate of the presiding bishop's Venture in Mission project simi-

larly illustrates the locus of the vital forces in the life of the Episcopal
Church. Originally conceived as a $100 million national fund drive,
Venture in Mission has been quietly taken over and transformed by the
several dioceses. It has become a collection of diocesan-level mission-
study and fund-raising enterprises in which local needs are included
along with national and international projects. On the positive side, the
project has harnessed the energy and enthusiasm of church members all
over the country. It remains to be seen whether the value of local initiative will be offset by a kind of provincialism that takes care of minor
local concerns before considering the critical needs of the church in
other parts of the world.

The ordination of women has already been accepted far more widely than most proponents had dared hope. Congregations actually exposed to women priests seem to adjust to the idea rather quickly. Even
those who disapprove are more likely to stay within the church while
staying away from ordained women.

Women will continue to experience great difficulty in finding full-
time work (or, rather, full-time salaries) in the church. I do not know
how this matter will be resolved. The church needs to expand its view
of what constitutes ministry and how ordained persons can be most
effectively employed. At the same time, those clergy and congregations that fought for the ordination of women priests have a special
obligation to find—and to create—employment opportunities for them.

In the immediate future, I expect to see the question of identity
occupying a prominent place on the church's agenda. Ecumenical involvement with both Protestant and Roman Catholic partners will force
the Episcopal Church to keep asking: What does it mean to be an
Anglican? What is special and peculiar to the Episcopal Church?

Episcopalians are becoming more aware of and more assertive
about their own heritage. The New Church's Teaching Series, a collection of seven volumes, is intended to be a resource to help the church
explore and affirm that heritage. Membership in the multinational,
multiracial Anglican Consultative Council helps to remind American
Episcopalians that "Anglican" is no longer to be equated with white,
English-speaking, established churchmanship. The diversity of worldwide Anglicanism—indeed, the increasing diversity of the Episcopal
Church itself—adds a degree of urgency to the question of what is the

particular contribution that this tradition has to make to the larger Christian enterprise.

Despite what Episcopalians may say about themselves, however, the identity of the Episcopal Church has always been quite clear to the outsider: it was the WASP establishment at prayer. But times have changed. With the decline of upper-class influence and the concomitant emergence of Anglo-Catholicism as the dominant force in the church, a new identity is beginning to emerge. What distinguishes Episcopal worship today is not the stately purity of Cranmerian prose but the vitality of eucharistic celebration. Word and sacrament are combined in a style of liturgy that has long been missing from both Catholicism and Protestantism. At the same time, the church is coming to grips, intelligently and sensitively, with such explosive issues as sexuality and family planning, abortion, the role of women, economic justice and world peace. It may be that, in the American religious environment, there is a constituency of searchers who would find such a church attractive. The fact that the church is no longer identified with the Social Register may make it more congenial to ordinary folk who do not want their practice of the Christian religion to be contaminated by the suspicion of social climbing.

These considerations point to a reversal of those centrifugal forces which, in recent years, have driven the Episcopal Church's subgroups off into different directions, thus producing late-blooming Counter-Reformation traditionalists, middle-class Pentecostals and neo-Marxist radicals. Forces that make for cohesion will have to gain the ascendancy if the church is to continue to incorporate in its common life a commitment to the gospel, a loyalty to tradition and a confidence in human reason. The church's health depends on its capacity for keeping those commitments in creative tension.

We Episcopalians have discovered that living in this kind of tension can be uncomfortable to the point of being painful. But if we can bear the pain and tension long enough for the forces of cohesion to prevail, we may discover that the church is stronger and livelier and more faithful because of the struggles it has gone through.

2

The Mormons:
Looking Forward and Outward

The Latter-day Saints are journeying toward a
destination totally different from that posited
by more traditional Christian doctrines.

JAN SHIPPS

The recent 150th anniversary of the formal organization of the Mormon
Church was observed with carefully choreographed ceremonies telecast
from the gigantic Tabernacle in Salt Lake City's historic Temple
Square. Distinctly separate ceremonies were conducted in the 10,000-
scat auditorium in Independence, Missouri, the center-place and headquarters of the Reorganized Church of Jesus Christ of Latter Day Saints
(RLDS). And in a variety of less-well-known places the members of an
astonishing array of Mormon splinter sects commemorated the beginning times of their faith. Though "Come, Come, Ye Saints" rang forth
from the mountains and "The Spirit of God Like a Fire Is Burning"
welled up from the plains in sesquicentennial celebration in the spring
of 1980, the birth of Mormonism actually preceded the April 6, 1830,
date which marked the creation of the church. The first Latter-day
Saints gathered around Joseph Smith, the Mormon prophet, as the
Book of Mormon came into being; the Mormon field has been "white
to the harvest" for more than a century and a half. For that reason,
1978 was as much a year of jubilee as 1980. But in any case, this is a
fit and proper time to make inquiry about the nature of modern Mormonism and then to ask, "Where from here?"

*Dr. Shipps is associate professor of history and religious studies at Indi-
ana University–Purdue University at Indianapolis.*

Amazing Growth

Although surveyors of the religious scene have been mentioning the Mormons for almost as long as Mormonism has been in existence, their reports have always placed the Saints outside the mainstream, treating them as a sort of aberrant footnote to the nation's religious life. But if Mormonism continues to grow at its present 5 per cent per annum rate for a few more years, this situation is bound to change. Already there are more Mormons than Presbyterians; by conservative estimates, the LDS church, as the Utah body is often called, will soon have upward of 4.5 million members. Between 250,000 and 300,000 more Saints can be added when all the Mormon groups are counted in. The sum total suggests that while the Mormons are definitely not moving toward the American religious mainstream, that mainstream could well be moving toward them.

That Mormonism might ever become the national religion seems farfetched. Yet in view of its amazing growth in its first 150 years, it is not without interest to note that an LDS mathematician recently made a half-joking but statistically correct projection that "if Mormonism continues to grow in the United States at its present rate, and if the U.S. population continues to grow at its present rate, then in another 150 years when Mormonism celebrates its tricentennial, all the nation's citizens will be Mormons."

The perils of ecclesiastical success and the difficulty of predicting the birthrate make questionable the accuracy of that extrapolation. Yet Mormonism has clearly arrived as a religious force—and not just in the United States. Growth is, in fact, proceeding faster outside the U.S. than within the nation's boundaries. Practically every Saturday the Mormon publication *Church News* reports the organization of new stakes, wards, branches or missions (the basic units of the LDS system) beyond the boundaries of this country. Significant Mormon populations exist in Mexico, in many Central and South American nations, in the South Seas and in Europe. LDS temples nowadays are almost as likely to be built outside as inside the United States. And ever-increasing numbers of converts made in foreign lands by that portion of the church's 25,300-member full-time missionary staff stationed outside the U.S. seem to many Mormons to presage a time when their church will be the church universal.

The New Revelation

Whether such will ever be the case or not, a crucial obstacle which almost certainly would have prevented the LDS church from ever being a universal church was removed on June 9, 1978, when the Lord, it was reported, confirmed "by revelation" to church President Spencer W. Kimball and his counselors "that the long-promised day had come when every faithful worthy man in the church may receive the holy priesthood." Signaling the elimination of the barrier which had kept black men of African descent from holding the LDS priesthood, this revelation was an event of extraordinary importance to Latter-day Saints. It was widely and rapidly reported in the American press and electronic news media, where many accounts, elaborating on the official announcement, suggested that the revelation was, in the words of the *New York Times*, "another example of the adaptation of Mormon beliefs to American culture."

Despite the seductive persuasiveness of this interpretation, the June 9 revelation will never be fully understood if it is regarded simply as a pragmatic doctrinal shift ultimately designed to bring Latter-day Saints into congruence with mainstream America. The timing and context, and even the wording of the announcement of the revelation itself, indicate that the change has to do not with America so much as with the world.

A revelation in Mormondom rarely comes as a bolt from the blue; the process involves asking questions and getting answers. The occasion of questioning has to be considered, and it must be recalled that while questions about priesthood and the black man may have been asked, an answer was not forthcoming in the '60s when the church was under pressure about the matter from without, nor in the early '70s when liberal Latter-day Saints agitated the issue from within. The inspiration which led President Kimball and his counselors to spend many hours in the Upper Room of the Temple pleading long and earnestly for divine guidance did not stem from a messy situation with blacks picketing the church's annual conference in Salt Lake City, but was "the expansion of the work of the Lord over the earth."

Most especially, the black man's having been "cursed as to the priesthood" had made for difficulty as the church expanded in South America. In many cases there, determining who has African ancestry and who has not presents serious problems. If a pragmatic reason for the revelation must be found, it is better found in the fact that on October 30, 1979, an LDS temple was dedicated in São Paulo, Brazil—and making sufficient determination as to which Mormons were racially acceptable to enter the holy place could have proved a horrendous task. Since revelation now has established the doctrine that worthy men of any race can hold the priesthood "with power to exercise its divine authority, and enjoy with [their] loved ones every blessing that flows therefrom, including the blessings of the temple," such difficulty has been avoided. At the same time the way is opened for stakes and wards to be organized where adequate local priesthood leadership might have proved a problem heretofore, and the path is cleared so that LDS temples may be built in any place in the world and universally used by all worthy Mormons in the area.

Predicting the impact of the June 9 revelation on the growth pattern of the church would be risky. But the fact that this revelation came in the context of worldwide evangelism rather than domestic politics or American social and cultural circumstances is yet another indication that Mormonism can no longer be regarded as a 19th century religiocultural artifact and dismissed as a footnote to the story of American religion. Mormonism is here to stay. Where did it come from? And more important, how and why is it growing at such a rapid pace?

Telling the Mormon Story

"How much do you know about the Mormon Church? Would you like to know more?" These are the "golden questions" asked every day by thousands of Mormon missionaries, mainly young male members of the Utah-based LDS church. Notwithstanding enough affirmative responses to lead to 167,939 convert baptisms in 1977, the missionary task is not always an easy one. Fresh-faced, clean-cut, neatly dressed, these young people often find a warm welcome in the homes of "golden" families already committed to investigating the Mormon gospel. But in straight-line tracting, the strategy of knocking

on every door in a specific area, they are invited to come in only nine out of every 1,000 times. It is not difficult, therefore, to understand the discouragement recently revealed during an impromptu interview by a very young and obviously inexperienced LDS elder. He was homesick, lonely, and quite evidently dismayed at his lack of success. But his principal complaint was the somewhat unexpected lament that "everyone knows the Mormon story already."

Doubtless this pleasant young man soon found someone unacquainted with *Joseph Smith's Testimony,* that ubiquitous missionary tract which contains the official account of the prophet's visions and his discovery of the ancient record chronicling the lives and times, vicissitudes and final destruction of a Hebraic people whose patriarch immigrated to America with his family in 600 B.C. But whether he found someone to hear his message or not, it is easy to appreciate the young missionary's fear that everyone already knew the Mormon story. Mormons all together—RLDS and LDS—have some 31,000 missionaries in the field worldwide. In addition, the Utah church is actively engaged in spreading the LDS message via official and quasi-official publications, television and radio programs and spot announcements, visitors' center activities, local ward open houses and genealogy classes, and even by using billboards, bumper stickers, and multipaged advertisements in the *Reader's Digest.*

Certainly large numbers of Americans are familiar with the general outlines of Joseph Smith's story. They are not always sensitive to it, however, for knowing the story and comprehending its significance are two very different things. The tale of an unsophisticated farm boy who found some engraved metal plates and used "magic spectacles" to translate therefrom a thousand years of pre-Columbian American history appears so incredible to many non-Mormons that they simply dismiss the prophet's visions as hallucinations, regard his "golden bible" as a worthless document, and wonder how any intelligent person could ever accept it as true. Serious critics look at the Book of Mormon more closely. Using as evidence its obvious parallels to other 19th century accounts tying the American Indian to Israel's lost tribes, its descriptions of situations, incidents and characters suspiciously like those within Joseph Smith's ken, its echoes of Masonic lore, its Isaiah passages and its bountiful supply of anachronisms, they conclude that the work is not only worthless but a fraud. In either case, efforts to explore the implications of the book's content are missing.

A Usable Past

The book is cast in the form of a historical narrative. Having something of the style and flavor of the Old Testament, it claims to be the story of what happened when God's people came to the Western Hemisphere. It is a history, and it has functioned—as history tends to function—as a binding agent, melding disparate individuals together into a single people by giving them a common past. The Book of Mormon provided the Saints with a usable past and a common set of expectations—in much the same fashion as did the book that was pulled together by the Jews as they sat down by the rivers of Babylon and wept when they remembered Zion. An unorthodox reminder of their Judeo-Christian heritage, Smith's book told them that the Lord's song had been sung on this side of the Atlantic and explained how it might be sung again. Defined as truth by the prophet whose raising up was prophesied therein, the book became true for those who believed, in much the same way that the entire body of Christian Scripture has become true for biblical literalists.

Those persons who have considered Smith's book simply as an ordinary historical account have found much to criticize. Yet critics find it well-nigh impossible to discount the way the Book of Mormon, appearing as it did at a time when all America seemed set adrift in a bewildering new world, furnished Jacksonian believers with a reassuring sense of time and place. In that uprooted society it supplied a very real connection with the Ancient of Days, an extremely useful Abrahamic lineage, and a universe of story and metaphor so powerful that it continues to tie together a good portion of the human race, even in this era when alienation and anomie threaten to predominate. Without accepting the work at face value, it is nevertheless possible to regard the Book of Mormon as the product of an extraordinary and profound act of the religious imagination. It lent legitimacy to Joseph Smith's prophetic career and, by tying America to Israel, gave credence to the claim that in these latter days America is the Promised Land and the Mormons are the Chosen People.

The book's Hebraic influence was intensified in the lives of the

Saints by the peculiar form of Christianity instituted with the organization of the LDS church. A primitivist of an unusual kind, Smith harked back to a form of Christianity which repudiated the outcome of the Jerusalem conference described in Acts 15. Adopting a position not unlike that of St. Peter before a vision taught him not to despise the Gentiles, the prophet held that would-be Christians would first have to choose to be chosen. This meant that before they gained access to God's grace they would have to repent and be baptized into the (Mormon) Church of Christ because old covenants had been done away with when God executed a new, perpetual and exclusive contract with the Latter-day Saints in 1830.

As Christianity was God's gift to his own people, and as the Mormons were that people, so membership in the Church of Jesus Christ of Latter-day Saints became the new covenant sign. And the work rolled forth, carried forward by Christians completely convinced that they had taken possession of that special relationship to God which had once been the sole property of the Jews.

Asserting that God and Jesus are literally father and son, that Jesus and Jehovah are one and the same, and that even the Holy Spirit is somehow located in time and space, these new Saints clothed the mystical body of Christ with the real flesh of Mormonism and started out to build up Zion, drawing biblical parallels every step of the way. They had such a vivid perception of themselves as God's people that the past and present were joined. Prosaic and matter-of-fact, they made the symbolic so tangible that a direct link was forged between their own day and the days described in Old Testament and New. Mormon theology's emphasis on the family as the redemptive unit, its system of patriarchal blessing in which each individual's membership in the household of Ephraim or Manasseh or Judah was solemnly intoned, and its "restored" priesthood all worked to strengthen the Hebraic connection.

The process of cultural integration was accelerated as the 19th century progressed. Persecution and kingdom-building pushed and pulled the Saints together, giving them a firm LDS identity. Then shared memories of those early years plus present participation in Mormonism's corporate life completed the transformation. Now Mormons are not simply members of an unusual ecclesiastical corporation. They are a neo Judaic people so separate and distinct that new converts must undergo a process of assimilation roughly comparable to that which has to take place when immigrants adopt a new and dissimilar nationality.

Today the Mormon world intersects the larger one at a multiplicity of points, and when the two fail to converge the difference in direction is often very subtle. Still, there is no denying that the Mormons inhabit a radically different world from the one outside, and that — for the most part — theirs is an orderly world wherein questions have answers and people know who they are and where they stand.

Mormon Fundamentalists

If the 19th century was a time of cultural integration, it was also a time of internal division. The church split apart in the aftermath of the prophet's murder in 1844, and it remains divided today. Sometimes the sheer size and visibility of the Utah-based Church of Jesus Christ of Latter-day Saints cause it to be thought of as the "real" Mormon church. But close to 150 other LDS organizations are or have been in existence. While most of these can be described as splinter groups of small membership and minimal importance, there are presently two major exceptions, the new Mormon fundamentalists and the Reorganized Church of Jesus Christ of Latter Day Saints.

One of the more visible manifestations of early Mormonism's identification with Old Testament times was the institution of plural marriage (polygamy), which was openly practiced in Utah from 1850 to 1890. In response to terrific outside pressure, the practice was banned by the church in 1890, but continued to be officially condoned until 1907, when it was banned absolutely and made a cause for excommunication. Plural marriage persisted on the underground nevertheless. In the past decade it has reappeared as the major tenet of an undetermined number of LDS fundamentalist sects with a total membership estimated to be somewhere between 3,000 and 20,000.

In accounts of contemporary Mormonism, the new polygamists are often highlighted too much just because they make such good copy, especially when they kill each other off. Yet these modern Saints who have elected to live in plural marriage as the most dramatic and satisfying means of demonstrating total commitment to the fullness of the gospel are clearly a part of the picture. As today's influential LDS leaders idealize the monogamous nuclear family and make it the center of the faith, plurality's extended households are a necessary reminder of the enormous extent to which Mormonism deviated from the U.S. norm in the not-too-distant past.

The 'Reorganization'

Much more important than the fundamentalists, the Reorganized Church stands at the opposite end of the Mormon spectrum. Rather than being "more Mormon" than the Utah Mormons, its members so closely resemble their mostly Protestant midwestern neighbors that some Salt Lake Saints claim that the RLDS church is Protestant in everything but name. In this they are mistaken. It is true that in 1972 the RLDS church formally recognized as revelation the basic principle that "there are those who are not of this fold to whom the saving grace of the gospel must go." But the acceptance of a position which much of Protestant Christianity regards as axiomatic does not make the Reorganization a Protestant church. The RLDS membership retains a distinctive Latter Day Saint identity, which should not be surprising since the roots of the RLDS form of Mormonism are to be found in the very beginnings of the Mormon movement.

Mormonism changed dramatically between 1830 and 1844. Starting out as a variant form of New Testament primitivism, it became increasingly Hebraic as time passed. The prophet's charismatic authority kept the church together during his lifetime, but in the years after Smith's death, Saints scattered in all directions. Although many of the Mormons—perhaps a majority, but no one knows for sure—accepted the leadership of Brigham Young and the Council of the Twelve and followed them to Utah, many others stayed behind. Remaining true to Mormonism despite a decade-long interruption in the continuity of the prophetic leadership line, many of the Saints who stayed away from Utah were reunited under the leadership of Joseph Smith III in 1860.

The "Reorganization" pulled together those Saints whose understanding of the Mormon message was more closely tied to traditional Christian primitivism than to the neo-Judaic Christianity of Mormonism's last few years in Nauvoo, Illinois. This is not to say that the members of this group were no longer tied to Old Testament history and prophecy. However, despite what might be called their Hebraic connection, they refused to accept plural marriage, the idea of the political kingdom, and temple worship, as well as the more esoteric LDS doctrines such as plurality of gods and baptism of the dead. So they reestablished the church according to their own gospel interpretation, preserving in Mormonism that strain—present from the beginning—which saw the church first as the Church of Christ and after that as the Church of Latter Day Saints. Although the demise of polygamy and the political kingdom removed two of the most potent symbols of division between the RLDS group and the Utah Mormons, no ecclesiastical rapprochement has occurred. None is really expected since members of the two churches have apparently irreconcilable conceptions of what Mormonism means.

An ecumenical movement has arisen among LDS historians, however. During the past decade the Mormon History Association and the John Whitmer Historical Association have been established. Their meetings are occasions when professional historians from both traditions associate freely, sharing with each other information about the past. Despite an easy camaraderie and close fellowship which minimize faith commitments, it is nevertheless increasingly obvious that the two groups are taking separate approaches to their history-writing tasks. Whereas Utah Mormon scholars are making a close examination of the past in order to uncover and integrate every possible bit of existing information so that the official picture can be completed and clarified, RLDS scholars are looking at that same past with an eye to discovering not so much particular truths as universal ones.

Impelled by a need to find the roots of their form of Mormonism, leading historians of the Reorganization have embarked on an exercise in higher criticism, subjecting to close scrutiny Joseph Smith's story and Mormon scripture as well as the two official versions of church history. While the long-range outcome of this activity is hard to predict, what seems to be happening for these Saints is a reversal of the 19th century process whereby the metaphorical was translated into literal terms. The RLDS church has always maintained the now clearly unrealistic position that the prophet was not involved in plural marriage and that the Mormon religion was somehow drastically changed after Smith's death by Brigham Young and the Mormons who went to Utah. If the admittedly risky enterprise of taking the real stuff of the Mormon past and finding in it a meaningful body of symbolic truth is a success, a firmer foundation for the church could be the result.

Meanwhile, most RLDS activity goes on virtually oblivious of this intellectual and spiritual ferment. Plans are afoot to build a "temple school" for the training of new church leaders, but no major expansion of the church is presently contemplated even though, with a current membership of 213,399, the Reorganization is larger than it has ever been. The growth rate, the meaningful statistic in making future plans, is down now to slightly less than 1 per cent per year, and it seems likely that the RLDS church will continue as a modest but important ecclesiastical establishment, providing Latter Day Saints with an alternative to Utah Mormonism.

Mainstream Mormonism

Conventional Christianity paid little attention to Mormonism as long as LDS proselytizing was done mainly by pairs of young missionaries sent out from Salt Lake City. But now that large numbers of local Mormons are joining the "happiness is Mormonism" chorus, the churches are beginning to show some concern. A few are reacting by underwriting the publication of slightly modernized versions of early anti-Mormon tracts, but most Christians are simply asking questions, trying to find out exactly what—in the name of Jesus Christ—is really going on.

Multiple and sometimes contradictory answers often confuse the questioners. More than anything else, it helps to know that the Latter-day Saints are journeying toward a destination totally different from that posited by more traditional Christian doctrines. It is also crucially important to recognize that their journey is going forward along a road which closely parallels the road not taken by St. Paul and the first century Christians. As a result, Mormonism cannot be neatly placed in any one of the Catholic-Protestant-Reform categories or along the liberal-conservative-fundamentalist continuum developed to deal with the diversity of normative Christianity.

As its official name implies, the Mormon Church sees itself as a Christian body. At the same time, it is an elaborate priesthood organization which is similar in some respects to Masonic priesthood organizations. It is also an ecclesiastical domain with an administrative structure so intricate that a much-involved Latter-day Saint once predicted that, on the morrow of his death, he will have to confront a flow chart with arrows drawn in to indicate the lines of administrative authority in the celestial kingdom. But Mormonism is more than all that. It is a peculiar people with a distinctive mind-set and behavior pattern. And it is a collection of stakes being strengthened to support the tent of Zion.

A change in emphasis has occurred in Mormonism during the past few decades. Now the family unit rather than the priesthood quorum is the most important organization in the church, and support for families is the central thrust of today's church program. The local ward (parish) is a community of families; ward activities, standardized throughout the nation, are planned to engender family solidarity. Home teaching and church welfare programs provide mutual support. Genealogy serves to tie in the family from past time, and stress on the eternal marriage covenant takes the family into the distant future. Temple ordinances then sanctify family relationships so that the entire Mormon experience can be said to uphold the integrity of the LDS family. Because the missionary message is also built on what the church can do for families, conversion is often a family affair, and every LDS ward seems to be filled with new families being "fellowshipped" into Mormonism.

Problems and Prospects

The church's commitment to the traditional nuclear family as the foundation of stable society as well as of the church program led LDS leaders to conclude that the Equal Rights Amendment posed such a danger to family life that the church must place itself on record as standing against its passage. Following its clear articulation of this position in 1976, the church worked against the ERA in several direct and more-or-less official ways. Church publications emphasized LDS support for the anti-ERA position, and that support was demonstrated unmistakably during several state International Women's Year conventions. Some disagreement exists regarding exactly how important in determining the outcome of state ratification battles LDS influence has been, but there is abundant evidence that the church's opposition played a significant role in the defeat of the ERA in Utah and Nevada, and perhaps in Florida and Virginia.

Its decision to oppose ERA is not the first instance wherein the church has assumed a clearly defined political position; it has objected to the passage of right-to-work legislation for many years, for example, and following World War I, the church supported U.S. membership in the League of Nations. This is the first time since the early days of Utah statehood, however, that the church's assumption of a political position has engendered among its own membership the sort of active and open opposition as that recently made manifest by "Mormons for ERA." Rather than being satisfied with the more usual Mormon pattern of working for change from within, this Washington-based group, which claims to have 500 members nationwide, made a concerted effort to use the media to bring public opinion to bear on the church's ERA position. Although the intent was to persuade church leaders that the church ought to change its position, the confrontation strategy employed by the pro-ERA Saints is so alien to Mormonism that, instead of producing the desired change, it led to the excommunication of "Mormons for ERA" leader Sonia Johnson in an ecclesiastical media event which may very well make it the most celebrated excommunication since Savonarola's day.

As a result of the hullabaloo, a representative of the church's Public Communications Department was assigned the task of putting out the fire before it could burn out of control and destroy the positive public image which seems to have been developing in the wake of the changed status of blacks in the church. Appearing before the press, this church spokesman made it clear that Mrs. Johnson was not haled before a church court because she supported the ERA. The church does not object, he said, if individual members support ratification of the amendment. The concerns of Mrs. Johnson's accusers were doctrinal error and the more pragmatic matter of the negative effect she might be exercising on the LDS missionary program; the accused was unable to defend herself against these charges and so was cut off. The charges, it was emphasized, were brought in a local ward, the case was tried there, and appeal is possible.

While the Johnson case will likely continue to garner media attention until the appeal process is completed, historical precedent suggests that the efforts of "Mormons for ERA" have little chance of forcing a change in the church's official attitude toward passage of the amendment. On the other hand, historical precedent also suggests that, by pushing the question into the public arena, Sonia Johnson and the Mormon sisters who stand with her could well have attenuated to a serious degree the extent to which the LDS Church will be able to exert its influence in the future in behalf of political movements whose intent is to block the ERA.

Television and press coverage magnified Sonia Johnson's excommunication out of proportion. If the public has the notion that the men who sit in the councils of the mighty in Salt Lake City are spending most of their time discussing ways to deal with Mrs. Johnson and "Mormons for ERA," then the public is likely very wrong indeed. Finding the means for translating the LDS scriptures into every language, developing appropriate missionary programs and proselyting materials for cultures unacquainted with the Judeo-Christian tradition from which Mormonism sprang, building local priesthood leadership to enable the church to develop indigenous strength all over the world—these tasks take an enormous toll on the time and attention of church leaders. What happens to Mormons in the United States is not unimportant, of course, but the internationalization of Mormonism so crowds the LDS agenda that it is altogether probable that when policy is made, the ERA question sometime pales in significance to the point that it really does appear to be a local matter.

The LDS church is dynamic and changing. Though the Johnson case is one in a long line of examples of the multifarious problems which arise to keep the Saints from being able to say with certainty that "in Zion all is well," Mormonism is clearly on the move. The gospel is being spread around the world, and growth is becoming the normal condition. The church's administrative machinery is being stretched to the limits of its capacity and is undergoing constant alteration as the general authorities try to find ways to stay close to the Saints. Naturally there are many perplexing and difficult matters with which Mormons at every level must be concerned. While the growth of the church seems to be gratifying to all Mormons and the direction in which the church is going is generally approved, Sonia Johnson and her sisters are not the only ones who are apprehensive about the way things appear to be headed.

Some Saints worry that individuals are being shunted aside or left out in the rush to idealize the Mormon family. Others worry that the church is encouraging early and/or ill-advised marriages and fear that the rigidity of LDS sex roles may inhibit the flexibility which life in the modern world demands. LDS liberals—and contrary to popular belief, that is not an oxymoron—not only are concerned about the church's stand against ERA, but are disturbed to see the church acting as a political adjunct to Phyllis Schlafly's Eagle Forum. Although they are thrilled that the priesthood is no longer denied to black men, liberals are uncomfortable as leaders of the church express conservative social, political and economic positions in such a way that they become official.

There is a current of uneasiness, especially among Mormon academics, about what will happen if Ezra Taft Benson becomes church president and carries his right-wing political views into office with him. Intellectuals in the church—and that's not an oxymoron either—are bothered by the drift toward rigid orthodoxy in the spheres of both behavior and belief. For various reasons, a good many Saints feel constrained by the church's standardized program. And so many Saints are weary with much attendance at Mormon meetings that the church, in order to leave its members time to participate in the activities necessary to the building of strong and lasting families, has eliminated some meetings and consolidated its program in a number of areas.

But the importance of these concerns for the future pales almost to insignificance beside the grave problems the church will have to face as it continues to grow and develop into a truly international body. Notwithstanding the rosy picture of a world filled with Mormons which is being projected by the *Church News* and the official *Ensign*, the power of the LDS gospel to sustain communities of Saints throughout the world without requiring them to adopt peculiarly American attitudes and stereotyped life styles has not yet been fully proven. The essence of Mormonism awaits distillation, and while that long and

painful procedure is under way, the church will have to exercise
enough control over its growth to allow time for each new LDS cohort
to complete the acculturation process and to begin to establish what
being a Latter-day Saint really means before the next cohort arrives.
Otherwise the peculiar Mormon identity will dissipate, and, like some
other Christian churches, this one will divide.

For all that, however, Utah's form of Mormonism is anticipating
the future with confidence at the time of its 150th anniversary. Neither
looking backward in the fundamentalist fashion, nor inward in the
manner of the Reorganization, the Church of Jesus Christ of Latter-day
Saints is looking forward and outward with a view to telling all the
people in the world about their opportunity to live out their lives inside
the covenant beneath the tent of Zion.

3

The Black Church: A New Agenda

The black religious community is recognizing that fervent evangelical piety is an incomplete response to human need.

LAURENCE N. JONES

The term "black churches" denotes congregational structures "owned and operated by blacks"—some affiliated with established denominations, countless others freestanding or loosely affiliated. Numerous black congregations identified with predominantly white denominations may properly be included in the term "black churches," but it is not with these that I am concerned here. The focus of my discussion will be the future of the black church from the perspective of its historical development within the black community and its impact upon both its participants and society as a whole.

Cautionary Notes

Several caveats need to be stated at the outset. First, broad generalizations are difficult because black churches are highly diverse. Though yoked together by ethnic identity and a common history of racial oppression in America, they differ in doctrine, worship, faith commitment and the Christian life. Second, the spontaneity with which black congregations proliferate makes it difficult to speak with assurance about trends in black church life. Churches spring up as a result of migratory patterns, economic circumstances, and the commitments of individuals and groups, often without reference to historical groupings.

Dr. Jones is dean of Howard University's school of religion.

The storefronts and house churches in urban areas testify to this diversity. What appears to be a trend in a given geographic/ demographic area may be barely discernible elsewhere.

Third, since black churches have developed only limited central bureaucracies, it is difficult to assemble statistical data. Official statistics on membership, contributions, property holdings, and monetary allocations to various aspects of missions are not widely published or distributed. In addition, the collection of accurate statistics is rendered virtually impossible because of the number of congregations that are freestanding and unrelated to organized ecclesiastical bodies.

There are further complications among churches with congregational polities that approve affiliation with several national bodies. For example, a Baptist congregation may belong to the National Baptist Convention, U.S.A., and to the Progressive National Baptist Convention or the American Baptist Churches. Moreover, congregations under a particular denominational umbrella may accord primary allegiance to local, state or regional groupings, or to a body whose reason for being is some aspect of mission (e.g., educational, foreign or eleemosynary). These specific loyalties often predate the founding of national bodies and are sustained through participation in corporate structures and financial support. It is fair to say that black congregations have tended to be more ecumenical through their involvement in common mission than through their participation in structures. They have been more active in the life and work of the church than in its faith and order.

Major Bodies

These cautionary notes are designed to provide a prism through which the statistics that follow may be viewed. The majority of black Christians are Baptists. Their total number may exceed 8 million. The oldest black Baptist denomination is the National Baptist Convention in the U.S.A.; organized in 1895, it traces its roots to the 1840s. J. H. Jackson has been president of this group since 1952. The convention carries out its mission through nine boards and agencies, including the Foreign Mission Board, the Home Mission Board, the Sunday School Publishing Board, the Baptist Training Union Board, the Education Board, the Evangelism Board, the Laymen's Movement, the Women's Auxiliary Convention, and the National Sunday School and Baptist

Training Union Congress. Latest estimates place convention membership at 6.3 million, organized into 27,000 congregations.

The National Baptist Convention in America, organized in 1915 after a rupture with the National Baptist Convention in the U.S.A., has approximately 1 million members, led by James C. Sams, president, and T. B. Boyd, secretary-treasurer of the Publishing Board. Its structures nearly parallel those of the older group.

The Progressive National Baptist Convention, organized in 1961, similarly derived from the National Baptist Convention in the U.S.A. Its 750,000 members represent 1,534 churches, and it is presently headed by William Jones of Brooklyn, New York. The Progressive body has not developed as elaborate a structure as its counterparts. It functions principally through a Department of Christian Education, a Home Missions Board, a Foreign Missions Bureau, and a Congress of Christian Education.

Though the African Methodist Episcopal Church traces its beginnings to 1787, it was not formally organized as a denomination until 1816. Today its membership in the United States is approximately 1.5 million (2.5 million worldwide). It is organized into 13 episcopal districts and has congregations also in the Caribbean and Africa.

The first congregation in the African Methodist Episcopal Zion Church was organized in 1796, but the denomination did not sever all ties with the Methodist Episcopal Church until 1821. Its current membership is approximately 1.2 million, comprising nearly 7,000 congregations.

The Christian Methodist Episcopal Church, organized in 1870, has 480,000 members in 2,542 congregations. All of the Methodist bodies have developed quite broad structures in which they embody their witness and service.

Completing the roster of major black denominations is the Church of God in Christ, headed by Bishop J. O. Patterson, which traces its origins to 1895, and which today has approximately 400,000 members in the United States, and claims a worldwide constituency of 3 million. While it should be reiterated that these statistics are only realistic approximations, they nevertheless constitute a dependable index of the significant power of the black churches and of their enormous potential for shaping black life in the years ahead.

Origins of Black Congregations

The first institutions organized by blacks were benevolent societies designed to provide for the physical and educational needs of the sick, the widowed and the orphaned. The membership of these societies often constituted the nucleus of what were to become independent black congregations. For example, the Free African Bethel Society, organized in 1787 in Philadelphia, eventually spawned the African Methodist Episcopal congregation and the St. Thomas Protestant Episcopal congregation.

Mission, rather than creed, was the primary motive that impelled blacks to withdraw from historically white church bodies. There were, of course, other reasons advanced for separation. Sometime after Richard Allen, Absalom Jones and other blacks marched out of the St. George's Methodist Episcopal Society in Philadelphia, they offered three reasons for their radical and precedent-setting action: (1) They felt that their very presence in the St. George's congregation was an offense to some whites; (2) they felt inhibited in their worship by the obvious disfavor with which their enthusiasm in worship was greeted; and (3) they believed that they could minister more effectively to other blacks if they did not have to explain the "unchristian" conduct of some members of the Methodist society.

These reasons and others were present in virtually every instance in which black congregations came into existence. Invariably they were yoked to a concern for the abolition of slavery and a desire to provide educational opportunities for blacks, for whom the larger society was making little or no provision. In the first half of the 19th century, a zeal for foreign missions emerged among black churches as well as an interest in political action aimed at assuring the rights of the African diasapora. After the Civil War, the concern over slavery was displaced by issues related to segregation, discrimination, and economic, social and political oppression. In cooperation with the Freedmen's Bureau and several northern church bodies, black churches were the primary agents in the founding of schools for black people at the elementary, secondary and collegiate levels.

Culture and Education

From their inception, the churches were the center of life in most American communities; but, as the society matured economically, socially and politically, alternative institutions arose which lightened the church's load of secular concerns. Black churches did not relinquish their secular roles, however, and continue to retain them even today, in contrast to the roles played by their white counterparts. Since the late 18th century, black churches have been assembly halls to which the community has had ready access and, as such, have served as cultural and political centers.

The worship service provided a captivated audience to whom varied good causes could be advanced. W. E. B. Du Bois remarked during the 1920s that the NAACP could not have survived without the black churches. And though the NAACP has drawn support from a broad spectrum of social and fraternal organizations, the churches continue to provide an indispensable segment of its constituency. No knowledgeable black office seeker ignores the churches and their leadership if he or she wishes to gain visibility and patronage in the community. Among primarily religious, political, economic and social institutions, only the black churches have sustained an uninterrupted presence and acquired access to a large, stable constituency.

Education has been a constant concern of black churches, and in this respect they have maintained a similarity to their white counterparts. Even prior to the Civil War, education was high on the agenda. In some instances, Sunday schools served also as elementary schools for members. By the end of Reconstruction in 1877, churches had contributed in excess of $700,000 to educational purposes. At the time they initiated their educational activities, blacks were excluded from all but a few educational institutions, both public and private. At the turn of the 20th century, black Baptists were supporting 80 elementary schools and 18 academies and colleges, while the AME Church was underwriting 32 secondary and collegiate institutions. The smaller AME Zion Church was supporting eight colleges and institutes, while the CME Church, only 30 years old, had established five schools and colleges. There has since been a generalized decline in the number of

institutions depending primarily upon churches for support. Close examination shows this decline to be a direct result of the rising cost of
higher education, the lack of resources within the churches which can
be applied to these concerns, and the centralization of administration.

Structures and Budgets

Several references have been made to the absence of strong centralized church structures. This reality is partially a consequence of the
accidents of history, patterns of church growth and development, and
an inability to knit uniting bodies into unified structures. But the most
important single factor inhibiting the development of bureaucratic
structures has been the economic deprivation of black communities.
Churches have reflected the poor economic health of the overwhelming
majority of their members and have not found it viable to establish or
maintain national headquarters. Both positive and negative consequences have resulted from this action. Positively, it has tended to
make congregations and local judicatories mission-conscious and has
fostered a sense of involvement in the work of the church. Negatively,
it has inhibited the growth of the universality of the church in mission
and has made it difficult for churches to cooperate effectively in matters of broad import.

The generalized economic deprivation of blacks in America has affected church life in other ways also. It has been reflected in compara-
tively modest budgets for the funding of overseas missions, higher
education, theological education, church expansion, and support of national priorities in home missions. On the home front, it has meant that
local congregations have only limited possibilities of receiving assistance from central judicatories. Each congregation, with notable exceptions, is a "tub resting on its own bottom" in such critical areas as
building funds and salary support. Thus, in the area of finance, a de
facto congregationalism is the operational polity of the majority of
black Protestant institutions.

Black churches have not developed forums or structures for formu-
lating and developing consensus around important social, political, economic, religious or moral issues. This absence of the "sense of the
church" has the effect of depriving the churches of the information and
guidance that are important ingredients in effective mission and wit-

ness. This lack is critical in a religious community in which as much as 70 per cent of the leadership has not had the benefit of formal theological education. The African Methodist Episcopal Church has taken initial steps in this direction with the recent issuance of its *A.M.E. Working Papers,* which treat such subjects as abortion, the black family, homosexuality, capital punishment, women's rights and the like. Some of these issues are discussed in national denominational meetings, but any decisions made seldom achieve the status of official church pronouncements. Local and regional groups frequently take positions on local issues, even on political candidates, but at the national level it is most often the power, influence and prestige of top leadership that determine the weight of the guidance provided on matters debated in the public arena.

Another important consequence of black churches' restricted economic resources has been their failure, as denominations, to develop viable retirement programs for clergy. This lack has meant long tenure by incumbents, thus severely restricting access to positions of leadership by younger men and women. A survey conducted several years ago by a faculty member at Payne Theological Seminary revealed that the average age of AME clergy was between 58 and 60. Under such circumstances, one would suppose that the opportunities for placement of younger ministers would be abundant, but that is not the case. Limited upward mobility has diminished the attractiveness of the ministry as a vocation for many promising young men and women who are reluctant to accept cash salaries at or just above the poverty line.

The number of black women formally enrolled in theological education is growing, though not to the same degree as that of white women. One reason for this slower rate of growth is the reluctance of some Baptist bodies to ordain women. The exclusion of women from ordination limits women's access to the ministry in proportion to the black churches' numerical affiliation with Baptist denominations. Black Methodist bodies historically have been more open to the ordination of women.

There have been black congregations in America for nearly three centuries. But the role of the churches has been evolving and becoming increasingly more complex. It is clear, for example, that the resources available in average congregations are insufficient to address the massive social and economic needs of urban communities. It has become obvious that this historic expression of mission is now, to a large degree, palliative and stopgap. Moreover, the social welfare programs of the government and of private and community agencies are far better resourced and programmatically more comprehensive. The priority benevolent activity of churches now is to assure that eligible persons gain access to available benefits.

In the matter of church-supported education, no such clear conclusion can be drawn. Despite the broader access by blacks to public secondary and higher education since *Brown* v. *Board of Education* (1954), it is still not self-evident that church-related institutions should close their doors.

Confirming Personal Worth

The thrust of our discussion up to this point has been to emphasize the mission of the church in the world, but this is not the whole story, and perhaps not even the most important part of the story. There has been an intimate and continuing link between the history of black people and their churches. Though membership statistics indicate that approximately 60 per cent of the population is affiliated with religious institutions, the impact of the Christian faith has been felt far beyond church membership. The churches' ministry has been shaped by the social, economic and (until the last decade) political isolation of the majority of blacks.

This isolation has meant that a great deal of church energy has been expanded on priestly and pastoral concerns. The churches have confirmed the personal worth and significance of black persons in a social and in a divine sense. They have provided an area for personal growth, expression, development and social recognition, and for the exercise of leadership gifts and talents. Moreover, the churches have been the only viable, readily accessible vehicle for expressing group concerns in forms which are, at the root, religious. In the midst of an environment experienced as dehumanizing and overwhelmingly negative, the church has pronounced an overwhelming Yes to its communities. Rooted in the gospel of Jesus Christ, the community of believers has found an incentive to struggle with the inequities of this world and to hope for the vindication of God's righteousness here on earth. Humane black survival is inextricably linked with the gospel and with the churches through which it is proclaimed.

Looking to the Future

The future existence of black churches is not in jeopardy. They will continue to be the lone institution accessible to the majority of black persons in which one's worth and sense of belonging are confirmed and consistently reinforced. What is in question about black religious establishments is the capability of congregations to sustain their attraction for significant numbers of urban dwellers while reflecting a rural ethos and social context in their worship patterns and message.

The most significant phenomenon affecting the churches in this century has been the migration of blacks from the farms to the cities of the north and south. The cities are now populated by a generation of young people who have had no exposure to the warm evangelicalism which was characteristic of rural religion. This generation is much more secularized in outlook and much more aware of the ways in which black people's lives are shaped by structures and institutions they do not control. Moreover, young people are more likely to expect, if not demand, that religious institutions be active agents of social change. Churches may no longer anticipate with confidence that this generation of urban blacks will return to the fold as they mature—many have not had affirmative encounters with either the gospel or the churches.

It is dangerous to assume the role of a prophet, but it seems clear that if black churches are seriously to take account of the radically different social, political and economic realities that have matured in post–World War II America, they must operate on a much more sensitive and sophisticated scale than before. The new agenda will have both new and old items. As long as racism continues to color American life, black churches will need to sustain in individuals a conviction of their value under God and among persons, and congregations will need to continue to be accepting and sustaining communities that are at once spiritual and substantial. It will be tragic if there is a diminution of the proclamation of the gospel enjoining individual commitment to Christ, firm in its faith in a loving, actively concerned and forgiving Father.

One perception growing out of the civil rights movement of the

'60s was that of the systemic nature of racial oppression. While individual acts of charity have their own inherent worth, it is manifestly evident that they are ineffectual to address structures of injustice. The black religious community is only now becoming conscious of this reality. It is also recognizing that fervent evangelical piety is an incomplete response to human need. While the gospel is being faithfully proclaimed, it must be embodied in mission and in strategies calculated to accelerate the achievement of justice in society. In pursuit of their carefully determined mission objectives, congregations inevitably will have to marshal their considerable human and monetary resources to the end that they are demonstrably yoked to the purposes of God for his creation. To be avoided at all costs is the hazard of bifurcating reality into sacred and secular spheres, and of separating life in the spirit from life in the world.

The rising consciousness that human beings have a right to participate in structures that wield great influence in their lives will be reflected in demands for fuller participation in governance in ecclesiastical bodies. If black congregations are to attract and retain well-informed laypersons, the long tradition of clergy domination of churches must be reformed. Parishioners will remain in the churches only if they share in policy formulation and are enabled to utilize their talents in significant service.

A New Agenda

Paralleling increased involvement of laypeople in the life, mission and order of the church must be the development of a well-trained, deeply committed, and secure clergy. There are already signs that this is taking place, but the pace is tortuously slow. Increasing the supply of qualified clergy is not simply a matter of increasing the numbers of seminary graduates; it also involves the strengthening of regional and national structures supportive of clergy and congregations. There are a number of areas that would benefit from immediate attention:

1. Attention should be given to the development of programs of nurture within the churches to address the consciousness, realities and urgencies of contemporary urban life. The nurture of young persons is especially critical in light of the pathologies of urban life to which they

are regularly exposed and by which some are victimized. The Christian education programs of the churches need to be "indigenized" to the urban environment and must bring the gospel to bear upon life in the real world. Christian education must become bilingual (i.e., capable of understanding the language of the world and translating the gospel so that it is intelligible in that idiom). God-talk is not understood on many streets of the city. Christian educators must be bifocal in vision. They must not lose sight of heaven, but they must also see the world at hand and seek to enable persons to live meaningfully within it.

2. Churches qua churches must find the means for enlarging and coordinating their attack on the systemic problems which afflict large parts of their constituencies. Individual churches may have limited channels for addressing high unemployment among black youth, but churches together might make a significant economic and political impact. They must begin to engage cooperatively in strategy and planning so as to multiply their impact. Thus, black churches must become more ecumenical for the sake of effective mission and stewardship of resources. The hard fact is that black religious institutions must shed much of their naïveté about the world. They must become knowledgeable and wise—secular experts, if you will. They must be wise about the ways of the world without succumbing to the temptation to act in worldly ways.

3. There must be continuing attention to moral values; support must be offered for family structures. Deterioration of the quality of life in urban areas is emerging as a concern of the churches, and this awareness should be reflected in all aspects of church life. Many black youth do not belong to any social group that provides guidance and support for them in their efforts to achieve.

4. There is increasing evidence that persons, particularly the young, wish to recover spontaneity and individual participation in worship. Churches must devise means for accommodating this interest without derogating from the claims of the gospel for transformation of lives and continued commitment to the will and purpose of God.

5. The churches' historic concern for education must continue. The question which now must be addressed is not that of providing basic institutions, but of discovering the ways in which the institutions that

already exist can provide quality education that communicates humane values and commitment to service.

6. The concern for vitality is not restricted to the worship service alone. It applies also to issues of mission, life style, morality, and integrity of commitment. Churches must be aware that their significance as institutions is being challenged with increasing intensity. They are being arraigned for their failure to address the problems of economic, social and political injustices endemic in urban society.

7. Perhaps one of the most critical items on the churches' agenda is that of institutional administration and the management and allocation of resources. Because of the radical congregational polity of black churches and the lack of centralized regional and national structures, it is virtually impossible to marshal the economic resources of the churches. One black denomination has 341 congregations in a southern state. The average congregation's Sunday offering in 1976 was $300.00. In the course of a year these churches handled in excess of $5 million. If these funds had been deposited in a single banking institution, the influence of that church with respect to loan policy could have been quite significant. Churches might also consider the possibilities for cooperative purchase of supplies, printing services, insurance and the like. The potential in this area is considerable but as yet unexploited.

8. Another matter pressing for attention in the councils of black churches is the relatively small size of the majority of congregations. Small size and limited financial resources have a negative impact both upon a congregation's ability to attract and retain effective qualified ministerial leadership and upon its ability to be engaged in mission. Herein lies a paradox. The black community needs small churches because only in small groups can "somebody know one's name." In effect, the need of individuals for affirmation and for community works against successful corporate involvement in mission. A church must be large enough to be viable, but it cannot be so large that its members become nameless faces. The immediate problem is how to retain the intimacy of the small congregation and yet develop sufficient linkages so that the combined strength of the churches can be applied in mission.

Favorable Signs

The agenda of the black churches for the decades ahead is a large and complicated one, but there are important harbingers that bode well. Increasing numbers of bright young people from all denominations are seeking theological training; they are exerting pressures on schools and seminaries to prepare them to be resources to their communities as well as competent leaders of religious institutions. National church leadership apparently is increasingly aware of the changed situation of the churches and is seeking to respond to newly emergent realities. It is encouraging too that church membership has been holding steady and that middle-class defection has not been as great as some had predicted.

At the local level, there is increased participation of laypersons in the governance of the churches. Many clergy are finding their own power limited by constitutions and by-laws of local churches where the former pastors were virtual monarchs. Churches are also giving evidence of a continuing sense of social responsibility. Another favorable sign is the broadening effort to provide basic training for church leaders who are not formally qualified to pursue graduate theological education. This training is both theological and practical and will have significant impact.

Ecumenical Participation

Black churches have not been heavily involved in the formal ecumenical structures of American Protestantism. Their absence has been due in part to limited financial resources, but mainly to a preoccupation with survival and issues of social and economic import. Neither has ecumenism flourished among black churches themselves. There are no major national ecumenical bodies in the black community, though in urban areas there are often ministerial groups involving persons across denominational lines, and some congregations participate in local and regional ecumenical bodies.

A July 1978 meeting in Indianapolis may have been the harbinger of change. Attending the meeting at the invitation of John Adams, bishop of the AME Church, were representatives of the National Baptist Convention in America, the National Baptist Convention in the

U.S.A., the Progressive National Baptist Convention, the African Methodist Episcopal Church, the African Methodist Episcopal Zion Church, and the Church of God in Christ. The consultation identified four priority areas which the churches might address collectively: theological education, evangelism, communications and unemployment. The group has held additional meetings since. A significant aspect of this consultation is its focus on mission rather than structure, and the fact that it has addressed denominational differences only for the purpose of facilitating cooperative involvement in mission. The group has adopted the name "Congress of National Black Churches." Bishop Adams is chairman, and Bishop German Ross of the Church of God in Christ the secretary.

The Congress of National Black Churches is not the only ecumenical effort being pursued. John Satterwhite, formerly associate general secretary of the Consultation on Church Union (COCU), has called together members of the Methodist bodies on several occasions to investigate the possibilities of church union among the AME, AMEZ and CME churches. This long-sought goal is not yet within reach, but the dialogue continues.

One outgrowth of the crisis in the cities and the emergence of black-power ideology was the establishment in 1966 of the National Committee of Black Churchmen. Its name was subsequently changed to National Conference of Black Churchmen. NCBC, which meets annually, is currently headed by Charles Cobb of the United Church of Christ, with Mance Jackson of the Interdenominational Theological Center as its executive director. The conference agenda reflects the social, economic and political concerns that served as midwife to its birth. Its membership is drawn from a broad spectrum of church people, both lay and clergy. NCBC has not fulfilled its earlier promise of being a focal point at which blacks from all sectors of the religious community might meet to share share common concerns and strategies. Nevertheless, its existence points to the persistence of the problems that called it into existence.

In addition to denominational leaders, a whole company of clergy are prominent on the national scene: Jesse Jackson of Operation PUSH; Walter Fauntroy, U.S. congressman from the District of Columbia; William Gray, congressman from Philadelphia; Benjamin Hooks, president of the NAACP; Leon Sullivan of OIC; Joseph Lowery, president of SCLC; Andrew Young, former ambassador to the U.N.; and James Joseph, undersecretary of the interior. All provide leadership to constituencies larger than the churches with which they are identified, but they have not abandoned their clerical identities.

Black churches owe their origins to the institution of slavery. The Christian faith was promulgated among blacks and more often than not was "gerrymandered" to serve the interests of the slavemasters. The black churches took the gospel and appropriated its meaning for themselves. For them that gospel has been the means of salvation. It is my conviction that this will continue to be the case in the foreseeable future.

4

Peace and the Peace Churches: Re-examining a Heritage

The push for ecumenical wholeness among the Friends, the increasing desire of Mennonites to be involved in mission, and the heritage revival among Brethren may mean a kairos time for fresh examination of the theology of peacemaking.

DALE W. BROWN

Mennonites, Quakers and Brethren have worn the label "historic peace churches" only while attempting to weather the tides of violence, statism and industrialism in the 20th century. The assumption of a more self-conscious identity with the peace stance as integral to discipleship has accompanied a greater erosion of this testimony among us. The label may suggest a greater degree of common history and joint ministries than is actually the case. It may be applied too narrowly, as Schwenckfelders, Moravians and some Holiness groups have fit the "peace church" identity at one time or another in their histories. To call some bodies "peace churches" must not suggest a monopoly, as many other Christians share the peace testimony. If we omit the word "historic," there are communities which can more accurately be designated as peace churches than many with pacifist rootage.

Still, Mennonites, Quakers and Brethren have lived, gathered, talked and fought together enough to suggest a common family. Our histories and theologies have intersected enough times to convince us that we have a common witness—one which finds killing and war in-

Dr. Brown is professor of Christian theology at Bethany Theological Seminary in Oak Brook, Illinois.

compatible with the gospel and which affirms that the power of the
risen Christ makes possible obedience to the way of suffering love even
amid the exigencies of contemporary life. Our corporate statements almost universally reflect this testimony. At the same time, we are aware
that the consensus of our large meetings is not shared by many in our
smaller meetings. Thus, we continue to struggle with the question of
identity. We are sometimes comforted, sometimes deflated, to discover
that an intense seeking of who we have been in order to project who we
shall be is a quest similar to those going on in many other places.

At Peace with the World?

Some of us are greatly disturbed with the world. Others enjoy a
comfortable truce with the world. Some are disturbed at the peace
which others have made with the world. And we experience being
tossed to and fro by many of the same winds of doctrine that disturb
our Christian neighbors. Our identity crises focus on whether we are at
peace with the world, with ourselves, and even with the idea of peacemaking itself.

As with other groupings, the peace churches have known what it
means to be caricatured and classified by articulate members of mainline traditions. The most common typology has connoted a negativism
in relation to culture or the world. Max Weber and Ernst Troeltsch
called this quality "withdrawal." Though this term has been appropriate at certain times and places, the missionary zeal and confrontative
activity of the early Anabaptists and Quakers would have prompted
their opponents to wish that the Weberian and Troeltschian classifica-
tions had arrived earlier.

Many echo H. Richard Niebuhr in citing the peace churches as an
exhibit of the "Christ against culture" type. We are confident that had
he consulted with members of these churches, he might have formulated something like "Christ the servant of culture" as a paradigm for
those attempting to participate in God's suffering for the sins of the
world. It is true that the conjoining of *exousia* (power) with
servanthood by pacifists is confusing to those who identify culture almost exclusively with those at the top. In rejecting structures that kill
and oppress, it is still possible to retain world-affirming motifs such as
proper stewardship of the land, a concern for the welfare of neighbors

and a humanitarian concern for enemies, as well as an affirmation of the positive functions of the state.

The rejection of tribalism, nationalism and militarism stems not only from a higher loyalty to Christ but also from a vision that affirms a concern for the peace and unity of all peoples. Personally, I first experienced a strong sense of tension with culture not just because we were taught that we *should be* different but because the message that Christ died also for Japanese and Germans *made* us different from those around us. All of which is to maintain that the "against" is a fruit of the "for."

The traditional typologies are accurate, however, in pointing to a genuine tension that continues to be experienced in relation to much of our culture. Even prior to the contemporary focus on minorities, peace-church folk knew what it was to live with a minority psychology. We have experienced the kind of acceptance that declares: "Some of my best friends are pacifists." In ecumenical and academic circles I have often received the compliment, "We need your kind around," accompanied by patronizing connotations that it certainly would be expecting too much for anyone to take my views very seriously. As nuclear and ecological analyses become more apocalyptic, however, we find ourselves resonating with fellow pilgrims in surprising places and surprising ways.

At the same time that some have felt more existentially involved with our traditional stance of nonconformity, we are aware that as a people we are perhaps more acculturated than ever before. We are engaging in some breast-beating for our lack of boldness during the Vietnam era. The earlier efforts to tone down our peace testimony in order to minister "effectively" to larger numbers in our communities may have meant that we missed opportunities for a larger harvest which might have come with greater faithfulness to our "scandalous" witness. Our more radical voices tell us that our credibility is at a low ebb. We are far from being who we say we are. Though others may still look to us for theological explications on peace and ecumenical input concerning disarmament, we are so indistinguishable from middle-class America as to make us anemic in terms of marshaling a consistent attack on the roots of injustice and violence in our world.

Amid such despair about our condition, other observers among us cite the tenacity of the peace-church tradition which remains to come alive and *is* coming alive even after the popular peace movement fades in our memories. Significant remnants of the legacy of the late '60s and early '70s, such as the evangelical Sojourners community, utilize peace-church theology while shying away from close structural relationship. Three Brethren authors—Edward Ziegler, Art Gish and Vernard Eller—have written fairly popular books on the simple life as old peace-church themes suddenly become relevant to our ecological and energy crises.

Quakers' reconciling concerns, such as their long-held insistence that Americans should listen to both sides in the Middle East, are currently finding congenial listeners. John Howard Yoder's biblical politics is gaining a wider hearing in radical, evangelical and liberal circles. A visitor from Australia, who was commissioned by Christian communities to interview Anabaptist theologians, shared deeply of the worldwide interest in peace-church thought and life. The ascendancy of many of our traditional concerns, or of a label like Anabaptism, to the status of a theological fad evokes mixed feelings of satisfaction and typical suspicion about ourselves whenever we gain this much acceptance.

At Peace with Ourselves?

While ferreting out our roots, we have been battered by and forced to deal with such questions as ecumenicity, abortion, ordination, divorce and remarriage, prison concerns, world hunger, human rights, more simple life styles, tax resistance, the lettuce boycott, nuclear disarmament and the Panama Canal treaties. Along with mainliners, we are learning from and attempting to learn how to deal with our charismatics and evangelicals. The homosexual issue is just around the corner. The Quakers were early pioneers in terms of sexual equality, but American sexist culture refuses to take a holiday in many Friends meetings. Early Anabaptists modeled a remarkable egalitarianism in their life together. Nonetheless, Mennonites and Brethren are waiting patiently and impatiently for their German patriarchal heritage to catch up with their official pronouncements and their increasingly integrated theological schools. Modest yet increasing numbers of women are being added to pastoral directories. Cara Cole, administrative secretary of the Friends United Meeting; Ruby Rhoades, newly appointed executive of the World Ministries Commission of the Church of the Brethren; and Gloria Martin Eby, chairperson of Congregational Ministries of the Mennonite Church all represent at least a beginning in the assumption of top leadership roles by women.

We have known losses through both fundamentalist defections and the attrition of many liberals, and we seem in spots to be hopelessly divided. We have been graced and judged by new converts from the Vietnam ethos who know more what we should be about than we can articulate for ourselves. Though in general our churches are not growing in numbers, there may have been some cleansing and solidifying of membership records. Historic communal practices such as footwashing among the Brethren are supplemented by the current popularity of hugging and embracing and an infatuation with genealogy to indicate that the identity crisis is taking concrete shape in a desire to recapture the reality of the extended family which was so much a part of earlier generations. Recent conferences and other gatherings have been characterized by a familial festival atmosphere such as to give one reason to stop and think about the status of mission.

In small and significant ways there are efforts to incarnate our increasing theologizing about caring and sharing communities—a vital part of our believers' church tradition. The house-church movement is growing even when not consciously recognized as such. The Amish and other tightly knit groups in the conservative wing of our tradition no longer seem as strange and irrelevant to the rest of the family. Kindred intentional communities are becoming less separatist, while we have become less defensive. The Society of Brothers, for example, in reuniting with many Hutterian communities, is also reaching out in greater communication with other peace churches. Reba Place in Evanston, Illinois, another of the largest and oldest communal groups established in the 20th century, has recently gained congregational status with both Mennonite and Brethren bodies. As other communities follow this lead, an option is presented to those who wish to maintain ties with the older traditions while at the same time living in community. New Covenant Fellowship in Ohio is yet another example of a new community wishing to be in but not entirely of the Church of the Brethren.

Quaker Voices

The most exciting thing happening in the Society of Friends today is the Faith and Life Movement. This movement has constituted a fruitful dialogue among a variety of contemporary Quaker groups, ranging from the strongly evangelical through the primarily humanist. The humanist wing still struggles with such questions as whether a Quaker needs to be a Christian, while evangelicals debate their propensity to give priority to Holiness theology over Quaker thought. Real possibilities for rapprochement are occurring as more "liberal" Friends move from the humanist-mystical interpretation of early Quakerism of a Rufus Jones to the more christological analysis of a Lewis Benson. At the 1974 Faith and Life Conference in Indianapolis, keynoter John McCandless confessed: "I did not join the Quakers to find Christ, but since I have become a Friend, he has found me." At the same time evangelical Friends such as Arthur Roberts and Don Green are appropriating anew the historic and biblical peace concerns. If a radical center emerges between the best of humanism and fundamentalist Christianity, much credit should be given to the Quaker theological discussion group inspired by people like T. Canby Jones and Hugh Barbour; that group has provided an ecumenical forum through the periodical *Quaker Religious Thought*. Another significant bridge has been the Earlham School of Religion, pioneered less than two decades ago under the leadership of Wilmer Cooper. Though there are presently few Friends of national prominence except Elton Trueblood, there are new voices giving promise for the future. The mood at both leadership and "grass-roots" levels ranges from discouragement about aging membership and dwindling numbers to optimism about a new era of Quaker ecumenism and rediscovery of a holistic Quaker message.

Mennonite Ferment

Outwardly the Mennonites, even with their varieties, appear more stolid and solid. Their insistent biblicism and ethnicity combine with a more self-conscious and coherent theology to present a picture of cohesiveness. Though not strongly cooperative in terms of participation in councils of churches, the Mennonites have been ecumenical in the etymological sense through the worldwide missionary activity and impressive service programs of the Mennonite Central Committee. These growing ministries retain a greater consciousness of rootedness in the gospel and of "being the church" than is usually the case with similar programs. Associated Mennonite Biblical Seminaries at Elkhart, Indiana, provide a vital ecumenical center and forum for Mennonitism.

Some Mennonites would be uneasy with the preceding description. They would testify to many of the same stresses that are experienced by others. They have, for example, their own charismatic movement. For a long time they have experienced the struggles between those who have joined and those who have refused to join an Anabaptist biblicism with a more popular biblicism of either revivalism or American evangelicalism. Since the story of Anabaptist historiography has been so significant in signaling the cohesiveness I have described, some basic tensions can be discerned through the varying responses to the work of John Howard Yoder. His writings, including the widely read *Politics of Jesus,* constitute an important ecumenical contribution, for they embody the fruition of the recovery of the Anabaptist vision of his predecessors John Horsch, Harold Bender and Guy Hershberger. The modified kingdom theology, combining the more traditional theology of the cross with stronger accents on a theology of prophetic witness and service, has gained an enthusiastic acceptance in many circles.

Mennonites, who adhere to a more pronounced church-world dualism, judge Yoder's work as opening the door to the inroads of a secular pacifism which departs from the way of biblical nonresistance. Liberal transformationists and fundamental accommodationists, though differing sharply with each other, would share a mood which regards Yoder as too stubbornly refusing to be open to any new light which does not come through an Anabaptist filter. In agreeing with Yoder's strong peace concern, others emphasize that such a stance must be worked out in a realistic context. They point out that through educational institutions, missionary endeavors and service ministries, Mennonites have become involved in culture as never before while lacking an adequate theology for such involvement.

Voices such as Gordon Kaufman, J. Lawrence Burkholder and Edward Stoltzfus are calling for a greater recognition of the activity of God beyond the church, a theology of creation, as well as relevant nonviolent participation in a world where simple nonresistance is no longer a possibility. Whereas Yoder's well-reasoned and biblically documented position offers an attractive option for both Mennonites and non-Mennonites looking for a theology of community combined with a prophetic theology of witness, some of these other voices feel that Yoder's position is one which keeps too much of the cultural isolation of Anabaptist sectarianism. Such an oversimplification of contemporary ferment should signal, if nothing else, the continuing vitality of Mennonite life as well as that tradition's important theological contributions.

Brethren Leadership

In the 20th century, the Brethren more quickly shed many of the accouterments of their Anabaptist image and became more churchly and ecumenical. Following the Quaker lead in service ministries, the Brethren found they were more willing to lose their name institutionally. In this way Brethren leadership spawned and has remained instrumental in structures such as Church World Service, the Heifer Project Committee, and CROP (Christian Rural Overseas Program). As the Progressive Brethren found themselves in the evangelical camp and the Old Orders remained a separate people, the larger body, Church of the Brethren, found an increasing identity with mainline Protestantism. In recent decades liberal leadership has practically dominated national, district and seminary structures. In the immediate past, however, the denomination has felt the growing influence of the Brethren Revival Fellowship and of a charismatic network inspired by the leadership of Russell Bixler.

Along with others, the Brethren have discovered that the unsettling effect of a greater pluralism has been accompanied by an interest in their roots. The current Brethren heritage fad first became visible in an articulate way at the Louisville Conference in 1966. This emotionally charged gathering was a turning point in the continuing identity crisis. Radicals, conservatives, evangelicals and "grass-roots" Brethren joined together in an 80 per cent vote to overrule the desire of the liberal leadership to become full members of the Consultation on Church Union.

Since Louisville, many Brethren heritage materials have flowed from denominational headquarters, and joint curricular efforts have been undertaken with the Mennonites. Youth have known more empathy with and attraction to their grandparents' style, while seminarians and young pastors have attempted to reinterpret and apply the essence of the Pietist-Anabaptist dialectic. Donald Durnbaugh has worked at the translation of the recovery of the Anabaptist vision for Brethren. The recent appointment of Robert Neff, popular Old Testament professor at Bethany Seminary, as general executive of the denominational board points for some to a possible shift from a bureaucratic-liberal model to a more familial and biblical model, but one that does not forsake the strong ecumenical and social involvements of the Brethren. Veteran peace statesman M. R. Zigler, now in his 80s, is at work rallying a stronger peace consensus through On Earth Peace.

At Peace with Peacemaking?

Since the peace witness has been not a peripheral concern but one integral to our interpretation of the gospel, it has provided the focus for both the continuities and discontinuities among the three traditions. It has often been the ingredient that has brought us together during times of war, conscription and forced immigration. At the same time it has highlighted fundamental differences, as when Anabaptist realism about the nature of the state confronts a greater Quaker optimism about the possibilities of transforming the structures of society. The nature of the present push for ecumenical wholeness among the Friends, the increasing desire of Mennonites to be involved in mission, and the recent heritage revival among the Brethren may mean a kairos time for fresh examination of the theology of peacemaking.

Such a milieu surrounds the New Call to Peacemaking, initiated by the Friends' Faith and Life Movement and undergirded by the encouragement of evangelical leadership. It was decided that the call should be extended to and then proclaimed by the peace churches. Regional gatherings of Mennonites, Brethren in Christ, Friends and Brethren took place during 1977-78. The discussions focused in part on the efforts of task forces dealing respectively with biblical and theological bases, peacemaking life styles, and concerns for disarmament. The steering committee, led by Friend Robert Rumsey, presided over the culmination of regional meetings at a large gathering at Green Lake, Wisconsin, in October 1978. The enthusiasm was such that another large gathering was scheduled for Green Lake in October 1980.

The New Call is fostering dreams that our internal unity may be strengthened both within and between our constituencies as we encounter the Mennonites' biblicism, the Friends' optimism concerning the power of the Spirit, and the Brethren's reconciling mood. There is the projection that a sound biblically and theologically oriented theology of peacemaking can be boldly proclaimed in Christendom. From one of the many circulating epistles related to the New Call comes the reminder of Friend Dean Freiday:

> The Brethren who were harassed in the Palatinate, the more than four hundred Friends who gave their lives in 17th century jails in England in faithful witness to their Risen Lord, the thousands of Mennonites who were impaled, drowned, hanged, and tortured in every inconceivable fashion testify to the power of these theologies to evoke commitment.

Theologically, we are aware of basic issues with which we need to grapple. From the many that are being discussed in the joint meetings wherever the three traditions are found, the following questions may be illustrative of the nature of our tensions: Should the primary concern be for biblical purity and faithfulness or for efficacy in strategy and action? Do we have to choose between the Niebuhrian characterization of the pure passive love of Jesus and the more political paradigms of nonviolent resistance? Is pacifism (peacemaking) as biblical as nonresistance? Might there be a third way between staying home from Washington altogether and being political like everyone else?

There are expectations that the New Call might bridge some conservative-liberal polarities. Since to be a conservative in a peace tradition is to be a radical pacifist and to be liberal is to imbibe concerns for peace and justice, mutual dialogue and action should be possible. There are hopes that a proper theology of *shalom* can eliminate the false bifurcation between evangelism and peacemaking, the personal and the social gospel. Peace-church theologies may be so bold as to wish to transcend both Protestant individualism and Catholic institutionalism through a social strategy which maintains that the proclamation of the kingdom of peace and justice to the world must begin with the reality of some signs of the first fruits within the communities of faith.

In dreaming large dreams, why not add that both premillennialism and amillennialism can be transcended by an expectation of the kingdom coming which empowers the faithful to begin to live in the kingdom in the present? Within the peace-church tradition there are many persons hoping to bring together the desire of Mennonites and Brethren to "pick up the pieces" after disasters and the more reconciling ministries and social-justice concerns of the Quakers.

In attempting to speak for more than a dozen denominations, I need to beg forgiveness of my brothers and sisters for any wrong information, inferences or focus. With painful and exhilarating identity crises and new calls and programs in our common life, it is impossible to predict what's ahead. I enter an agnostic plea in reference to futurological analyses. As our discipleship heritage has helped us give priority to the Way over the most brilliant wisdom of ethicists, so should we give priority to promises about God's future over the most sophisticated analyses of the futurologists. We cannot know the future of our own efforts or those of our own communities. We *can* know that hope which lives by the faith that the Way of the Prince of Peace, for which God called out our ancestors, will survive and continue until that day when the kingdoms of this world become the kingdom of our Lord and of his Christ.

5

Lutheranism: A Quest for Identity

The majority of Lutherans seem to be moving, however haltingly, toward a fresh conception of just what
it means to be Lutheran. The new awareness is being
spoken of as 'evangelical catholicity.'

RICHARD E. KOENIG

It is a sobering fact that the three major Lutheran bodies constituting
the Lutheran Council in the U.S.A. have fewer members now than they
had ten years ago. The hemorrhage, while not as severe as that experienced by some of the other mainline denominations, has obviously
worried church leaders in view of the continued expansion of the general population. But despite their losses, Lutherans have recently appeared, if not ebullient, at least more hopeful. For two years in
succession, the reported losses have been low enough to lead the statis-
ticians to announce bravely that the slide may be "bottoming out."
The significance of the forecast lies more in its determination to read
the figures favorably than in its accuracy. After some of the most bewildering and potentially dispiriting years in their history on the American continent, Lutherans seem bent on turning things around.

At the same time, however, members of the Lutheran family are
continuing a critical, often painful engagement with questions of theology and, to use the current expression, denominational identity. The
more positive, less anxiety-ridden outlook will serve the churches of

*Mr. Koenig is a staff member of the Division for Professional Leadership
of the Lutheran Church in America and editor of* Partners, *a professional
church workers' magazine of the LCA.*

the Augsburg Confession well at such a moment. The present period may result in a Lutheranism which, though unable to achieve unity of organization, will be better shaped to serve both the larger church community and the world.

The Question of Lutheran Union

Ten years ago Lutherans were still riding the surge produced by the unprecedented institutional revival of the '50s. Although there were warning signs that the lines on the graphs would not continue upward forever, few anticipated either the suddenness with which the situations would change or the shifts in consciousness and morale which would accompany the change. Not only had the churches grown to nearly 9 million souls (if the smaller denominations are taken into account), but Lutheranism appeared finally to have achieved some genuine breakthroughs with respect to problems that had long frustrated its life in North America. The most important of these had to do with the question of Lutheran union—the dream of one, united Lutheran church in the U.S.

Given the political realities that obtained in Europe from the Reformation on, there was virtually no possibility for Lutherans of Scandinavia, Germany and other countries to unite their several national or territorial churches in one body or, indeed, even to consider the matter seriously. In America it was different. Untrammeled by any ties with the state and later animated by a powerful revival of Lutheran confessionalism, the Germans, Swedes, Norwegians, Danes, Finns and other national groupings were allowed the hope that, on this side of the Atlantic at least, a common theological confession might result in a common structure under which all Lutherans might share the fellowship of the gospel.

Now that era of hope is over. In a historic consultation at Overland Park, Kansas, in September 1977, mission specialists and top executives of the three largest U.S. Lutheran denominations candidly admitted that "there is no meaningful union of Lutheran churches in the United States in prospect." (A Canadian union may be on the horizon. Hence the careful reference to the United States in the forecast.)

With the adoption of the Overland Park statement, representatives of the majority of American Lutheranism formally closed what historian Richard C. Wolf has described as their period of "increasing unity and increasing union" without, so it appears, giving any evidence of the pain that must have been felt. Later the Association of Evangelical Lutheran Churches—Lutheranism's newest church body, born out of a schism in the Lutheran Church–Missouri Synod—would issue a poignant call for Lutherans to press on toward that earlier goal. The limp reaction which the call received serves only to corroborate the judgment reached at Overland Park. For the time being at least, Lutherans seem resigned to circumstances that have put further attempts at organic union on hold.

The somewhat offhand abandonment of such a noble objective ought not to be allowed to obscure the enduring results which earlier Lutheran efforts at union did achieve. Given the contentiousness for which Lutherans are deservedly notorious, the accomplishments are the more remarkable. Within a short span of some six years, from 1960 to 1966, a great deal of the organizational fragmentation afflicting Lutherans in America was overcome. Two new national church bodies, the American Lutheran Church (ALC) and the Lutheran Church in America (LCA), were formed where eight had existed before. With the creation of the Lutheran Council in the U.S.A. (LCUSA) in 1966, even the Lutheran Church–Missouri Synod (LCMS), historically the most isolationist of the major Lutheran bodies, became involved. Organization of the council meant that more than 90 per cent of American Lutherans were linked in at least a limited way for theological study, consultation and certain types of ministry. Many assumed that the council would prove a way station to further Lutheran mergers that would realize the goal of one Lutheran Church in the United States.

Union for Lutherans has proved as elusive as it has for the Arabs, leaving Lutheranism a contender for the distinction of being the most divided major denominational family in American Protestantism. It is common knowledge that the terminus declared by the Overland Park meeting came chiefly as the result of the Missouri Synod's de facto withdrawal from further involvement with other Lutherans. Because of that and for reasons of its own, the ALC has signaled a reluctance to pursue further moves toward any Lutheran merger at the moment, despite mounting pressure from the LCA and AELC. Apparently, even the ALC-LCA union predicted by former ALC president Kent Knutson (whose tragic death in 1973 is still keenly felt) is by no means certain. For the time being and foreseeable future, Lutherans seem to be frozen in denominational patterns which they have neither strength nor vision to overcome.

Missouri's retreat from participation with its sister churches in the quest for Lutheran union came as a result of the highly publicized reaction within its circles against the increasingly moderate course the Synod pursued until 1969. The Synod's spectacular performance in publicly disemboweling itself before the full gaze of the media makes it easy to misconstrue its experience. Ostensibly the schism which produced the Association of Evangelical Lutheran Churches, now numbering about 112,000 members in 265 parishes across the country, resulted from irreconcilable positions on the nature and authority of the Bible.

Viewing it another way, as many observers did, the controversy between moderates and conservatives in the LCMS was a struggle over what it means to be Lutheran. That is to say, in newer terminology borrowed from the social sciences, the Missouri Synod's civil war was a particularly wrenching example of Lutheranism's search for identity in a culture as different from the 16th century as an astrolabe is from a computer.

The Rediscovery of Identity

The notion of "identity" is somewhat slippery. To the LCMS, Lutheran identity is simply equivalent to the doctrinal content of the historic confessions, but other Lutherans regard such an assessment as too simplistic. For a confessional family which views justification by God's grace through faith alone as the heart of the gospel, there is no doubt that the doctrinal component in the question of identity will be of special significance. As LCA theologian Philip Hefner has written, "[No] Lutheran church to date has formulated a theological conceptuality which allows for the *sola fide* to stand alongside of a plurality of other centers of truth."

But there are ways by which identity can be called into question other than by formal declension from the confessions. This reality is what worries ALC historian E. Clifford Nelson. Nelson learned that "large numbers of Lutherans in all age groups and all social and economic strata have difficulty in articulating the central thrust of Christianity (the doctrine of justification)." His assertion was based on research done by the ALC's Merton Strommen on the actual beliefs of midwest Lutherans of all denominations. Nelson warns: "If it is true that justification is 'the article of a standing and falling church' . . ., the Lutheran churches in America are in no little spiritual danger." A similar deterioration was discovered by LCA seminary professors Robert Jenson and Eric Gritsch after measuring Lutherans against the same standard. Jenson and Gritsch conclude:

> The Lutheran denominations live—or do not live—by the same mixture of fundamentalism, helplessness before every wind of doctrine, tag-ends of denominational tradition, and occasional saving theological and proclamatory miracles as do the other American denominations.

So much for any latent Lutheran triumphalism. Seldom has a theological tradition been turned on itself with sharper or more unsparing candor.

But to interpret such warnings and excoriations as a summons to a new type of Lutheran chauvinism would be a serious mistake. Rather, they are evidence of unrest with current forms of church life in the interests of integrity, renewal and the rediscovery of identity in the midst of a pitilessly secular culture. For some Lutherans, however, the task of rediscovering an identity lies not in concentrating on what Lutheranism was but on bringing Reformation theology into a more creative contact with the scientific world view and changed conceptions of reality, whatever the risk to the tradition. A larger group, the considerable number of excellent biblical scholars which the Lutheran churches have produced, are busy with research that has yet to be integrated satisfactorily with familiar Lutheran motifs.

Meanwhile, the folks in the pew have been doing some questioning of their own. Lutheran congregations are supposedly noted for their theological alertness and denominational loyalty. Yet many a congregation reflects the impact of the startling rise of American evangelicalism and the charismatic movement. Some of the foremost figures of the latter phenomenon remain on the clergy rolls of Lutheran churches. One has to be taken aback at the sight of 10,000 rank-and-file Lutherans with arms upraised, speaking in tongues at a mass gathering; but scenes such as this are taking place on an annual basis. Many other Lutherans report that they have been "born again" along lines prescribed by leading evangelical exponents.

How many of the faithful have been touched by the new pietism is hard to say. Some Lutheran leaders believe that a lot of the folks aren't telling their pastor what is going on—a singular departure from the traditional relationship between pastors and people. Not all the Lutherans who disappear from the rolls, so it seems, enter the ranks of the unchurched. The perennial struggle between more churchly forms of piety and those that accentuate personal experience—a conflict which Lutherans have engaged in throughout their history—continues.

'Evangelical Catholicity'

As Lutherans look ahead to the observance of the 400th anniversary of the Book of Concord (the collection of doctrinal statements first published as a unit in 1580), the variety of ways with which they are choosing to deal with their confessional tradition would seem to reduce any talk about Lutheran identity to an exercise in fancy.

Such a conclusion, it seems to me, would be off the mark in two ways. First, while the doctrinal element is indispensable, the thing called Lutheranism includes more than a list of approved teachings The Lutheran tradition expresses itself also as an ambience, culture, style, point of view, much of it ethnic in origin but much of it the creation of the justification-by-faith doctrine in its encounter with the lands and the people where Lutheranism took root. It is therefore possible to detect a Lutheran identity despite divergences in the forms in which the doctrinal tradition is cast.

Second, though no theological giant is presently on the scene to help them sift and make creative use of their theological tradition (even the great Luther renaissance that so nourished the previous generation of church people has run its course), the majority of Lutherans seem to be moving, however haltingly, toward a fresh conception of what it means to be Lutheran. The new awareness is being spoken of as "evangelical catholicity," a term first made popular by the great Swedish Lutheran Archbishop Nathan Söderblom (d. 1931). The "ability to experience one's self as something that has continuity and sameness," as Erik Erikson defines identity, does not doom an individual or a theological tradition to rigidity. To be alive and to participate in history means to change.

While attempting to maintain vital contact with the primacy and graciousness of grace ("evangelical"), Lutherans more and more, it seems to me, want that evangelical core to be blended with the life of the wider church and the world ("catholic"). Much of this development is occurring among Lutherans almost intuitively as the churches pursue their mission and ministry from day to day amid a pluralism that tempers even the most determined absolutist.

Social Concern, Evangelism, Ecumenism

The '60s changed many things, including the consciences of Lutherans. The social issues debated with such passion in that decade provoked an impressive set of statements by national assemblies of Lutherans which had varying but undeniable influence on the congregations. It is widely anticipated that one of the chief concerns of Lutherans in the immediate future will be questions of family life and patterns of sexual behavior. While some Lutheran bodies, notably the Missouri Synod, continue to hold the line against the ordination of women to the ministry, both the ALC and LCA and some of the smaller churches have adopted changes which permit women's ordination. The number of women in preparation for the ministry forecasts a sharply revised ratio of males to females in the near future. Women are gradually beginning to assume positions in the decision-making processes of the churches. While other Americans may be losing interest, Lutherans continue attempts at racial and economic justice and carry on ministries to the poor, especially the hungry. Viewed in the light of Lutheranism's alleged quietism, these changes in attitude and commitment to the questions of social justice are noteworthy.

The same applies to the task of evangelism or, as the current emphasis is being called in some of the churches, "evangelical outreach." Practically all Lutheran groups are stressing some kind of evangelistic program, with only modest success in reaching lapsed and unchurched neighbors. Lutherans will never duplicate the effectiveness of the Southern Baptists in the creation of new Christians—first, because they are not good at it, and second, for the obvious reason that their theology is tilted against getting people to make a "decision for Christ." The chief beneficiaries of the new commitment to outreach will be Lutherans. The introduction of new members will help break down vestiges of Lutheran insularity left over from the past, forming Lutheran churches into the more inclusive fellowships that the Overland Park consultation said their confessions intend them to be.

A similar kind of secondary benefit is noticeable as a spin-off from the ecumenical activity in which Lutherans engage on both the local and national levels. Since 1963, representatives of Lutheran churches have conducted an ambitious series of conversations with counterparts from Reformed bodies (twice), the Roman Catholic Church, the Orthodox churches, the Episcopal Church and the United Methodist Church. Conversations with Jews are also being held on a regular basis. Revived attention to the Holocaust has made Lutherans more sensitive than ever to the necessity for deepening ties between their people and Jews.

The official report from LCUSA on the results of the various dialogues gives the impression that the commissioners were chagrined at the minimal response their efforts seemed to have evoked. The conclusion is unwarranted. Lutherans, like most Christians, appear to be incurably parochial, but they are not antiecumenical. The Lutherans who hold to the conviction that theirs is "the [only?] true visible church of God on earth" are a curiosity to their fellows. Most striking are the changes in attitude toward Roman Catholics. It has been proposed that the quadricentennial of the Book of Concord should be highlighted by intensive discussions and encounters with Roman Catholics on both the official and parish levels.

A Common Book of Worship

Social concern, evangelism and ecumenism are three areas in which Lutherans are exhibiting or experiencing a more "catholic" church life under an evangelical commitment. Perhaps the clearest expression of the new consciousness Lutherans are developing is to be found in the *Lutheran Book of Worship*, the new hymnal and service book which has recently appeared for use by congregations in both the U.S. and Canada. Ironically, it was the Missouri Synod which in 1965, at the height of its brief experiment with meaningful inter-Lutheran cooperation, put forth the proposal that a common hymnal be published for use by all Lutherans in North America. A common book of worship has been the cherished hope of Lutherans ever since Henry Melchior Muhlenberg, the patriarch of American Lutheranism, produced the first one in 1748.

In order to grasp the radicality of Missouri's proposal, the non-Lutheran will have to understand that for the majority of Lutheran laypeople, the hymnal, not excluding its color, was and is an important key to what branch of Lutheranism they belong to, whether Missouri and its satellites (blue) or the more moderate churches such as the LCA or ALC (red). More significantly, the hymnal is a principal means by which Lutherans develop whatever "feel" they come to possess of what it means to be Lutheran. The way the church worships not only expresses but informs belief.

The latter observation, true of any religious tradition, is of peculiar importance for Lutherans, who might be said to constitute the largest ethnic bloc in Protestantism—the terminal moraine, as it were, of the massive North European immigrations of the 19th century. There were Lutherans in America prior to the American Revolution, of course, but the largest number arrived in the middle of the next century—so many, in fact, that had the Lutheran churches been able to retain them all, Lutherans would easily make up the second largest Christian communion in America. For Lutheran immigrants and the churches they founded, Lutheran identity and ethnicity became inextricably bound together. Truth to tell, the ethnic heritage, now fast fading, has provided, up to the present time, a good deal of the capital from which Lutheranism lived, as the names on congregational and clergy rosters will attest. But now that the immigrant boats have stopped coming, as LCA theologian William Lazareth says, Lutherans have arrived at a moment in their history when their sense of commonality will have to be fed more from other sources—one of the most important being public worship.

Lutherans may therefore be more blessed than they realize in giving everyone a chance to "go green" (the color of the new *Lutheran Book of Worship*). Despite its flaws, the new book can serve to bring them together, perhaps even re-ignite the desire for one Lutheran church, while at the same time providing them a means to express their faith in more contemporary—and more catholic—terms. While retaining the traditional Lutheran emphases on the preached Word and the gospel as the forgiveness of sins, the new liturgy presents these elements in more pronounced coordination with the sacraments of holy baptism and the Lord's Supper in the context of the congregation as the active community of faith.

The new hymnal is both a product of the '60s and an ecclesiastical compromise, which is to say that it is by no means of uniform excellence or unfailing delight. Not even the able Inter-Lutheran Commission on Worship, which labored so diligently for over a decade to bring the project to fruition, would deny its shortcomings. Yet the hymnal's obvious advantage over present worship resources is instantly recognizable. The collection of hymns reflects a broader range of concerns than Lutherans have traditionally voiced in their worship, and with better music and improved texts. The various liturgies, particularly that of the holy communion, call for wider congregational participation and set forth more plainly the nature of the congregation as the gathered people of God.

That is partly what I mean by catholicity. The neoisolationist Missouri Synod was officially quite correct, therefore, no matter how churlish, in refusing to endorse the book which it helped so greatly to produce. The *Lutheran Book of Worship* is sure to have a profound influence in the development of that evangelical catholicity in which the majority of Lutherans in America are coming to recognize themselves.

A Spiritual Challenge

Using a frightening image, Malcolm Muggeridge avows that the great traditions of Christendom are in a state of visible "decomposition." Lutheranism may be a denominational family in transformation, but it is not a church decomposing. The old ethnic heritage is eroding, and with it a great deal of what Lutheranism was. There is a note of sadness—and peril—in that observation, but like other pilgrim people of God, Lutherans cannot look back, nor should they care to.

In place of the former ethnic and confessional exclusiveness, something new is emerging. Lutherans are re-forming themselves around an identity in which they will live as intentional Christians both evangelical and catholic. That process calls for hard theological work and dedicated churchmanship on the part of all the people of God who call themselves Lutheran Christians if they are to make the most creative use of the moment. The Reformation heritage summons Lutherans to make new excursions into the mystery and surprise of God's grace in order that they might re-present it compellingly in today's world.

Ultimately the principal challenge for this faith community is spiritual; for churches, like individuals, are not saved or motivated by the latest managerial techniques or group dynamics—or even by episcopal figures! The rediscovery of identity is a spiritual event which opens the future. Given the direction of Western culture, Lutherans will not find evangelical catholicity a sure-fire formula for success, but the clearer and more committed Lutherans become in their self-understanding, the less threatened their future will be. You can handle a great number of problems when you know who you are.

6

The Holiness and Pentecostal Churches: Emerging from Cultural Isolation

Holiness and Pentecostal folk are busily engaged in creating all those agencies and patterns of church life that their maverick forebears found too confining.

DONALD W. DAYTON

The Holiness and Pentecostal churches, the youngest of the ecclesiastical families examined in this book, are often overlooked and sometimes avoided by their elder brothers and sisters in Christendom. Notice, however, is especially appropriate now because the rest of this century will see the culmination of a continuing process as these churches emerge from sectarian isolation into broader American church life as vigorous ecclesiastical traditions.

Distinguishing the Families

No single article can easily discern the dynamic and project the future of this constellation of churches. Holiness churches, largely a product of the Methodist tradition, follow those who in the ethos of the 19th century camp meeting preserved a variation of the Wesleyan doctrine of "Christian perfection," emphasizing a postconversion experience of "entire sanctification." Distinctly "Holiness" churches do not speak in tongues; they are among the sharpest critics of the practice. Pentecostal churches teach that Pentecost is a repeatable experience available to Christians in all ages and usually that its appropriation is

---

Mr. Dayton is librarian and assistant professor of historical theology at Northern Baptist Theological Seminary in Lombard, Illinois.

"evidenced" by speaking in tongues. Something of the difference may be seen in the caricature that Holiness churches emphasize the "graces" or "fruits" of the Spirit while Pentecostal churches place greater weight on the "gifts" of the Spirit, especially "divine healing" and glossolalia.

Yet there is an appropriateness in treating the two traditions together. Historians increasingly agree that Pentecostalism emerged at the turn of the century largely from a radical wing of the Holiness movement emphasizing "divine healing" and the imminent return of Christ. At that time Holiness leaders were attempting to interpret Pentecost as an experience of "entire sanctification" until the emergence of tongues-speaking Pentecostalism prompted them to purge features that might cause confusion. The lines are also blurred by large segments of Pentecostalism (especially in the south and among blacks) that are also "Holiness" in that they teach "three works of grace"—conversion, entire sanctification and a "baptism in the Spirit" with speaking in tongues. And Holiness and Pentecostal churches share much in ethos, hymnody and social/cultural experience.

This wing of Christendom encompasses incredible diversity. Both branches were movements before the formation of denominations. Thus the Holiness family includes pockets of influence within Methodism (many camp meetings and some educational institutions), pre–Civil War perfectionist antislavery radicals like the Wesleyans and Free Methodists, such products of the National Camp Meeting Association as the Church of the Nazarene and the Pilgrim Holiness Church, social-service movements like the Salvation Army, a synthesis of Holiness theology and a Campbellite-like ecclesiology in the Church of God (Anderson, Indiana), as well as a host of smaller bodies.

Pentecostalism is even more diverse, especially ethnically and theologically. Pentecostals range from the most developed Assemblies of God churches (increasingly taking on the shape of wider Protestant church life) through southern Holiness-Pentecostal churches, the intensely sectarian "Jesus only" unitarian Pentecostals, and large black and ethnic churches, to the uncharacteristic extremes of Appalachian "snake-handlers," all too often the only public image of "holy rollers."

I will grossly oversimplify this complexity by speaking primarily of three broad groups: (1) the largely white Holiness churches, especially those in the Christian Holiness Association (CHA); (2) the white Pentecostal churches in the Pentecostal Fellowship of North America (PFNA); and (3) a more diffuse grouping of ethnic Pentecostal churches dominated by black Pentecostalism.

Growth and Vigor

We can only estimate the extent of these churches. No one knows the size of the Church of God in Christ, the largest black Pentecostal church. Guesses range from a very conservative half-million members to 2 or 3 million. The CHA claims to represent a total membership of perhaps 2 million, while American Pentecostalism would probably exceed twice that figure.

But such numbers do not tell the whole story. Until surpassed by the Southern Baptists, the Methodists were the dominant religious body in America, at a membership of about 10 million. The United Methodist Church, however, now lists a Sunday school enrollment of only half its membership, and on a given Sunday has only about a third of its membership in church. By contrast, the Church of the Nazarene claims a Sunday school enrollment double its half-million membership and attendance larger than membership totals. The Wesleyan Church often has double its membership in attendance. This suggests that on a given Sunday roughly as many people are in Holiness churches as in United Methodist churches.

Thus the picture of Holiness and Pentecostal churches as they enter the 1980s is largely one of youth and vigor. These new churches are flexing their muscles as they enter maturity riding the crest of fantastic growth. The *1977 Yearbook of American and Canadian Churches* identified the Salvation Army as the fastest-growing religious body in America. The Church of the Nazarene has nearly tripled in size since 1940, while the Assemblies of God have more than quadrupled and the Church of God (Cleveland, Tennessee) has more than quintupled. According to National Council of Churches statistics (which appear not to include Pentecostal churches), five of the top eight denominations in per capita giving are Holiness bodies. Free Methodists, for example, average about four times the giving of United Methodists, Lutherans or Episcopalians.

At the same time, such growth is now leveling off. Thus the Nazarenes grew only 1.4 per cent in this country in 1977 and dropped by more than 20,000 in Sunday school enrollment. Similar patterns obtain among Pentecostals. This leveling off is correlated with other important changes. Holiness and Pentecostal folk are busily engaged in creating all those agencies and patterns of church life that their maverick forebears found too confining. Within a variety of polities, the weight of authority is being shifted away from congregations toward denominational structures. Thus the most heated debates in recent General Councils of the Assemblies of God have centered on efforts to qualify local sovereignty in favor of district and national councils.

One ominous result of this bureaucratization is that all sorts of decisions are being made primarily on the basis of political and institutional requirements without the theological and ecclesiastical controls that exist in other contexts. Thus one problem facing these churches in the next couple of decades will be to find ways to open up the decision-making processes to responsible theological reflection and wider accountability. This task will not be easy—to judge, for example, by the resistance met recently in the Assemblies of God by various "sunshine" resolutions designed to open up administration in the wake of charges about high-level financial indiscretions.

Maturing Scholarship

One of the most significant facts about both the Holiness and Pentecostal churches is the rapid and recent growth of seminary education. Though some Holiness seminaries go back further (especially Asbury Theological Seminary and Anderson School of Theology), the late 1940s saw the beginnings of their real growth and the founding of the Nazarene Theological Seminary and Western Evangelical Seminary. The Pentecostals are just now entering the field. The first Pentecostal seminary was founded by blacks—the C. H. Mason Theological Seminary in Atlanta's Interdenominational Theological Center. The Assemblies of God have now launched in their Springfield, Missouri, headquarters a graduate school of theology. And to a certain extent, one must see in this line such recent efforts as the more technically "charismatic" or "neo-Pentecostal" Melodyland School of Theology and the projected school of theology at Pat Robertson's CBN University (of the "700 Club") in view of their tendency to build faculties on a flowering of scholarship within the Assemblies of God. And mirroring its founder's evolution out of the Holiness wing of Pentecostalism into Methodism is the school of theology at Oral Roberts University.

Such developments have naturally led to a burst of scholarly and theological activity. The Wesleyan Theological Society (WTS), representing the Holiness churches, is now 15 years old and claims a thousand members. A smaller but initially more vigorous Society for Pentecostal Studies (SPS) was founded in 1970. The increasing sophistication of theological work in these traditions may be traced in emerging journals: the *Wesleyan Theological Journal* (edited by Lee Haines of Marion College), now in its 14th year; *Spirit: A Journal of Issues Incident to Black Pentecostalism* (edited by James Tinney of Howard University), now in its second volume; and the new SPS journal *Pneuma* (edited by William Menzies of Evangel College).

The influence of this maturing scholarship is being felt outside the denominations involved. Mainstream churches and educational institutions have had in the past a disproportionate share of leaders who were reared in Holiness and Pentecostal contexts but whose theological development led them into other ecclesiastical fields of service. With the maturation of their own churches, more of these scholars are maintaining their identification with Holiness and Pentecostal bodies. Perhaps the greatest symbol of this trend for the present generation has been Timothy Smith, who in addition to his work at Johns Hopkins University has continued to pastor Nazarene churches and on occasion to preach "special meetings." This tendency is especially prominent among Pentecostals, who have begun to move into the evangelical seminaries. Thus text critic Gordon Fee of the Assemblies of God teaches New Testament at Gordon-Conwell, and several Pentecostals serve Fuller Seminary. Perhaps more interesting are such figures in the ecumenical centers. Union Theological Seminary (New York) now has Old Testament scholar Jerry Sheppard of the Assemblies of God and black homiletician James Forbes of the United Holy Church of America.

Theological Ferment

This maturing scholarship is growing in impact, and the strains of theological reformulation are already being felt. Both traditions suffer from a reductionism in which distinctive teachings have been elevated out of proportion. Part of the theological problem faced by each is to recover perspective and balance. The Pentecostal teachings have been more easily translated into other contexts, as the rise of the charismatic movement indicates, and the most creative Pentecostal theology is taking place in that dialogue. Holiness doctrines present a greater problem of reinterpretation, and recent years have seen a variety of theological methods applied to the task. Really persuasive restatements have not yet emerged. Probably most influential for a new generation of Holiness scholars has been the work of Nazarene theologian Mildred Bangs Wynkoop, especially her book *A Theology of Love: The Dynamic of Wesleyanism* (Beacon Hill, 1972).

The most explosive issue in Holiness thought today is being fought out primarily in the Church of the Nazarene. Increasing historical sophistication has revealed the discontinuities between classical Wesleyanism and late 19th century Holiness thought in which the doctrine of "entire sanctification" was expounded from the accounts of Pentecost in the Book of Acts. This doctrine of "Pentecostal sanctification" not only has been shown to have shaky exegetical foundations but appears also to have been repudiated by Wesley. This tension forces Nazarene theologians into two camps—those wishing to reaffirm classical Wesleyanism and those defending the 19th century developments. Such discussions are tremendously threatening. They not only challenge the consensus of several decades but also suggest the historical conditioning of Holiness theology, raise questions about the varieties of theologies in the New Testament, and focus issues about the historical and theological relationships between Holiness and Pentecostal traditions.

Among white Pentecostals the pressure comes from the charismatics, who are shedding certain classical Pentecostal doctrines, particularly "the baptism of the Holy Spirit" and its being "evidenced" by speaking in tongues. The most sophisticated debates center on the hermeneutical problem of how "historical precedent" determines doctrine in the case of the narratives in Acts. The controversies around the "evidence doctrine" are not about the validity of "tongues" as such, but only about the experience as the necessary evidence of having received the baptism. Ultimately, classical Pentecostals will have to follow the charismatics in discarding some of these claims, but the process will be slow because these teachings have been so central to identity that most classical Pentecostals are unable to see what might lie beyond them.

For black Pentecostals the theological issues are often different. Their theology is more fluid and less rigidly committed to the formulations agitating white Pentecostals. More important, however, at least for the theological avant-garde, is the fact that black Pentecostals identify as much with the black church experience as with white Pentecostals. Some interesting developments are taking place at C. H. Mason Seminary in Atlanta, where certain themes of liberation theology are being incorporated into Pentecostal thought.

Such ferment signals an emerging theological pluralism also evidenced by the rise of a number of irreverent "Young Turk" journals. The most spritely is *Agora*, originating in the Assemblies of God but broadening into a "magazine of Pentecostal opinion." *Agora*'s agenda includes "promoting an intellectual tradition," building bridges with charismatics, and articulating a prophetic word on social issues. The shock to the Pentecostal establishment is indicated by the fact that the General Council of the Assemblies of God voted to revoke the ministerial credentials of the editors before thinking better of it and backing away.

Several Holiness denominations have similar journals. The *Listening Post* pursues "renewal" and related issues within the Free Methodist Church. *Colloquium* explores such issues as race, urban ministry and the role of women in the Church of God (Anderson, Indiana). A common strategy of these journals is revealed in the name of the *Epworth Pulpit*, centered in the Nazarene seminary but aspiring to broader Holiness impact. The "Epworth Pulpit" was the tomb of John Wesley's father from which the son preached in the churchyard when locked out of the parish church in which he had been reared. Today's editors seek to speak to the modern Holiness movement from the more socially committed positions of the forebears.

Fundamentalist Forces

The meaning of all this is not yet clear, but the older Holiness traditions may indicate what lies ahead for both traditions. One analysis a few years ago from the right wing identified three major tendencies among Holiness churches: a dominant push toward acculturation, called into question from two sides—a young, theologically innovative and socially aware minority on one side and those attempting to hold to the old Holiness ways on the other. The latter tendency is already well established. Since World War II bits and pieces of the Holiness bodies have been pulling off to form the "conservative" Holiness movement committed to resisting cultural accommodation by holding on to the ethos of the camp meeting and the taboos against television, wedding rings and so forth.

I would suggest that the future of Holiness and Pentecostal churches will take shape as issues are fought out along four major axes. One of the basic questions facing these churches is whether they will align themselves with fundamentalism. Both traditions began to reach beyond an earlier sectarianism just as the post–World War II "postfundamentalist evangelical" coalition was beginning to emerge. Founders of the National Association of Evangelicals (NAE) sought to broaden their base just as the Holiness and Pentecostal churches were reaching for wider acceptance. The impact of this relationship was profound. In the wake of the founding of the NAE, the Pentecostal Fellowship of North America was set up along similar lines, and the Christian Holiness Association was restructured to match. The PFNA, and to a lesser extent the CHA, adopted the NAE statement of faith, inserting in each case an additional article on distinctive themes. The Wesleyan Theological Society and the Society for Pentecostal Studies were successively founded in imitation of the Evangelical Theological Society. The key issue for the fundamentalists was the inerrancy of the Scriptures, and one may trace under NAE and ETS influence a rush to beef up Holiness and Pentecostal statements on Scripture. In short, as one Pentecostal historian puts it privately, large segments of the Holiness and Pentecostal movements were "captured" by fundamentalism.

Recent years have seen some reassessment of this tendency in the Holiness churches, where its impact was less in the first place.

Churches like the Wesleyan and the Free Methodist were readily incorporated into NAE, but other large segments of the Holiness movement, especially the Salvation Army, the Church of the Nazarene and the Church of God (Anderson, Indiana), have shied away from such identification. The forging of a full Holiness coalition in the CHA has required a blunting of fundamentalist rhetoric and doctrines like premillennialism and the inerrancy of the Scriptures. Both the CHA and the WTS have quietly excised "inerrancy" formulations over the past decade or so, and the future probably lies with the Nazarenes, whose leaders and scholars describe themselves as "conservative" and say they are as distant from the fundamentalist "Battle for the Bible" as from the dominant schools of biblical criticism. At any rate, most Holiness schools tolerate restrained forms of biblical criticism and modern theology as yet unacceptable among "evangelicals."

The situation is different among white Pentecostals, whose identification with fundamentalism is much stronger. Despite blasts from *Agora*, the Assemblies of God appear to be moving toward the official adoption of a tight formulation of "biblical inerrancy." Church leaders have begun quietly to purge faculties of those with broader sympathies. Though complicated with political battles of another sort, such issues were also at the root of the recent struggles at Melodyland School of Theology that led to a split in which many of the noninerrantists went into exile.

Black Pentecostalism is another story. Largely excluded from the PFNA when the whites were joining the NAE, and more likely to find solidarity with the other black churches than with the white Pentecostals or evangelicals, these churches are much less tempted by a fundamentalist identity. Ironically, earlier patterns of exclusion and oppression have left the black and ethnic Pentecostal churches in the place of providing more creative theological leadership.

The Charismatic Movement

A second force shaping both Holiness and Pentecostal churches is the charismatic movement. There is a spiritual vulnerability produced by third- and fourth-generation ambivalence toward ecstatic religious experience in traditions trained to expect it. I am told that perhaps only 50 per cent of the youngest generations of Pentecostals cultivate the distinguishing mark of speaking in tongues. And in many Holiness churches it is difficult to find contemporary preaching of "entire sanctification." Under such circumstances the dynamic of the charismatic movement is a special threat particularly for the Pentecostals, who earlier felt compelled to withdraw from traditional churches. To grant the validity of the charismatic movement undercuts their very rationale for existence.

One of the most creative forces, however, in building bridges between classical Pentecostals and charismatics has been historian and church leader H. Vinson Synan of the Pentecostal Holiness Church. Synan goes so far as to suggest occasionally that the primary purpose of classical Pentecostal churches in the providence of God was to preserve and mediate the Pentecostal teachings to the rest of Christendom. He therefore relates openly to the charismatic tradition, participates in Vatican dialogues with the Pentecostals, and so forth.

Much of the struggle has been focused in the Assemblies of God. Mavericks in the denomination broke through the anticharismatic taboos to build large and powerful churches by incorporating the charismatic impulse. These churches are creating new relationships between Pentecostals and charismatics and have drawn together in a distinct party that finds its voice in *Restoration* magazine. Such forces toward greater openness were given additional impetus recently when church leaders were caught off guard by the passing of a General Council resolution calling for more interaction in the future.

The issues are different for the Holiness bodies, which see the charismatic movement as only the most recent manifestation of an old enemy, Pentecostalism. Holiness teaching usually denies flatly the existence of glossolalia understood as ecstatic utterance. Some Holiness churches, notably the Church of the Nazarene and the Wesleyan Church, have seen high-level administrative rulings against the charismatic movement whose enforcement means virtual excommunication for those professing charismatic experience. On the other side has been the founding in 1977 at the large charismatic gathering in Kansas City of a Wesleyan Holiness Charismatic Fellowship. This group had its first convention in January 1979. The beginnings were small, mostly a handful of disspirited ex-Nazarenes, but the mere existence of this group represents a major challenge and a nagging reminder of unresolved issues.

Social Witness

To analyze and project the response to social questions during the rest of this century is a difficult task filled with irony—but such response is a third major issue that will shape the future of these churches. I would resist an analysis of the social impact of the Holiness and Pentecostal churches based solely on the styles of social witness that have dominated the major denominations in the past two decades. One could argue that these churches have been at their best socially, at least historically, in dealing directly with the radical dissolution of personal and family life under the pressures of oppression, personal vice, and the like. Still today the Pentecostals often have better success in dealing with problems of drug addiction and alcoholism through conversion and spiritual discipline than the supposedly more sophisticated programs launched by the government and various social agencies. And one should not overlook the sustaining power of Pentecostal life and worship in maintaining identity and an alternative vision of reality in the face of racial and economic oppression and deprivation. The irony is that such styles and concerns are less characteristic of these churches as they rush to adopt the styles of the mainstream.

In fact, on many social issues the Holiness and Pentecostal churches have a better historical than current record. Two Holiness bodies, the Wesleyan Methodists and the Free Methodists, were antislavery and radically reformist in the pre–Civil War founding—and into the 20th century maintained very active "reform" committees on the district and national levels. Many turn-of-the-century Holiness bodies, archetypically the Nazarenes and the Pilgrim Holiness Church, understood their special calling to be ministry to the poor, especially those in the inner cities—and this impulse was epitomized in the Salvation Army. And early Pentecostal church life reveals striking illustrations of racial integration—such as whites worshiping in the black Azusa Street (Los Angeles) mission that launched the international Pentecostal revival, or integrated worship services in the south at the height of the Jim Crow era.

Such concerns are, however, largely absent today. The Holiness reform impulse is largely evaporated, and often in the recent identification with the "evangelical" world even repudiated as inappropriate for a properly "spiritual" and "evangelistic" church. Pentecostalism as well is now sharply split along racial lines with little evidence of interaction.

A similar pattern may be discerned with regard to women. A recent NCC study found one-third of all ordained women in this country in Pentecostalism and another one-third in paramilitary groups like the Salvation Army. Had Holiness bodies been properly grouped with the latter, several hundred more women ministers would have been identified and the fact discovered that perhaps 50 per cent of all ordained women are in Holiness churches.

Ironically, the institutionalization of these churches is pulling them in the opposite direction. The Church of the Nazarene, for example, had 20 per cent women ministers at its founding, but only 6 per cent by 1973. And the Salvation Army now less consistently applies its earlier feminist principles. But there is some push among the younger generation—partly in response to the wider feminist currents—to reaffirm and reappropriate this heritage as both a source of role models and a powerful tool in moving today's church leaders.

One reason for the scant interest in social issues in the past few decades is that energies have been more absorbed in issues of personal ethics. The generations that matured in the 1940s, 1950s and even 1960s struggled with a legalistic code of taboos in behavior and dress. These battles are largely over. I was teaching in a Holiness college in the mid-1960s when the prohibition against movies and the theater fell. Now the issue is more likely to be alcohol, and the avant-garde in Holiness and Pentecostal schools are experimenting with restrained social drinking. If such patterns of accommodation continue, Holiness and Pentecostal folk will become even more indistinguishable from other Christians.

A Longing for the 'Good Life'

Probably the greatest temptation facing these churches today is materialism. Marginality, both cultural and economic, has produced its opposite in successive generations—the push toward "respectability," a strong desire to be close to the centers of power, and a longing to enjoy the "good life." One result is the lavish style of conspicuous consumption that dominates such institutions as Oral Roberts University and the Christian Broadcasting Network, where it has become normative doctrine that the pious will prosper. A black Pentecostal bishop recently confided that such currents are the greatest threat his church faces. As Presiding Bishop J. O. Patterson observed at the 1975 "Holy Convocation" of the Church of God in Christ: "God has blessed us to ride in the best automobiles, live in the best homes, wear the finest minks and exclusive clothing, and to have large bank accounts. Our churches are no longer confined to the storefronts, but we are building cathedrals."

Such movement is obviously out of step with the broader church interest in discovering and defining a ministry to and with the poor. Holiness and Pentecostal folk are still fleeing the life of the poor. But as one might expect, there are third- and fourth-generation efforts to reverse this pattern, especially among those coming to maturity in the 1960s and 1970s. Thus Free Methodist Howard Snyder, author of the popular *Problem of Wineskins* (InterVarsity, 1975), has called his church to recover its early ministry of "preaching good news to the poor" via a return to ministry in the central cities. Nazarene Tom Nees recently left a prestigious Washington, D.C., pulpit to found the Community of Hope, with links with the Church of the Saviour and the Sojourners community. His work, especially a project of "Jubilee Housing" that attempts to involve the community in the reclaiming of slum housing, is having wide impact in his denomination. And Ronald J. Sider of Eastern Baptist Theological Seminary, the major force behind the "Chicago Declaration of Evangelical Social Concern" and "Evangelicals for Social Action," holds ministerial credentials in a Holiness denomination, the Brethren in Christ.

I expect such themes and ministries to gain force in Holiness circles in the years ahead. A strong history of social concern and the nagging presence of the Salvation Army help keep these themes more alive than in Pentecostal and evangelical contexts. The 1974 annual convention of the Christian Holiness Association became the largest body to adopt the "Chicago Declaration" as a resolution—despite some concern that such action would admit too much complicity in recent evangelical failures in this area.

Among Pentecostals such themes are more muted—though one must recognize the ministries modeled after the work of David Wilkerson's "Teen Challenge" with urban youth and the role of Pentecostals in the Hispanic community in New York City. The merging of Pentecostal power and enthusiasm with social concern is an exciting possibility, repeatedly promised but not often achieved. Perhaps the most significant work in this direction will come from the blacks and other minority Pentecostals whose history of oppression and alienation has given them a different consciousness that may yet have a significant flowering.

And with the cultural broadening of these churches we may expect a move toward greater political involvement. The Holiness churches have had more of a history in this area, having often been involved with third-party presidential campaigns from the antislavery era to Prohibition. But more recently the typical Holiness and Pentecostal political attitude has been either apolitical or reactionary. Signs of what lie ahead are the increasing involvement of persons from these churches in local and state politics.

There is some statistical oddity (as well as ideological irony) in the fact that President Eisenhower had close ties with the Holiness and pacifist Brethren in Christ, while Richard Nixon's roots were among the Holiness Quakers. George McGovern grew up among the Wesleyan Methodists in the Plains states. His autobiographical statements reflect a deliberate rejection of his background in favor of the "social gospel," but one cannot help wondering about some "Holiness" roots of his "populist egalitarianism"! Senator Gary Hart graduated from a Nazarene college, and U.S Commissioner of Education Ernest Boyer maintains contact with his Brethren in Christ roots. I expect that such examples are harbingers of future Holiness and Pentecostal political figures, especially as recent cultural shifts permit more open identification with such "evangelical" traditions.

Ecumenical Trends

Finally, I would notice some trends in interchurch and ecumenical relations. Here again, the terrain is complex. Though little noted on the outside, Holiness and Pentecostal churches have been involved in numerous mergers in the 20th century. Bodies like the Church of the Nazarene and the Assemblies of God were built up by a complex agglutinative process as various independent ministries, small groups, and local or state associations came together in merger. My own church, the Wesleyan Methodist, absorbed the Reformed Baptists in 1966 before merging with the Pilgrim Holiness Church in 1968 and voting in the merging conference to begin negotiations with the Free Methodists. Those talks have since foundered, but such activity led to some speculation, especially in the 1960s, about the emergence of a sizable new church in the Methodist tradition composed of Holiness bodies. I doubt that now, but I do predict a greater self-consciousness of a Holiness bloc of denominations grouped under the CHA, where there is already very close cooperation in such areas as publishing and preparing Christian education materials.

Internal Pentecostal relationships are more complex—with splits along racial lines, according to commitment to the Holiness doctrine of santification, and even more deeply over the issues of the "Jesus only" doctrines of the Trinity. Such variety even raises questions as to whether it is possible to find a common denominator other than that of speaking in tongues. Perhaps the most creative dialogue among these branches is occurring in the Society for Pentecostal Studies.

Relationships between Holiness and Pentecostal churches are almost nonexistent except in the National Association of Evangelicals, which incorporates some Holiness bodies and a good part of white Pentecostalism. Direct dialogue is confined to the most avant-garde academic circles, where representatives of the WTS and the SPS have been quietly slipping into each other's annual meetings. Something of the suspicion on the Holiness side was revealed recently by controversy that followed the discovery of a "Holiness-Pentecostal" scholar on the WTS membership rolls, or by the fact that a few years ago a WTS motion to send greetings to the fledgling SPS not only failed to gain any votes in support—the discussion was even stricken from the official minutes in embarrassment and confusion! But there is still some hope that even this sibling rivalry may in the distant future find some ecumenical resolution.

Relationships with the rest of the church world will probably move along a variety of trajectories. In some parts of the world, aspects of the Pentecostal movement and the Salvation Army have found it natural to gravitate toward the conciliar movements. In America the context of the fundamentalist-modernist controversy has skewered the identification in the fundamentalist and evangelical direction. We may expect the Salvation Army, the Church of the Nazarene, and the Church of God (Anderson, Indiana) to provide a center of gravity that will continue to pull Holiness identification away from the National Association of Evangelicals into some suspended position between the NAE and the National Council of Churches.

White Pentecostals will continue to find stronger identification with American fundamentalism and evangelicalism, despite the protests of some Pentecostal academics. In the early years of the NAE, the Assemblies of God made a clear choice to follow the lead of figures like Thomas Zimmerman into the NAE by disfellowshiping David DuPlessis, who reached toward the ecumenical movement. Black Pentecostals will find even more of their identity in being a part of the black experience, and the highly sectarian "oneness churches" will remain somewhat isolated for the time being. No uniform pattern emerges, but the variety will be a source of ferment as the Holiness and Pentecostal churches continue to assert themselves and to emerge from isolation to claim a significant place among other churches of Christendom.

7

The Unitarian Universalists:
A Church of Converts

There is evidence that the UUA's very real
stylistic freedom is accompanied by a
homogenous substance of beliefs and values.

ROBERT B. TAPP

For church watchers, the Unitarian Universalist Association (UUA) provides fascination. Formed in 1961 by a merger of Unitarians and Universalists, this relatively new denomination is small (its membership peaked at slightly above 200,000 during the bulge of the '60s); wealthy (43 per cent of its members earn more than $25,000 a year); and highly educated (42 per cent of them have at least a master's degree).

During the decade of the '60s the UUA suffered a net membership loss of 4.4 per cent as compared to population growth. Much of this loss occurred in New England, where Unitarianism and Universalism had their origin; only in Canada did the growth rate exceed the rate of population increase. UU sermons and pamphlets fondly quote Thomas Jefferson's expectation that his young contemporaries would all be Unitarians before they died—a prophecy that was not to be fulfilled. In many ways the pattern of UU membership resembles that of the large mainline denominations. During 1969-74, for instance, giving to local churches increased 28 per cent while allocations by those same churches to the UUA fell by 32 per cent. These fiscal constraints have sharply cut denominational staff and services.

Dr. Tapp is chairperson of the humanities program and professor of humanities and religious studies at the University of Minnesota.

Stylistic Freedom, Homogenous Substance

The most striking fact about the denomination is that nine out of ten of its members are "converts," having grown up religiously somewhere else. Given the lack of membership growth, it is clear that UUA churches are in some sense "revolving doors." Most of the newcomers have left some kind of liberal Protestantism behind. What we do not know is where those who leave go next. My guess is that some have simply lost the need for communal support for their values. This surmise is based on reasonably solid data that members moved into their present value-belief orientations *before* joining the UUA and that their length of time in those churches does not measurably alter beliefs and values. A somewhat parallel explanation is that parents are most active in churches during their children's school years. Before and after that stage in the life cycle, people apparently feel less need for support groups.

In recent years UU spokespersons have described their movement in such phrases as "the fourth faith," "America's real religion" and "religious liberalism." Along with such sectarian labels, however, they have stressed their diversity. In 1975 then-president Robert Nelson West could say: "Some are theists, some nontheists; some consider themselves Christians, others non-Christians." E. M. Wilbur's history of Unitarianism summarizes the movement's thrust as "freedom, reason, toleration." More recently, Sidney Mead has written of "faith in democratic method."

If we are accurately to situate the UUA among America's religions, however, we must distinguish style from substance. The rhetorics I have cited are an important part of Unitarian and Universalist *style*, past and present. There is clearly a pride in being creedless, in having open membership. On the international scene, the UUA forms a major component of the International Association for Religious Freedom, along with European "free Christians," liberal Buddhists and Shintoists from Japan, and liberal Hindus.

We must not assume, however, that religious freedom necessarily generates religious diversity. There is considerable evidence that the UUA's very real stylistic freedom is presently accompanied by a homogenous substance of beliefs and values. Perceptions of diversity are relative, of course, and members are sensitive to nuances that tend to escape outside observers.

A Consensus of Values

Of this present substance, we can speak with some certainty. I conducted a major survey of UUs in 1966 which was partially replicated in 1976. Robert L. Miller surveyed the value orientations of a sizable sample in 1974, and the denominational newspaper conducted a more limited survey in 1978. Certain benchmarks and trends can be noted. In 1966, only 43 per cent of the UUs described their personal religion as "Christian," and this segment had dropped to 26 per cent by 1976. If we turn to the question of nonbelief in personal immortality, the consensus becomes more striking. On value matters (sexual privatism, nondiscrimination, censorship), consensus is almost complete.

The 1976 survey identified ministers, directors of religious education and laypersons. Detailed analyses showed that there were almost no significant variations in the responses of these three groups. This consensus could be interpreted to reflect powerful socializing forces within UU churches or to indicate that the same kinds of persons are attracted to the pews, pulpits and classrooms of this denomination. I am satisfied that this latter is the case, since length of membership does not produce significant changes in responses.

The solidarity between members and professional leadership, coupled with the high degree of value homogeneity, points toward minimal conflict in goal-setting and goal-achieving. These factors also suggest that the intensive theological strife of earlier decades is over.

What do these UUs want from their local churches? Since this question was included in three successive surveys, the rank orderings afford some answers:

Rankings of emphases	1966	1976	1978
religious education	1	2	2
personal development	2	3	3
fellowship among members	3	1	1
social action	4	5	4
public worship	5	4	5

The continuing stress on the religious education of children makes sense: most of the members are new to this church, and to some extent they want their children to have what they, as children, did not have. But as the UU movement shifts "leftward" religiously, its members will more and more become a new "minority group." Like Quakers or Jews, they will feel strong needs to provide defensive islands for their youngsters.

More striking are the shifting responses regarding personal development, fellowship and social action. While the UUs are obviously part of the larger cultural scene and even to some extent share the ups and downs of the American religious scene, they often appear to march to "a different drummer." Their support for social action (measured by the percentage viewing it as "very important") has remained steady. During the '60s, when many denominations were moving *toward* social activism (at a high cost in terms of membership and contributions, as it turned out), the UUs were adding (almost prematurely) an emphasis on "personal development" to their activism. As other denominations retreated from activism to a more pietistic inwardness, the UUs were already feeling disenchantment with encounter, sensitivity and human potential movements. Most dramatically, they now seem to be increasing their emphasis on "fellowship," reflecting a new sort of ingroup solidarity.

This kind of descriptive generalization can sometimes conceal as well as reveal. If we are to assess the uniqueness of the UUs, we need to move to more specific data and to an examination of actual experiences.

A Liberal Agenda

Let me try to describe, empirically, the UUA's social conscience. We can use 1977 evaluations of a number of action areas in order to predict denominational agendas. UUs were asked if each of several issues had, over the past five years, become "more" or "less" important or had remained "the same." Ranking highest in the survey were ecology, criminal-justice reform, mental health, freedom of expression, and Third World development. An expanded list would include family planning, resistance to totalitarianism, and women's liberation. This overall agenda would not differ from those of most liberal Protestant or Jewish groups—except in the high level of consensus, and in the fact that the most important religious goal for UUs is "a community for shared values" (rather than theology or personal growth or social change or experiences of transcendence).

These shared values can have only personal impact until they flow through group channels. The polity of the UUA is intensely congregational. In the phrase of the UUA's best-known social ethicist, James Luther Adams, these churches and this denomination are "voluntary associations." Given the absence of family, ethnic and regional ties, the free coming/staying/going of persons becomes even more salient. The central denomination can *offer* services (religious education and worship materials, the certification of clergy and religious education professionals). But local churches can (and sometimes do) decline the offer. No effective sanctions prevent any local church from calling and ordaining anyone to its ministry.

Denominational power in the most visible sense rests in a well-attended General Assembly that meets annually. The assembly delegates elect a board of trustees, a president (usually a minister), and a moderator (usually a layperson). The assembly can also mandate policies, but actual expenditures must come from the board. This diffusion of powers can and does lead to unusual problems. Some of these will be evident as we turn to the actual business of the UUA in recent years.

Black and Gay Concerns

Black affairs. The Unitarians and Universalists have had a good track record in regard to civil rights (although most of their churches would have to be described as "open" rather than "integrated"). About one-third of all UU clergy went to Selma to march with Martin Luther King. This liberal consensus was sorely tested, however, by the emergence of a black caucus which was then challenged by an integrationist caucus. BAC (the Black Affairs Council) went before the 1968 General Assembly with a "black empowerment" program and a demand for $4 million. BAC termed integration a failure and viewed as "patronizing" any provisions for white representation in the spending of these funds, or any fiscal accountability. BAC was opposed by BAWA (Black and White Action), which also wanted money but wanted an integrated group to spend it for integrating purposes. Here was a classic confrontation that produced the deepest division in decades. Compromise was ruled out by BAC's refusal to participate in any solution that would also fund BAWA.

The delegates voted exclusive funding for BAC—$1 million to be distributed over four years. It remains impossible to assess the relative causal impacts of populism, white guilt, sharp ideological shifts and covert racism in this action. The board voted the first $250,000 to BAC, and those churches that disagreed with the assembly action began reducing their denominational contributions. BAWA, since it was not being funded, was free to make independent solicitations (which BAC could no longer do).

Technically, the long-term commitment was moral rather than binding on future assemblies, and raising and disbursing funds was a board function. Faced with shrinking funds, the board recommended one year later that BAC's additional funding be spread over a four-year (instead of three-year) period. This proposal only intensified the divisions, leading to a delegate walkout at the 1969 assembly. The board voted $200,000 to BAC (which was now selling bonds as an additional support for its programs). In 1970, BAC quit the UUA, the board dropped BAC from the budget, and the assembly recommended voluntary support.

In 1972, a seemingly feasible solution appeared. A fund controlled by a local church gave the board $250,000 for "racial justice," and the money was allocated to BAC *and* BAWA.

The next year, however, a split emerged within BAC (to avoid confusion, we have retained this single designation to describe several actual groups with overlapping memberships). One side feared the emergence of a separate, non-UU religious movement. The parties went to court, and eventually the funds went into receivership. By this time, $630,000 from the UUA and $250,000 from local churches had been raised. In 1977, a distribution plan for unspent assets (about 60 per cent) was implemented.

One result of this experience was a shift in denominational budgeting. There is now a "basis" budget which supports core staff and services and a "grants" budget for innovative purposes. The former is considerably insulated from assembly mandates. The problem, of course, is that this "rational" solution emerged only in the present inflationary period when any reserve for "grants" becomes highly vulnerable.

Gay concerns. A second area of of UU activities relates to gay persons. In some ways this issue resembles that of black affairs. But even "tolerant" persons seem to be only minimally tolerant of their gay neighbors, and UUs are no exception. In 1973 the assembly mandated an Office of Gay Concerns. This action was opposed by the president, and funded by a board vote of only 12-11.

The problem here, we must note, was one of priority rather than of principle. Money problems threatened the UUA's social-action and responsibility commitments; and an assembly mandate, while hard to resist, would probably transform such a fear into reality. There are gay UUs in ministry and seminary, and the moral-theological-principle issue that plagues other denominations simply could not arise within the UUA. The solution here was quicker and less divisive than that achieved with the black issue. There remains a staff position for gay concerns, now incorporated within an Office of Social Responsibility.

Other Agenda Areas

Sexuality. A 1973 multimedia education unit, *About Your Sexuality*, probably still represents the most comprehensive religious education contribution in this field. While the anticipated charges of "pornography" have dwindled, the unit is a landmark in helping young people understand and develop their own styles in sexuality. The UUs' religious marginality lets them view Catholic, Jewish and various Protestant positions as cultural factors rather than as norms; UUs support nonjudgmental terminology ("same-sex," "other-sex").

Marriage/divorce. Eighty per cent of UUs were married in 1966 but only 63 per cent by 1978. This radical shift suggests a very different set of religious needs and functions. While the number of never-married members has remained steady, the widowed have increased and the divorced have increased dramatically. An occasional "divorce ceremony" makes the news, and "singles' clubs" seem to be a standard UU function, but within the present denominational organization there is no way or place to reassess the meaning of this shift within the membership.

Religious education. Beginning in the 1930s, a flood of new curric-

ular materials was produced by Beacon Press. This premerger cooperative venture of Unitarians and Universalists was guided by Sophia
Lyon Fahs. While the philosophical spirit stemmed from John Dewey,
the results somehow satisfied theists as well as humanists. Jesus' birth,
for instance, was presented as an ancient "wonder story" along with
similar accounts about Buddha and Lao-tse. The Jewish creation stories
were set alongside speculations from India, North America and modern
astronomy.

Recent expansions of curricular materials, in addition to the sexuality unit, have moved into situational ethics, cultural anthropology, and
a very open exploration of biblical materials and works of religious
experiences. Unfortunately we do not have long-term evaluations. In
the most narrow sense, these materials, however excellent they might
be, do not seem to have produced "church loyalty" in the two generations of young people who have grown up with them. But that judgment may be premature. These materials may well have exposed large
numbers of children (and their parents) to the ideas and values of religious liberals. And they have clearly pioneered directions for other denominations that share some of the UUs' pedagogical and ideological
goals.

Women. The Universalists hold the honor of having ordained the
first U.S. woman minister (1863). Since then both denominations have
had a slightly better record than other churches in terms of women cler-
ics and leaders. But this is not saying much, and certainly not saying
enough in the current climate of transformed consciousness. The 1977
assembly mandated a Task Force for Women and Religion which may
speed matters.

Publishing. The denomination's Beacon Press has a distinguished
record in service to the intellectual community and in controversial
publishing (from Paul Blanshard's *American Freedom and Catholic
Power* to *The Pentagon Papers*). Beacon's religious, ethical and philosophical nurture has ranged far beyond parochial UU interests. Nevertheless, increasing denominational subsidies have been required,
attempts to sell Beacon Press have been made, and its future now
seems to depend on a much smaller, more strictly denominational
effort.

Death. The American mortuary scene has changed greatly since

Jessica Mitford and Evelyn Waugh opened things up. Memorial societies and simpler funerals, both significant ways of making death a more natural and rational event, are now widespread. Many of these societies began under UU church auspices, and this social change may well be the UUs' religious contribution to the larger society. By 1966, 16 per cent of UUs belonged to such groups. There can be little doubt that these pioneerings were rooted in their rejection of belief in immortality and the alternative liturgical practices that this rejection encouraged among their clergy.

Hymnody and worship. The definition of worship as "the celebration of life" was coined by Chicago's UU minister Von Ogden Vogt (who also guided the construction of a Gothic UU church freighted with symbolism but devoid of any traditional Christian symbols beyond the cruciform floor plan!). Universalists and Unitarians have produced numerous hymnals showing that their problem was with words and ideas rather than singing. Kenneth Patton has been the most prolific UU poet/liturgist/hymn writer in recent years. In the current UU *Hymns for the Celebration of Life*, Luther's "A Mighty Fortress Is Our God" appears with Patton's words "Man is the earth upright and proud." This is certainly not an intended parody, but the theological reversal is clear.

Vincent Silliman, reflecting on the 1963 hymnal in which he played a major role, recently described it as the first major liturgical attempt to treat religions as of equal standing and to view freedom as a major religious value. Nevertheless, though a generation has not yet passed, there are moves to update. Some are suggesting a loose-leaf hymnal and books of readings and services which would permit tailoring by local churches.

Laity and Clergy

Fellowships. I have used the term "church" to denote local units, though many of them prefer the less traditional name "society." In addition—and this may be a UU innovation—40 per cent are called "fellowships," indicating an absence of professional ministerial leadership. Some of these will grow into churches, some are spin-offs from existing churches, and some, despite large budgets and buildings, have no intention of securing regular ministerial leadership. There can be no doubt that the widespread responsibility of laypersons for the full activity of their local groups leavens the UUA in unique ways. Professional ministers have the burden to legitimate themselves by achievements rather than by an ascribed status.

Lay involvement. In comparing the UUA to other denominations, one is struck by the significant roles, paid as well as volunteer, assumed by the laity. This has been the case in religious education, social action, and even theological education. In part this lay leadership reflects the absence of any fixed tradition to be transmitted and defended by "inside" specialists. Liberal religion owes its real growth to the Enlightenment of the 18th century, and the continuers of that movement are found throughout the modern university—not only in theological seminaries. Precisely because the inspirations of modern religious liberalism now come from all quarters, the person in the pulpit is as likely to quote Erich Fromm as Theodore Parker, and more likely to quote either than Augustine or Aquinas. The educated layperson has at least as ready access to and understanding of these new sources as does the minister. This situation could be called one of shared leadership or of intellectual equality between pulpit and pew. The fact remains that it is a salient aspect of the UUA.

Ministry. UU parish ministers are unusually creative and well trained. At the time of merger, in 1961, the UUA spoke of its five theological schools. In the 1975 directory the ministers' school backgrounds included Meadville/Lombard (at the University of Chicago), 17 per cent; Harvard, 15 per cent; Tufts, 13 per cent; Starr King (in Berkeley), 10 per cent; and St. Lawrence, 10 per cent. Since then, both Tufts and St. Lawrence have closed. The figures cited indicate that 35 per cent of the UU ministers were trained in schools *not* funded by the UUA (Harvard, to be sure, is also not funded by the UUA, but there are some long-standing historical associations and loyalties). A significant number of this second group not only were trained in other schools but transferred from other denominations. Given the perennial waiting list of such would-be transfers and the role of Harvard, the funding of denominational schools has been problematic. Harvard has a better record than the denominational schools in the care and feeding of UU scholars—the other rationale for sectarian seminaries.

The UUA is now considering a controversial report urging the full ordination of a second ministry, the ministry of education. There are many highly competent directors of religious education who feel that their ministry deserves equal recognition and status. Many have not attended seminaries or have taken shorter programs when they did. In the absence of a clear-cut theological tradition, however, it is difficult to argue that this alternate route to ministry is inherently inferior.

Theological Climates and Personalities

The areas just sketched illustrate something of UU substance. At several points I have mentioned the value consensus of these contemporary UUs. To the extent that this theological core can be discovered, the particular items of present and future UUA agendas may reveal more coherence than appears on the surface.

The organizational boundaries of the UUA give some indications of this deep substance. On the "right," a few ministers have joint fellowship with the United Church of Christ. On the "left," ministers flow freely back and forth from Ethical Culture. In some cities and states, the UUs are part of Protestant church councils; elsewhere they are not, by a kind of mutual agreement. "UU Christians" meet and publish a journal, as do the "religious humanists." Two generations back, Unitarians and Universalists spoke of "humanism vs. theism"; in the 19th century it was "free religion" and "liberal Christianity," and before that it was "rational liberalism" vs. "transcendentalism."

The enduring affirmation, we would suggest, is the postulated linking of "reason" and "ethics." The problem is with the priorities. No wonder the persons most likely to be quoted from UU pulpits are Alfred North Whitehead, Albert Schweitzer, Martin Buber and Erich Fromm. This dual focus on reason and ethics similarly explains the close attention religious liberals have paid to the sciences—physics as a source for better cosmologies, and the biological and social sciences as a source for both ethics and philosophies of history.

The present and future theological contribution of the UUA is the legitimation of a post-Christian religious humanism. The UUA's late President Paul Carnes embodied this interest. An intellectual with charisma, he did not hesitate to articulate a new religious liberalism. (Upon Carnes's death early in 1979, Robert Senghas became acting president, serving until April 1979, when the board of trustees elected Eugene Pickett to serve until 1981.)

In a broader sense, the present period reflects the convergence of bureaucratic theology and movement theology. The social forces producing the convergence have been the membership growth and turnover since 1945, increased lay involvement, and (perhaps) the absence of theological giants who could prolong the twilight of waning theological fashions. What we have termed "bureaucratic theology" has dominated much of the UUA's theological education and political organization until recently, giving outsiders the impression that the movement was simply a very liberal continuation of Protestant impulses. The visibility of this New England–based faction obscured what was actually emerging.

The most coherent statements of this movement theology were being made by Sophia Fahs (as architect of religious education) and Henry Nelson Wieman (whose recognition by the UUs came largely after his retirement from the University of Chicago). The most sensitive contemporary articulator of this converging theology may turn out to be Joseph L. Fisher. An economist and ecologist, he was UUA moderator for 12 turbulent years (and is now a third-term congressman from Virginia).

A more explicit theologian, with UU identification and salience, is James Luther Adams, who has focused on social ethics and the religious role of voluntary associations. Three UU historians have also made a significant re-examination of the liberal past: Sidney Mead, George Williams and Conrad Wright. Since social activism has been a persisting and widespread UU characteristic, selection of representative figures becomes more difficult. Jack Mendelsohn certainly belongs here, as does Homer Jack. As an innovative theological educator, Robert Kimball must be noted.

Most of the persons of national visibility whom we have named are academics, and such a listing runs the very risk of contributing to the bureaucratic historicism we have decried. Movement history, on the other hand, is being shaped by those whose activities are more local or denominational. The creative thrusts in preaching, worship, music, education, social action and organization which will determine the UUA's future defy brief description or prognostication by their very variety.

What of the future—if we assume that membership shrinkage has stabilized, that fiscal stringencies have been effected, and that a theological convergence toward a religious humanism has not only occurred but has at last received official recognition? A possible pattern is that of the Quakers—smallness, integrity and influence. But the Friends' ethos and ways are difficult and must be learned—a kind of orthopraxy. A pattern of orthodoxy—precise beliefs, precisely enforced—seems even less likely. A third communal pattern could be based on shared values, both explicitly and implicitly religious—an "axiocentrism." This model seems to characterize today's UUs. Many of these shared beliefs and values are by-products of modernity and higher education. To the extent that U.S. culture is now tilting toward conservatism, those who hold such values may come to feel and act like a minority group—which seeks mutual support, recognizable ingroup styles, viable defense patterns.

Two factors suggest that growth might recur along these lines. The 1977-78 Gallup Report showed 37 per cent of the U.S. positive toward UUs and only 10 per cent negative. Not surprisingly, 53 per cent had no opinion. The UUs' most successful slogan in their most recent growth period was "Are you a Unitarian Universalist without knowing it?" That query, raised afresh, might well induce some of the positive viewers to become active churchpersons. Whatever happens, UU-watching will remain fascinating.

8

American Baptists: Bureaucratic and Democratic

The carefully nurtured fiction that the locus of authority in the ABC resides in 6,300 'autonomous' congregations has become increasingly difficult to maintain.

PAUL M. HARRISON

In October 1976, I received a call from a regional executive of the American Baptists. If he were in a church, he would be a bishop's coadjutor, but the Baptists have never determined whether they are a church, sect, denomination, association or convention. My friend was profoundly choked up over a proposal for the reorganization of the national and regional structures of the denomination.

Now every informant, even one in a friendly religious bureaucracy, must maintain anonymity, so he shall simply be identified as "Deep Choke." After the preliminaries, our conversation ran roughly as follows:

Paul Harrison: I'm not equipped to study the convention now. I dropped analysis of religious organizations years ago for moral reasons. I'm studying theological ethics.

Deep Choke: All the more reason. The ABC is centralizing without a center and rationalizing with insufficient rationale.

P.H.: You might need Woodward and Bernstein.

D.C.: The *Washington Post* isn't interested in the northern Baptists.

P.H.: They should be. If they could learn about Baptists, they could reveal the true secrets of Jimmy Carter.

D.C.: Let's be serious. Listen, I think the situation may be worse in the

---

Dr. Harrison is professor of religion and society at Pennsylvania State University.

convention than 20 years ago when your book was published. At least then we had some of the liberals and fundamentalists around. Today the people on the reorganization committees wouldn't acknowledge a theological idea if it were formally introduced to them.

P.H.: That sounds familiar, but I can give you the names of a couple of people who are working on this stuff all the time. They'd do a better job for you.

D.C.: Do they know the Baptists?

P.H.: No, but I think—

D.C.: Look, you're the one who helped us examine ourselves more critically. Now there are several of us who are deeply concerned. Why don't you check out the situation and tell us what you think? It wouldn't be a whole lot of work. All you have to do is look at the documents and write a paper or something before the biennial meeting in San Diego in June.

P.H.: That's all you want!

D.C.: Oh, come off it, Paul, I happen to know you analyzed SCODS in 1972 and gave an underground report at the Pennsylvania Association meeting.

P.H.: SCODS? I don't even recall your jargon. Anyway, it wasn't underground. The program committee said they couldn't find a time for it, so we held a seven o'clock breakfast meeting in an empty church.

D.C.: Sounds underground to me—SCODS was the "Study Commission on Denominational Structure."

P.H.: Oh, yes. I recall the title. It was about 200 pages of infinite trivia. That's another reason I don't study religious bureaucracy. I can't unravel infinity. . . . But suppose I did agree to do it, could you provide the material, find others for me to talk to?

D.C.: Definitely. Come to see us. Talk to others. Write what you want. No strings. Who knows? Maybe the *Post* will publish it.

P.H.: OK. I'll do it, but only if you get me the Rockefeller tapes. What that renegade Baptist had to say about Jimmy Carter could be helpful.

D.C.: I'll try.

The Bureaucratese of Reorganization

A few days after Deep Choke called, I received some material from him. As I glanced through the newest 265-page reorganizational report (called "SCOR" for "Study Commission on Relationships"), my eyes lit up at its gripping style. The following example may give the careful reader some useful information:

> The National Staff Council upon recommendation of the Executive Ministers Council (a professional organization of the Executive Ministers of the thirty-seven Region/State/City organizations) believed 1974 was the time for addressing a growing number of relational issues among the Affiliated Organizations and the ABC. The National Staff Council in November 1974 recommended this action to the General Board and the Board created the Commission.
>
> The purpose of SCOR is to integrate the 37 Region, State, and City offices and chief administration officers into the new structure which was imaginatively created by the Study Commission on Denominational Structure[SCODS].

The fundamental purposes of the convention have not altered in 70 years. Its chartered intention is "to bear witness to the Gospel of Jesus Christ. . . . To seek the mind of Christ on moral, spiritual, political, economic, social, denominational and ecumenical matters. . . . To guide, unify, and assist American Baptist churches and groups within the whole Body of Christ." The autonomy of the local church and the separation of church and state are still vaunted and familiar hallmarks of Baptist identity. But it has not always been that way.

Authority of Local Associations

Spiritual heirs of the Anabaptists—the religious revolutionaries of 16th century Europe—the Baptists we know today emerged from the Congregational and Presbyterian churches in the first decade of the 17th century. Baptist congregations in America were initially established in 1638-39 by Roger Williams in Providence and John Clarke in Newport. In 1707 the first (American) Baptist Association of Churches was organized in Philadelphia; by 1776 that association was composed of 42 churches in six colonies: Pennsylvania, Maryland, Virginia, New Jersey, New York and Connecticut. Other associations were formed throughout the new nation: at an association meeting in Kentucky in 1796, it was decided that the *authority of an association* derived from the command of God's word to assemble in his name for worship, counsel and union for mutual edification and assistance, and to cultivate uniformity of sentiment in principles and practice; most important, the association had power to regulate and govern itself as a body and to give advice to its several churches. Any church that agreed with the enunciated principles should be admitted, and those that opposed them should be rejected. Those principles were typical of the associations formed in America. They all possessed advisory and disciplinary authority in relation to the congregations. The idea of congregational autonomy was to appear much later.

The Massachusetts Mission Society, formed in 1802, was the first state convention. A foreign mission agency was organized in Philadelphia in 1813. The Home Mission Society was founded in New York City in 1832. The momentous schism between the "Southern" and "Northern" Baptists occurred in 1845 amid the growing debate over slavery and related issues. Missionary evangelism, educational work and publications continued in both denominations. In the north the various denominational boards and agencies increasingly found themselves in intensive competition for financial support from the churches. The Northern Baptist Convention (NBC) was formed in 1907, in great part to alleviate the fratricidal warfare for funds between the national mission agencies.

The Foreign and Home Mission Societies, the Boards of Education and Publication, the Women's Home and Foreign Mission agencies, and the Baptist Historical Society were the primary national institutions. Each maintained and jealously guarded its own autonomy; that is, each possessed freedom to govern its own affairs with separate officers, boards and executive secretaries who administered agency business in the interim between board meetings and annual conventions.

When the Northern Baptist Convention was formed in 1907, the mission agencies relinquished their fund-raising activities to the officers and executives of the convention. This style of operation survived for about 60 years. During this period, functional cooperation between the agencies was not emphasized, either horizontally (between agencies at the same level) or vertically (between churches, associations and agencies at various levels). The principal force that held the American Baptists together was a commonly declared but variously defined evangelical view of world missions and a *pragmatically organized* convention designed to further the mission enterprise more efficiently.

Today Baptists consider themselves to be the most radical proponents of congregational polity. The clarion call for "the autonomy of the local church" became a byword in the 19th century. Then it was affirmed that no ecclesiastical officers or agencies would ever govern the affairs of the autonomous congregations. The ironic result is that when such governance and control do occur, Baptists seldom recognize it since, on traditional and ideological grounds, they believe it cannot happen. Another irony is that *local associations* have sacrificed their own powers to state and national agencies. The local associations appeared to exert the greatest power and threat to congregational autonomy, so the Baptists gradually nullified the power of these groups, and thereby eliminated the most effective instrument for balancing the powers of the state and national conventions in their relations with the congregations.

Among both American and Southern Baptists, congregational independence remains a revered aspect of the inheritance. The emphasis is somewhat muted outside the Sunbelt because today few people in the north believe that the switch to God's light is found only in the local pew.

American Baptists believe that God's intention can be sought and followed in local congregations and other gatherings of Christians in associational, regional, national and world bodies as they receive from one another mutual counsel and correction [SCODS].

American Baptist Intentions and Realities

The broader mission of the Baptists, whether evangelizing the world for Christ or reaffirming the basic principles of human rights in every nation, remains firm and openly declared. Inside the conventions it is a different matter. The infighting is close. The unspoken purpose is to gather together as many uninformed delegates as possible and persuade them with evangelical fervor that one's causes are just, one's explicit intentions are righteous and the strategy should be to create a unity of purpose out of a babel of competing interests. If they know *anything* about the proceedings, the people from local congregations are bewildered by this welter of forces; if they know *nothing,* they are impressed or overjoyed by the "spirit of the meetings."

At present the American Baptists are the victims of the invisible gulf that exists between their own national and state bureaucracies and the individual congregations. For example, in the Pennsylvania-Delaware Association the executive minister is responsible for 475 churches (rural-metropolitan-suburban). True, within Pennsylvania-Delaware there are "area representatives" in the regional associations. Roughly analogous to district managers in a corporate enterprise, they possess *no* policy-making powers and have *no* independent budget. They are troubleshooters, paid to assist churches that have lost a minister, or are experiencing financial difficulty, or are not contributing to the mission programs of the state and national conventions.

If significant crises occur, the executive minister may call for assistance from the Ministers Benefit or the National Missions Boards, the Baptist counterparts of HEW; but when this happens, Baptists have made the inevitable move from local problems to nationalized solutions, and the churches once again taste the bitter medicine of dependency. In certain critical matters, the small and average-size congregations, acting in sincere covenant with the ABC, are hardly more independent of the actions of the ABC "headquarters" at Valley Forge than the communities of our nation are free of the actions of the bureaus of the federal government. The local churches and denominations in this land are clearly analogous to their secular counterparts. They offer, therefore, modest and perhaps unique social laboratories for the testing of programs and solutions that might later be applied to broader social spheres. It is a wonder that some expert in Washington has not called attention to these possibilities. For relatively modest sums the federal government could pretest hundreds of programs.

Pressures for Reorganization

The carefully nurtured fiction that the locus of authority in the ABC resides in 6,300 "autonomous" congregations has become increasingly difficult to maintain. In 1959 it was suggested that "there remain three principles of democratic procedure to which free church polity must give serious thought"—that is, free discussion, no exclusion from national office except on the basis of creed or ability, and legislation and policy-making executed in accord with methods of representative government (*Authority and Power in the Free Church Tradition,* by P. M. Harrison [Southern Illinois University Press, 1971], p. 162). These rec-

ommendations were acted upon with varying degrees of seriousness by
the SCODS committee; but the primary pressure that triggered reorganization of the convention was the ferment of the 1960s. Various
caucuses, notably the "Black American Baptist Churchmen," were organized, and the grosser forms of discrimination were duly remedied.
It was also admitted in the SCODS report that the annual meetings
were not representative with respect to the whole body of delegates.
The report said that the annual convention could not operate as a legislative body since the delegates "represent everyone and no one at the
same time."

The convention has *never* been a legislative body with delegated
lawmakers from the churches. There is a difference between delegates
and legislators, but that fact did not become evident to Baptists for
some decades. To this day, policy provides for 21,000 delegates from
the 6,300 churches. But an average of only 3,249 delegates has attended recent conventions. In 1971 68 per cent of the congregations were
not directly represented at all. It is not admitted that the constituency is
uninformed concerning convention operations or that the subsidized
Baptist publications offer only skimpy reports of denominational actions, well tempered by kudos concerning the beneficence of our leaders. That the bureaucratic leaders are beneficent has never been
questioned and is not the real issue; good and talented people can make
disastrous errors, and the market on self-deception has not been cor-
nered by intentional deceivers.

To remedy the situation at the annual conventions, the delegates in
1974 ruled that the annual American Baptist Convention would be
called a "meeting" of "the American Baptist Churches" and the meetings would henceforth be biennial. The annual spring ceremony went
the way of other religious rites in our time. The leaders could conduct
the business of the churches through the improved instruments of the
"General Board" and other agencies at the national level.

That was a good move but possibly in the wrong direction. The
annual conventions were crudely conceived and dominated for the most
part by a small parade of quasi-charismatic leaders. As a sideshow,
each board, agency, commission and committee hawked its wares, like
Tetzel selling indulgences at Wittenberg. Dominated by the politics of
personality, the conventions had been a recipe for the impotency of the

people. Finally, in the era of Watergate the Baptists recognized their condition, but in an era of untenable paradoxes they sought to remedy the past by building new structures of power on the shifting sands of independent churches.

The Mission of the Gathered Congregations

In-depth interviews at the San Diego meetings of the American Baptists in June 1977, conferences with executive ministers, discussions with a score of leading clergy and a few leading laypeople, and the study of a considerable body of official and unofficial materials uncovered an increasing discontent at the grass-roots level that most national leaders appear to ignore. Local clergy were disenfranchised by the reorganization of the American Baptist Convention into a biennial nonorganization called the "American Baptist Churches, USA."

The growing discontent is gradually giving rise to a variety of calls for reorganization *at the local level,* partially to offset the state and national powers, in part as a means to achieve more effective missions at *every* level. What follows is a compendium of tentative and prescriptive ideas expressed by several persons.

It is of critical importance to recognize that it is a perverse waste of time to blame the "bureaucrats" for this state of affairs. "We the people" have wittingly or unwittingly handed over the reins of authority, power and responsibility to others. We have done this for a variety of reasons, including ignorance, indifference, hypercompetitiveness at the local level, and a persistent romanticizing of the American version of the laissez-faire dream applied to religious organizations. It is clear that the secular and religious bureaucrats have often achieved their purposes as well as conditions have permitted. That executives and bureaucrats often act in a self-serving manner and with mixed motives needs no further empirical proof, but we in the grass-roots communities and churches do not have to continue to give our national officers the responsibility for solving everything and then condemn them for solving so little.

The prescriptions that follow are based on the assumption that missions, like everything else in the Baptist denominations, should be initiated and organized at the local level. In no other way are the congregations going to relearn what is involved in this aspect of the

Christian endeavor. In no other way can the people in the local churches become actively reintegrated into the polity of the denomination. In a word, national and world missions should grow out of and extend the local mission efforts.

The local congregations should be engaged in cooperative missions which involve united efforts to learn about the "secular" and "religious" needs in their own areas. Second, the churches could pool their resources for evangelistic and social action. The principle of missions should never be conceived as "foreign," as it has been for generations in the American churches. "Foreign" connotes "alien" or "different from" and inevitably results in all the misconceptions of paternalism and philanthropy; i.e., aiding those who don't have what we have and who need it. Missions should be conceived as Christian persons helping their neighbors and, in turn, learning from them and receiving aid from them. Mission work is then cooperative and indigenous, and "missionaries" become "ministers," not Christian strangers from a superior culture bringing a message of "truth" to a people steeped in religious, social and moral ignorance. The concept of missions as serving one's neighbor is particularly significant for the grounding of mission in the local churches and local associations.

So, etiologically perceived, the local churches may not exempt themselves from missions by engaging in them indirectly. When the denominational leaders fail to encourage local missions, they are leaving out the basic component and initiatory stimulus for all mission programs. When the local churches remain predominantly focused on missions as something that specialists do "out there," they are reneging on their basic responsibility to their immediate neighbors. The romanticism and moral irresponsibility of defining missions as service to people in faraway places needs to be critically re-examined by the American Baptists.

This romanticism is dramatically symbolized at the biennial meetings when gold emblems are pinned on the newly appointed foreign missionaries. These are the people perceived as truly going forth into the golden rays of the sun's light. This is a particularly significant theological distortion in a denomination that emphasizes the doctrine of the priesthood of all believers, wherein mediating priests are an anathema, except in mission activities.

Reorganizing the Local Associations

Assuming that reorganization at the national and regional levels through SCODS and SCOR is on the right track, it appears essential to look further—that is, toward revitalizing and restructuring the local churches and associations. Assuming further that a vital mission program involves the same complex of activities and structures that are now present at the national level, what should the local associations of churches do? What follows are merely "bare bones" suggestions.

First, the local associations should develop liturgical and celebrative activities. These associations should meet at regular intervals as a "council of churches," break bread and drink the cup together as neighbors one to another.

Second, they should elect officers and special boards and appoint a part-time "executive minister" from among the local clergy. There is no reason in principle why local associations should be bereft of staff executives, but such persons should not be appointed by higher judicatories at the state or national level. The first task of the local executive minister should be to serve his or her association.

Third, to enable this to happen, the local churches should be free to allocate their money in its entirety to the local association, if they so desire. Money could then be allocated by the association to the national and/or state conventions. Obviously, this would be local control "with a vengeance" and would involve risks of parochialism and the like. But many persons firmly believe that the majority of local congregations, though moribund, are constituted by mission-oriented Baptists; probably the only way to awaken them is to offer them new responsibilities, authorities and powers at the most immediate locus of need.

Fourth, delegates should be sent from each local church to the local association, following formulas that are now operative at the national level. It would be these people, numbering from 50 to 200, meeting quarterly or semiannually, who would determine the general policies and programs for the association. Their elected boards and appointed executives would refine and administer the policies and programs, as is now done at the state and national levels.

Fifth, the existing local associations should be geographically reorganized. In urban areas, the large associations of 100 or more churches should be divided into more manageable groups of about 25 churches. In sparsely settled regions where only a handful of Baptist churches are present, the mission should be ecumenically extended to include other denominations that share congregational practice and polity; e.g., the United Church of Christ, the Brethren, the Disciples, the Quakers. Ideally, these efforts would be applauded by the various denominational headquarters, even though no such programs are now on the drawing boards at Valley Forge.

Sixth, delegates from local associations would be elected to attend the state and national conventions. Thus a delegational process would be established which would enable persons to become familiar with every level of denominational organization and polity. Presumably, most of the state and national delegates, board members, and the higher-level executive officers as well, would be recruited from the ranks of those persons who had demonstrated most interest and competence at the local associational level. Since activity at that level is now insignificant throughout the denomination, recruitment for state and national office necessarily focuses on "successful" local pastors and active laypersons from the larger and more affluent churches.

Seventh, it has been suggested that no more than 400 delegates are necessary at the state and national conventions. With that number of persons, far greater participatory sophistication could be anticipated. The local congregations would no longer send delegates directly to the state and national meetings. The churches would be more effectively, although indirectly, represented by the delegates from their local associations. The 68 per cent of the churches presently represented only by their regional executive minister would gain more immediate representation by local delegates and executives.

Revitalizing the Middle

The 20,000 legally entitled delegates who can now, theoretically, be sent from local churches would then be eliminated. At present only about 3,000 uninformed delegates attend the biennial, ostensibly to represent 6,000 churches. The regional and national conventions would then be delegate-centered and business-focused. Visitors from the churches would be encouraged, but they would sit and participate from "the wings," as is true in every serious deliberative and legislative session in the world, except for meetings of the ABC. At the ABC meetings delegates and visitors may sit anywhere and everywhere, almost as though it were an intentional act of the executive leadership to render the policy-making and voting process as difficult as possible for the delegates, scattered as they are and mingled with the "visitors," who often outnumber them 5 to 1 in a business session.

Meanwhile, back at the local association of churches, the executive minister could cooperate fully with the local churches and their ministers to launch integrated mission programs for the area. There would be less need for regional or national administrators to decide on local budgets and to offer their guidance and program directives to areas they know almost nothing about. The national headquarters, however, could deploy functional specialists for various mission projects, such as building new churches, or organizing a local "war of the churches against poverty."

National and foreign mission programs would most likely be enhanced and strengthened by the new local activities. The local people would be more knowledgeable and perhaps more sympathetic to the problems and opportunities for the more extended missions; that is, to their neighbors in more distant areas of need.

Western technology and industry have had the effect of destroying or seriously wounding all of our primary and secondary institutions. This includes the family, the school, the neighborhood, the city, the local region and even the states and commonwealths. Few effective entities seem to exist between the individual person (who is often frantically reading books on self-help and personal integration) and the national or multinational forces. We need to revitalize the middle, the mediating institutions. The churches are no exception: They could become once again a beacon on the hill, a light to the nation and the world.

An Afterword

Upon reading the foregoing proposals, a person high in the councils of the ABC wrote to me as follows:

> Your suggestion that the associations take on new life is a good one, if they were also identical with election districts; and if election districts and associations could be constituted as functionally as well as geographically

similar, this might help. The election districts in some areas are not well put together, but this problem can be changed with time and experience. The election district from the point of view of ABC nationally is the first building block beyond the local church.

This topic opens a new can of worms. The election districts are a creation of SCODS, the intention being to create an instrument which would enable every area in the denomination to elect members to the General Board, 150 in all. Delegates to the biennial elect the remaining 50 members of the board.

People at the national level look to the election districts with fervent hopes, but there are problems. One issue is that in many states election-district members hold no office in local or state associations, so the associational workers are disenfranchised. The problem is that the election districts have gained authority before they have any power, and the associations have lost their power before they have lost their authority. The clear purpose seems to be to establish two centers of authority, the local churches and the national boards, with nothing in between.

As my friendly critic put it:

> In many ways the problem was and still is how to provide close representative connections between local churches and national policies: education curriculum, youth work, national ministries, and international ministries, etc., without the insights of the local churches *being filtered through* states and regions in a typical connectional system.

It is doubtful that the crux of the issue today is how to connect the local congregations directly to national sources of skill and power. The problem is to develop local or regional associations of churches with their own resources for policy and program. With the exception of a tiny minority of vital and mature congregations, the local church standing alone in relation only to national headquarters is a dependent rather than a viable and interdependent entity.

Let my correspondent have the last word, for I could not agree more: "The real issues facing us, as I tried to indicate, are how to keep necessary order from becoming tyranny, how to achieve a sense of unity without the stultifying overtones of sameness so that *people* are free to be and do what they really believe is important."

9

United Methodism: A Cautious Mood

The United Methodist Church is a great circus tent, with all sorts of sideshows going on underneath and around it.

JAMESON JONES

At its best, the United Methodist Church is a highly organized and effective action machine. Once its cogs mesh and its wheels begin to turn, the denomination can accomplish anything it sets out to do. Its resources, human and material, are overwhelming in breadth and depth. Probably above all else, United Methodists want to be relevant in the world. Their current malaise has resulted from failure to act. The problem: how to get the denomination moving again.

The Behemoth Slows Down

Until recently the largest single Protestant denomination in the U.S., the United Methodist Church is a great circus tent, with all sorts of sideshows going on underneath and around it. "Until recently" summarizes much of the story. Other denominations and church groups are growing; United Methodism is not. Leadership in the denomination has undergone many changes, with more to come. Sideshows around the tent have diverted the crowds from the main event—evangelism, effective social action, the unified program, the sense of movement within the denomination. The behemoth has been slowing down.

Size is an issue. United Methodism is a billion-dollar enterprise.

Dr. Jones is president of Iliff School of Theology, a United Methodist seminary in Denver, Colorado.

Almost a quarter of a billion dollars goes each year for clergy salaries. There are 38,795 organized local churches. At one time, there were more Methodist churches in the U.S than post offices. However, the postal service keeps opening new branches while United Methodism is closing down its smaller units. Some 51 churches were closed in 1976. Membership continues to decline. Since 1964, the denomination has lost almost 1.2 million members. In 1976, 36 per cent of all United Methodist congregations received no new members by profession of faith. Membership in the denomination now stands at 9.8 million in the U.S. and Puerto Rico. There are also some 600,000 members in Asia, Africa and Europe.

It's a huge denomination indeed. But things are not well with the followers of Wesley, Otterbein and Albright. The 1968 merger of the Methodist Church and the Evangelical United Brethren Church brought together English pietist and German pietist streams with a common concern: how to put new fires on ecclesiastical altars. United Methodism's current worry is that its own fire may have gone out.

The Bishops' Changing Role

The old picture of Methodism was that of a monolith—tightly organized, efficient and effective in service, with a host of people across the nation united in spirit, in commitment, in approach to issues and in mission. The Methodists' "bold new venture" in church journalism was named *Together,* a slick and colorful magazine launched in 1956 as a unifying vehicle. Both the magazine and the mood of togetherness are gone.

Heretofore, when bishops spoke the church listened and obeyed. When the president of the women's organization sneezed, 40,000 local women's group presidents reached for handkerchiefs. Youth and student organizations affected not only the denomination but countless other lives. Missionaries at home and abroad extended the influence and witness of Methodism. Now the mood is to pull back, conserve, talk rather than act.

Some old-timers think that the church moved when the bishops were in the driver's seat, but those days are gone forever. The image of the Methodist bishop as omnipotent autocrat has undergone radical change. Even in the powers of appointment, now subject to "consultation" with clergy and with churches, the bishop's role has become more limited and democratic.

Some think the church is no longer electing great bishops. In the words of one retired bishop, "All the tall pines have been cut down, and only saplings are left." Nostalgia always influences that kind of statement, and yet one remembers admiringly such episcopal giants as G. Bromley Oxnam and Francis J. McConnell. One can hope that a James Armstrong or a James S. Thomas will someday be remembered in like terms.

The 1976 General Conference saw a major attack on life tenure for bishops. One significant argument was that "term" episcopacy would encourage the election of bishops who would be relatively young, or female or of ethnic minority background. An interesting argument on the other side was that limiting the term of bishops would only increase the power of general church secretaries and agency executives. Whom do you like less, bishops or bureaucrats? Life tenure for bishops won (there were, of course, other reasons for the victory). United Methodist bishops do have life tenure in office, but their service as episcopal leaders in one geographical area has been cut to a maximum of eight years. The eight-year limit is gathering opposition from a number of bishops and other influential leaders.

Also in 1976, the retirement age of bishops was lowered by two years, so that a bishop must retire between ages 66 and 70. Some persons are hoping that federal legislation on retirement might negate that church action and enable bishops to stay on longer. Others doubt that federal legislation will affect church policy and say that even if it did, the mood of the church about its bishops was so clear that they would do well to retire anyway.

It is true that the Council of Bishops as a whole does not speak often to the whole church, nor with the same power and influence that it once commanded. Leadership is most likely to be exercised by a bishop within the bounds of his own annual conference. Slowly, the role of the bishop has changed from that of a great preacher and spiritual giant to that of manager and administrator.

Those who want bishops to be the church's leaders (in the best sense of that term, both as spiritual giants and as managers/administrators) must deal with a real problem. The legislation that re-

tires bishops as early as age 66 and apparently limits their assignment
to eight years in a particular area will result in the largest turnover of
episcopal leadership in memory. There are 45 active bishops in the
U.S. In September 1980, 16 of them must retire, 17 must move to new
areas, and only 12 can remain in their present leadership posts. The
effect of this turnover on the church's programs can only be negative.
It takes time for a bishop to become acquainted with churches and clergy and lay leadership, and to develop and implement effective policies.

Women in Leadership

The election of a woman bishop has long been predicted by United
Methodism, the only questions being who and how soon. For a time
the likely candidate was Jeanne Audrey Powers, assistant general secretary for ecumenical and interreligious concerns of the Board of Global Ministries. She had great support in the North Central Jurisdiction in
1976, but withdrew early in the voting with a powerful statement that
supported the cause of a woman bishop. Unless her sense of vocation
changes, she is not likely to be a candidate again. On July 17, 1980,
Marjorie Swank Matthews, 64, a district superintendent in the West
Michigan Conference, became the first woman bishop in the United
Methodist Church. Elected by the North Central Jurisdictional Conference after 29 ballots, she was assigned to the Wisconsin area. My best
guess is that the next woman bishop will be elected in the Western
Jurisdiction in 1984, and is likely to be Barbara Troxell, a district superintendent in the California-Nevada Conference.

United Methodism has a long tradition of women clergy. There are
now 766 women under appointment, 319 of them with full ministerial
rights and relationships, the others in process. Women make up about
25 per cent of all students in United Methodist seminaries (650 women
among 2,717 Master of Divinity students, 1,070 women among 4,350
students in all categories and programs).

Not all of the women students in United Methodist seminaries are
United Methodists. Moreover, the denomination looks more and more
attractive to women from denominations with a "call" system for fill-
ing pastorates, where it is often harder for a woman to find a place to
serve. Under the Methodist appointment system, once an individual
has been accepted into membership of an annual conference and or-

dained, he or she is guaranteed work as a full-time ordained minister. While some local churches still resist the idea of a woman pastor (women members are more likely to be opposed than male members), the appointment system does assure women of employment in ministry.

In other areas of the church's life, women have assumed new and important leadership roles. When women's work was independent and almost autonomous, the denominational women's organization was powerful and effective. Examples include its mission projects at home and abroad and its civil rights efforts during the '50s and '60s. Then women's work was "integrated" into the larger church, and women assumed more general leadership roles. More than a decade ago, Ann Porter Brown became general secretary of what is now the Board of Global Ministries, the first woman in any denomination to assume that kind of position.

A development which should surprise no one is the increase in the number of clergy couples (with both husband and wife ordained as ministers). Young people are not marrying as early as they were a few years ago. More single students, male and female, enter theological school, meet and marry without either one giving up a ministerial commitment.

United Methodism now has about 50 clergy couples, with the number sure to increase. A clergy couple presents problems for the appointment system. Should both persons be appointed to the same church? If so, as co-pastors, or one as senior and the other as associate? Or should they be appointed to nearby churches with one convenient parsonage? Or one to a church and the other to a specialized ministry?

Ethnic Identity

Probably in this denomination more than any other, issues of ethnicity and inclusiveness will be settled in ways that will certainly affect religious life and structures for the whole nation. Prior to 1964, the chief racial issue was the existence of the Central Jurisdiction, a nongeographical structure that segregated black Methodists. The jurisdiction was abolished, a victory for integrationists. Ethnic minority persons (black, Hispanic, Asian and native American) now represent about 5 per cent of total church membership.

One issue here is the desire of these persons to maintain separate identities as well as have guarantees of full representation and participation. Persons raised on the racial liberalism of the '40s and '50s tend toward inclusiveness and the absence of racial quotas. This struggle may yet become intense.

A second issue relates to "open itinerancy." Favored by ethnic pastors, such a policy would allow them equal consideration with white pastors for all churches; they would not be locked into their own ethnic churches. Yet some of these same ethnic clergy argue that white pastors are not competent to serve ethnic congregations. This stance is becoming increasingly popular: Hispanic pastors for Hispanic churches, Asian pastors for Asian churches, black pastors for black churches, and so on. Critically short of ethnic minority clergy, United Methodism must solve this problem in the near future.

A third issue is based on divisions between ethnic groups. Some blacks feel they are losing ground because other minorities are demanding more attention. Other minority persons say they are only seeking the conditions already attained by blacks. The oldest ethnic caucus, Black Methodists for Church Renewal, has been the most effective. At present, with some of its goals having been accomplished, it is rather quiet. One of the major goals of MARCHA (Methodists Associated Representing the Cause of Hispanic Americans) is yet to be accomplished—the election of a bishop of Hispanic background. If it happens soon, it is likely to be through Hispanic unity in the southwest, which did not obtain at the time of the most recent elections.

The first bishop of Asian background, Wilbur W. Y. Choy, was elected in 1972. Caucuses representing Asians and native Americans have been successful in sensitizing the church to their presence and needs (scholarship programs have been the most significant response to date to meet those needs).

A Pluralistic Stance

Highly visible, well organized and institutionally successful is the "Good News Movement," which identifies itself as "A Forum for Scriptural Christianity Within the United Methodist Church." "Good

News" publishes a bimonthly journal, as well as newsletters for women and seminarians; it sponsors large-group convocations and small-group "think tank" meetings, and has a major program aimed at making mission programs more "evangelical."

The president of "Good News" has called on those responsible for church school curriculum to produce a "track" of distinctively evangelical literature. The movement is considering publishing its own church school materials. It has already put out its own confirmation literature and has announced its first 13-unit study plans for adults and high school youth. United Methodist leadership is already more evangelical than Good News people think, but it will never be as evangelical as Good News people want it to be.

The word to argue over is "pluralism." At best, pluralism is the strength of the denomination, a reason for its vitality. Some see pluralism as a weakness, a sign of theological indifference. For a variety of reasons, leadership in office tends to welcome pluralism; grass-roots representatives tend to condemn it. As generally used, the term "pluralistic" accurately describes the denomination. That doctrinal stance was reflected in the 1972 General Conference's actions; United Methodism has refused to become a creedal church and instead continues to set Scripture, tradition, experience and reason in interaction with each other as sources for doing theology.

Two special-interest groups deserve mention. The newest is the United Methodist Renewal Services Fellowship, a charismatic movement formed as an outgrowth of the interdenominational Conference on Charismatic Renewal held during the summer of 1977 in Kansas City. The fellowship plans no office or staff, at least for now, but will have a monthly newsletter. One estimate is that some 230,000 United Methodists are potential members for a charismatic fellowship. If so, then there must be a million potential members for an effective social-action fellowship (and only the tiny and almost unnoticed Methodist Federation for Social Action exists to meet that need).

There is an organized fellowship of gay United Methodists, and some 100 persons, gay and straight, met in November 1977 for an "Education Conference on Homosexuality and the United Methodist Church." Then 24 males and one female changed their constitution to allow the election of a female along with a male to head the organization; they named the caucus "Affirmation: United Methodists for Lesbian and Gay Concerns."

At the 1976 General Conference the grass-roots level of the church expressed itself more clearly on the issue of homosexuality than on any other matter. The conference voted with the grass roots, saying "we do not condone the practice of homosexuality" and consider it "incompatible with Christian teaching." In June 1977 the Minnesota Conference revoked the deacon's orders of an acknowledged homosexual man and returned him to lay status.

The issue of homosexuality illustrates the sensitivity of the denomination to grass-roots opinion and the conservative nature of the denomination on matters of personal morality, no matter how liberal it might be on matters of public policy.

Firing salvos at bureaucracies is currently the nation's favorite pastime. United Methodist agencies are not exempted from becoming targets, having lost the status and prestige they once had. In years gone by, the denomination's program was set by these national boards and agencies, then communicated and implemented through effective channels of organization. The pattern was from the top down—and it worked.

After a massive restructuring in 1972, the denomination now has four major program boards: Church and Society, Discipleship, Global Ministries, and Higher Education and Ministry. A simplified, one-word description of each respectively: advocacy, nurture, outreach and vocations. Wherever these agencies are ineffective, one factor is the nationwide revolt against bureaucracy and centralized authority of any kind. Another reason is a decline in real dollars made available for the work of the boards (only 5.38 per cent of total local church giving goes to the national church for administration, ministerial support, benevolences and missions). A third cause of failure is the extensive turnover among the directors who establish policy and elect key staff of the boards.

When program council directors of annual conferences (links between national program and local churches) met in Miami Beach in November 1977, the major news was that directors and national staff persons had mended their fences. National staff apparently had seen these conference-level personnel as blocking the implementation of national programs. The point of that dispute was not where the blocks were, but the admission that national programs were not being implemented.

Organization and Ecumenicity

United Methodism, like any organized denomination or bureaucratic structure, bewails overlapping, duplication and waste. The former Methodist Church had established a Coordinating Council to exorcise these demons, but the council was never really effective. National boards operated with almost complete autonomy, subject only to quadrennial action of the General Conference. In the former EUB Church, coordination was far more effective through a national Council on Ministries. In the united church, the EUB structure was adopted. One current struggle at the national level is whether that pattern can be made effective among boards which continue to operate in the former Methodist (that is, autonomous) style.

The General Council on Ministries promises to give effective leadership in research and planning for the whole denomination; it has not, however, yet achieved an effective means to coordinate and evaluate the programs of the national agencies.

United Methodism is confused about ecumenicity. A number of influential leaders, for sound biblical-theological reasons, or because of experience in mission fields, affirm the ecumenical stance of the denomination and call it to responsible ecumenical participation and action. Some of United Methodism's own have played key roles in the ecumenical movement. Surely the late John R. Mott, founder of the World Student Christian Federation, must be mentioned first. The names of Bishop James K. Mathews, Robert W. Huston, Jeanne Audrey Powers and J. Robert Nelson come immediately to mind, as only the beginnings of a current list. Another United Methodist, Gerald F. Moede, is the executive officer of the Consultation on Church Union (COCU).

Yet United Methodists as a whole are not ecumenical for biblical or theological reasons. Basically, they are practical in their approach. If a task can better be accomplished together than separately, ecumenism is the order of the day. If there is no increase in effectiveness, no saving in effort or costs from such cooperation, then they will choose to go it alone.

Failures and Successes

For 1977-80 the denomination's program theme has been "Committed to Christ—Called to Change." There are seven vital concerns: deeper personal commitment to Christ, strengthening the local church, full participation by laypersons, concern for persons, values and ethics in public and private life, living as good stewards in an age of scarcity, and the future of church-related institutions. These are generalities that everybody can favor, so not much has happened. There are specific programs in three "missional priorities." Beginning in 1977, United Methodism set out to raise $2 million each year for world hunger, $1.5 million for the ethnic minority local church, and $125,000 for evangelism.

The denomination has done its best job in emphasizing and interpreting evangelism. It is a priority that calls for witness, not money. World hunger has touched the church's pocketbook as well as the creativity of its national agencies. The emphasis on the ethnic minority local church has been in trouble, with a very poor response in the beginning. The first year, giving to world hunger outpaced giving to the ethnic minority program by 12 to 1. Later, giving picked up considerably. The emphasis may yet "succeed," and "racism" is probably not the reason for its poor start. Reasons could include the structure of the financial program, the lack of information about the program as mission, and the refusal to disclose just where and how the money is being used (to avoid the embarrassment and paternalism which might result from disclosure). In an attempt to activate this priority, a new plan permits an annual conference to keep half the money it raises for use in ethnic minority local-church work within its own boundaries.

There are some success stories. One is that of Methodism as a world movement, with an increase of some 4 million members over a five-year period. Methodism's long list of world leaders has included José Miguez Bonino, able theologian and a president of the World Council of Churches; Bishop Abel Muzorewa, who played a key role in the transition from white-ruled Rhodesia to black-ruled Zimbabwe; and Bishop Bennie D. Warner, former vice-president of Liberia.

The U.S. denomination has committed itself to raise $6 million a year to support its 11 black colleges and one black medical school. The

Ministerial Education Fund seeks to raise $3.1 million a year for scholarships and ministerial continuing education within and by annual conferences, and $9.5 million a year for its 13 theological seminaries and for the work of its Division of the Ordained ministry. None of these financial goals has been reached yet, but the commitments themselves are very significant.

The mood of this denomination is cautious and conservative now —an up-with-the-grass-roots-and-down-with-centralized-bureaucracies mood. But that's the current mood of most major denominations and of the country itself, isn't it? The present problem is the plateau upon which United Methodism rests, uncertain how to get moving again. Certain sources of vitality have always characterized the Methodist movement: its able and competent leadership—a mixture of young and old, men and women, ethnic minorities and the majority; theological creativity; and perhaps most important of all, the very size of the denomination, its material and spiritual resources pointing to the possibilities of a major impact upon the nation and the world.

Once the cogs mesh and the wheels of United Methodism start turning again . . .

10

Southern Baptists: A Concern for Experiential Conversion

What Is 'Southern Baptist'—above all, missions and evangelism—takes precedence over even the authority issue, as big as it is for conservatives.

E. GLENN HINSON

Almost any observation one makes about Southern Baptists will be true and not true at the same time. This colossus of almost 13 million members is a burgoo into which the leftovers of yesterday have been thrown with abandon. It represents the whole crazy kaleidoscope of contrasts and conflicts in American religious life—conservative to liberal theology, isolationist to ecumenical ecclesiology, John Birch to Norman Thomas politics, laissez-faire to Marxist economics, pragmatism to idealism, evangelical pietism to social secularism, Phyllis Schlafly antifeminism to Bella Abzug feminism, and so on ad infinitum.

Given such vast contrasts, external observers understandably wonder what holds Southern Baptists together and explains their notable success. Southern Baptists often ask the same question. Insofar as I can see, the one thing which the majority have in common, apart from their humanity, is a fanatical commitment to the "Great Commission." They don't even agree on what this commission is — whether "mission" or "missions," evangelism or social ministry and action, proclamation or priesthood. Yet they agree that they have a job to do, and this agreement is undergirded by a mania, which many outsiders will find incredible, to discharge it. The best way to find out what makes

Dr. Hinson is professor of church history at Southern Baptist Theological Seminary, Louisville, Kentucky.

the Southern Baptist heart beat is to attend an annual convention—either local, state or national—on foreign missions night. There the sternum is split, and the heart itself, beating for all it is worth, lies before one's eyes.

Lacking a Clear Self-Image

It is evident even to a casual observer that the Southern Baptist phenomenon is a shoot far removed from the original Baptist root. There is debate, of course, as to what the original root was. Some see it in European Anabaptism; others, including myself, in English Puritan separatism. If the root was Anabaptism, then Southern Baptists have little besides the practice of believer's baptism to show for it. If it was English Puritanism, they can claim still to have conserved in a grand way the basic character of the root—a "zeal for souls," meaning a concern for experiential conversion. Indeed, they can envision themselves as the premier specimen of this central Puritan concern. "Mr. Puritan," Richard Baxter, would have swelled with pride to see so many preach "as dying men to dying men."

This is not to say that Southern Baptists have conserved the whole Puritan heritage. Far from it. In their century-and-a-third of existence they have managed to accommodate nearly all other principles so as to serve the one great end. One or two examples will illustrate the point.

First, taking a lead from such English Baptists as Andrew Fuller and William Carey, they have steered around that part of the hyper-Calvinist theology of the Puritans which disputed "the use of means" for conversion. Many Southern Baptists, of course, still espouse Calvinist theology—i.e., in its current fundamentalist or "evangelical" shape—but they do not let that get in the way of the grand endeavor. Ironically, the most Calvinistic of them will often employ the *wildest* means imaginable to win adherents—giving away bicycles and television sets for group attendance prizes, dispatching a fleet of buses 100 miles in order to pack the pews back home, singing 135 verses of "Just as I Am" until somebody staggers down the aisle or all drop from exhaustion, applying psychological gimmicks to effect conversions ("Every head bowed. Every eye closed. Those who love Jesus, put your hands up. You put your hand up; now come forward and give your heart to Jesus. There are no *secret* believers."). The "new lights" of the Great Awakening in America debated similar uses of means, but once Baptists in the south, who came largely from the "new light" group, resolved the issue for themselves, they entertained few further reservations about them.

Second, Southern Baptists have managed in a striking way to surmount or circumvent possible problems posed for missions/evangelism efforts by the strict congregationalism of the English separatists. Scarcely any factor could have throttled the drive to the big goal more quickly than a conviction that a local congregation is the only legitimate expression of the church, for this view could have prevented the development of structures—societies, boards, commissions, agencies—to effect the mission in its broader sense. Throughout much of their history Baptists have battled over this issue.

In the colonial era Baptists in America often dragged their feet in the formation of associations and societies, lest a hierarchy develop and restrict personal or congregational freedom. In the north they never fully dissolved such apprehensions. In the south, however, Baptists shoved doubts aside at the outset in the formation of a Foreign Mission Board and a Home Mission Board to carry out the larger mission tasks not connected with local congregations. Despite strong antiorganization sentiment, in subsequent years they added a Sunday School Board, charged with publication, and vast numbers of other structures set up to discharge other tasks.

More significant still, in 1919 they launched a huge unified fund drive (the $75 million campaign); in 1924 this drive was continued as the Cooperative Program, which comes very close to being the key to the immense programming effort of the SBC. In 1927, realizing the value of coordination of effort, they formed an Executive Board. Again, the irony is that all of these structural developments have occurred while Southern Baptists have persisted in reaffirming their congregational heritage. They have overcome antiorganization sentiment in the process by reassuring themselves that each local congregation is "autonomous" (which is true in practice), and that what goes on beyond congregations is a product of voluntary cooperation (which is also true).

In the future, critical problems will emerge out of the very success Southern Baptists have had in such accommodations for the sake of meeting their chief goal. All of these developments have taken place so unselfconsciously and pragmatically that Southern Baptists have a limited awareness of their present identity. Those who are conscious of the problem often want to define their identity in static terms—Anabaptist or separatist origins. The fact is, however, that Southern Baptists can never roll the process backward. They are what they have become in the crucible of history. They will have to work out their identity, therefore, in terms of their present state.

That undoubtedly will be done with reference to the Bible, to which most Southern Baptists have a slavish attachment. But this brings them face to face with the problem of interpretation. Only a small segment of the constituency is ready for modern historical interpretation, and a struggle over its use has been going on for a number of years.

All of this means that Southern Baptists find themselves in roughly the same situation most other large denominations are in: minus a clear self-image. Like most others, they present a mottled picture in trying to be or do what they think the church is to be and do.

From a purely statistical standpoint, the SBC is one of the more vital and exciting denominations in the United States. Each year the aggressive evangelistic efforts of its 35,000 churches net several hundred thousand new members. For 1977-78 the convention allocated over $54 million to its various boards and agencies from its Cooperative Program and supplemented these funds through two additional offerings for home and foreign missions. Moreover, convention leadership is readying and motivating the churches for a "Bold Mission Thrust" which may augment the growth rate and income still more. In the past several years Southern Baptist seminaries have registered a marked upsurge in enrollment, the six seminaries now reporting over 9,000 students in 1978-79.

Save for individual congregations in certain areas, there are few signs of decline or decay. Southern Baptist leaders are skillful planners, organizers, directors and promoters, and so long as they can devise plans which excite their constituents at the grass roots, all systems are "go." The grass-roots laypeople seem, at this juncture, to lend enthusiastic support to efforts to get them caught up in missions and evangelism, those magic words which kindle Southern Baptist imagination as few others can. Leaders generate contagious enthusiasm with an often extravagant self-assurance, sometimes based on previous successes; but there is no end to Southern Baptist optimism.

Areas of Conflict

There are, of course, some areas of conflict which the leadership usually opts to back away from or circumvent rather than plow into directly. The most critical one at the moment has to do with interpretation of the Bible. This issue has been fermenting for a long time. Although Southern Baptists sill possess a faded sense of the well-known Baptist commitment to toleration, conservatives created enough waves to cause the firing of Ralph Elliott, a professor at Midwestern Baptist Seminary, in 1963, and subsequently to force the revision of a 1925 confessional statement and the withdrawal and rewriting of a commentary on Genesis in *The Broadman Bible Commentary* "with due consideration of the conservative viewpoint."

A small splinter group calling itself "The Baptist Faith and Message Fellowship" has kept churning the issue, agitating for removal of seminary professors or workers in other agencies who will not subscribe to the plenary theory of biblical inspiration which they espouse. In 1979 ultraconservatives rallied sufficient votes at the annual convention, which met in Houston, to elect as president on the first ballot Adrian Rogers, a pastor often identified with their position. By exercising his powers of appointment to the full, Rogers could change the balance on boards of trustees which govern SBC agencies. However, he cannot control the convention as J. A. O. Preus does the Lutheran Church–Missouri Synod. Continued agitation may lead to a split, but I suspect that the ultraconservatives will draw out a very small group, for the intense sense of mission most Southern Baptists possess has a centripetal effect.

Southern Baptists are addressing and will continue to address themselves to the social issues most other denominations confront—racism, poverty, world hunger, the energy crisis, aging, crime, pornography, women's equality. Typically they will proceed with caution and do less than their considerable resources might allow. There are various reasons for the slow pace: (1) their long heritage of hesitancy in tackling social or political issues; (2) the fact that southerners, still the vast majority in the SBC, are conservative socially; (3) the diverse and democratic character of the denomination, which makes broad consensus impossible; (4) a conception of leadership which emphasizes service to the constituency more than prophetic guidance.

Conservatism notwithstanding, however, they have acted and will act. For instance, Southern Baptists have made giant steps toward strengthening ties with blacks. In 1968 the convention, meeting in the space-age environment of Houston, leaped a major hurdle in directing its agencies, specifically the Home Mission Board, "to take the leadership in working with the Convention agencies concerned with the problems related to this [racial] crisis in the most effective manner possible" and called on individuals, churches, associations and state conventions to join the SBC "in a renewal of Christian effort to meet the national crisis."

From Houston on, one may discern a cautious escalation of attention to the social implications of the gospel, even though the phrase "social gospel" is still anathema among many Southern Baptists. Agencies such as the Christian Life Commission sensitize the constituency to major issues. Although they come under frequent and severe attack from social conservatives, the size and institutional complexity of the SBC insulates them enough to allow a fairly prophetic ministry. I predict slow but steady progress in each of the areas delineated above.

Among these, the role of women in church and society is an urgent issue now. Since the late 19th century, women have played a significant role in the SBC, particularly through the Woman's Missionary Union, an auxiliary to the convention. Convention boards, commissions, schools and other agencies, moreover, have employed many women as teachers, writers, editors and consultants. Further, the number of women functioning in roles not requiring ordination—music, Christian education, campus ministry, et al.—is high.

To date, however, Southern Baptist congregations, which hold the authority for ordination, have ordained only about 50 women, and only a handful of these function in a directly pastoral role. Even these ordinations are being hotly contested. In Kentucky, for instance, an association has withdrawn fellowship from a congregation which ordained a woman. Thus far, women have not pushed hard for ordination, but that is coming. Increasing numbers of women, now about 5 or 10 per cent of the total, are entering the seminaries with pastoral vocations. The problem will become more and more vexed, but the diverse character of the SBC will allow some churches to ease the tension while the rest catch up with the times.

An Affluent Corporation

It is difficult to characterize the leadership of the Southern Baptist Convention, for it is undergoing a major evolution in style as a new generation comes to the fore. Twenty years ago, a number of remarkable pulpiteers stood out, but that generation of "charismatic" types is giving way to "executive" types. Because of the congregational polity of the convention, the visible leaders are usually pastors of jumbo-size churches. At least 161 SBC churches claim more than 3,000 members, and over 3,000 churches claim 500-800 members. The current president of the convention, Adrian Rogers, is pastor of a church reporting 11,000 members. Pastors of such churches are appointed to committees and boards which make major policy decisions. Of these the Committee on Boards, Commissions and Standing Committees may have the biggest effect, for it selects members for these policy-making organizations.

The very size of the SBC and the complexity of its organizations, however, mean that denominational staff persons who plan and guide meetings and then implement their decisions can and do exercise immense power, even if southern nicety and political tact encourage them to disclaim it. The heads of such agencies as the Foreign Mission Board, Home Mission Board, Sunday School Board, the seminaries and the Executive Committee play strong leading roles.

Beyond pointing to these positions, I hesitate to name names of influential leaders and "comers" in the SBC, not so much out of fear of offense as out of recognition of the power structure's complexity. The convention, despite the town-hall air in the annual meeting, operates in the fashion of a giant corporation in which the power is spread out and hidden. Southern Baptists, of course, like to imagine that they operate still on a democratic model, in which the local congregations determine what happens. Realistically, so complex and far-flung an organization cannot function efficiently in that fashion, and Southern Baptists have a frenzied concern for efficiency.

In the corporate model, power is wielded by the heads of various companies and departments (in this case boards, commissions and agencies) and only nominally by the stockholders. When some 25,000 "messengers" of the churches gather for the annual convention, they make a lot of noise, but they, representing the stockholders, can do little besides rubber-stamp what their skilled force of executives, managers and other experts has decided after prolonged consideration. Even persons privy to the major policy meetings probably could not tell who really decided what. If forced to pinpoint a single body with the greatest overall clout, I would point to the Executive Board of the SBC and the committee which does its staff work. They decide who gets how much money from the Cooperative Program, and in this affluent corporation the power of the purse is a mighty one.

Faith and Theology

It is almost as difficult to name outstanding theologians as it is to name key leaders, and for a similar reason. There are many competent and well-trained theologians spread around the whole Southern Baptist landscape—in churches, boards, commissions, agencies, colleges and seminaries. Once again, however, in the complex body one will discern more by looking at institutions than at persons. Begging pardon for a mild bias, I believe it is fair to say that Southern Baptist Seminary in Louisville, the oldest of the denomination's six seminaries, has produced the majority of the convention's more productive theologians and can claim to have made a difference in Southern Baptist perceptions. For example, 75 per cent of the contributors to *The Broadman Bible Commentary*, a major milestone for Southern Baptist progress in biblical interpretation, either received their training at Southern or teach there.

In a field filled with "stars," however, there are few "superstars" comparable to A. T. Robertson, John A. Broadus or E. Y. Mullins in an earlier day. To be quite candid, many Southern Baptist theologians suffer from an inferiority complex which seriously inhibits the contribution they could make. Hypersensitive to the way they are either heard or ignored outside the convention, they have failed to address themselves as creatively and helpfully as they might have to the problems of their own constituency.

Southern Baptist faith and theology revolve around a single axle, the Bible. If Southern Baptists agree on any theological point, it is that the Scriptures, especially the New Testament, should be "the sole rule of faith and practice." As to what emerges from interpretation and application of these to life, however, Southern Baptists will give as many and varied answers as the Scriptures themselves contain, or as there are Southern Baptists. Although the majority probably fit the fundamentalist stereotype which many outsiders ascribe to them—plenary verbal inspiration, virgin birth, blood atonement, literal second coming, and bodily resurrection—15 or 20 per cent will have genuine appreciation for contemporary theology and theologians. In the seminaries ministers receive training as up-to-date as that found in other denominations. Furthermore, the rise in the urban and cultural index of Southern Baptists will increase further the number who appreciate critical theology.

Something similar is happening in worship, education and publication. No longer a denomination of predominantly rural and small-town folk, Southern Baptists show the world many faces. Worship ranges from informal, spontaneous styles to highly formal, liturgical ones. Education varies from near-illiteracy to postgraduate. Southern Baptists have established and offer modest support to 45 senior colleges and eight junior colleges, some of which (Baylor, Furman, Mercer, Richmond, Samford, Stetson, Wake Forest, William Jewell) have good-to-excellent academic reputations. The SBC provides tuition-free education for ministry in its six seminaries, a factor which helps partially to explain the surplus of students and also the remarkable growth of the denomination in recent years.

Publication is, by design, nearly as diverse as the constituency of the convention. The Sunday School Board bends toward the conservative side, but in recent years it has diversified its products so as to pacify if not please all except the extreme wings of the constituency. I doubt whether this middle-to-right-of-the-road policy will be altered in the near future, but one may see the board thrust a toe into more dangerous waters occasionally.

Ecumenically, Southern Baptists still are stand-offish. The typical Southern Baptist congregation, like that of most denominations, is a potpourri of denominational backgrounds—Presbyterian, Methodist, Episcopal, Pentecostal, and possibly even Roman Catholic, as well as Baptist. This fact helps Southern Baptists to feel comfortable with their fellow Christians. A large percentage of these congregations participate in joint social projects and occasional worship services with other churches. Fifteen or 20 per cent of Southern Baptists would vote for the SBC to join the National and World councils of churches, and one will even discover a few "ecumaniacs" in the SBC. But there is little prospect for more significant Southern Baptist engagement in structured ecumenism.

Among the many reasons for their aloofness, the most telling is success. The SBC as a whole and most congregations which belong to it don't see the value of ecumenical organizations for achieving Baptist goals, and they are too pragmatic to allow concern for unity to override evangelistic aims. They will cooperate with others to the extent that cooperation does not get in the way of the latter, but they will not get involved in organizations which even hint at inhibition of them. Interestingly, this view applies even to participation in the National Association of Evangelicals, with whom a majority of Southern Baptists might share theology and evangelistic zeal.

This keen denominational identity, if damaging to the ecumenical image of Southern Baptists, is mostly beneficial to them in one critical area. Whereas "evangelicals"—with whom Southern Baptists should not be too closely typed—are ripping themselves apart over the "battle for the Bible," Southern Baptists have thus far survived several skirmishes without a split and without erosion of support for their diverse programs. What is "Southern Baptist" — above all, missions and evangelism—takes precedence over even the authority issue, as big as it is for conservatives.

Pressing Issues

The preceding discussion has pointed to a number of pressing issues which confront Southern Baptists; others may be added. The principal ones are these:

1. *Identity.* The SBC no longer fits either the sectarian or the denominational type commonly cited. By virtue of its size and diversity, as well as certain other features, I would characterize it as a "catholic" type with both sectarian and denominational tendencies. The fact that many Southern Baptists have a strong aversion to "catholicism" (which they will equate with Roman Catholicism) interferes with a

forthright confrontation of the identity question. Some propose a return to the sectarian past, but that is impossible. Rather, Southern Baptists will have to decide what principles in their heritage are most essential and how they can be interrelated.

2. *Evangelism and* . . . Nothing is more evident than that Southern Baptists are committed to evangelism as the overriding concern. This commitment, however, poses problems of balance vis-à-vis other principles. It is urgent that they ask how evangelism jibes with

● historic concern for religious liberty and separation of church and state,

● social service and action,

● genuine spiritual formation and nurture of converts, and

● relationships with other churches and faiths.

3. *The Bible.* Since the Bible figures prominently in everything Southern Baptists do, they will continue to wrestle with the question of interpretation.

4. *Corporation Ethics.* The adoption of the corporation model as a pattern for church life and decision-making poses serious questions about means and ends. Some Southern Baptists will allow the end to justify any means. Others are asking how far both the churches and the denominational organization may go before the means subvert the end.

5. *Authority and the Spirit.* The very size and success of the SBC and its churches raise numerous questions regarding authority.

● Where will Southern Baptists find facilities for the growing throng who attend annual conventions? How will they justify the expense in terms of the actual effects? Can there be deliberation in such massive assemblies?

● Given the dominance of the corporation model, can Southern Baptists retain any semblance of democratic decision-making beyond the congregational level? Or should they just drop the charade and admit that they are concerned chiefly with efficiency?

● In the corporate model how does the Holy Spirit enter into the decision-making? Does the Spirit automatically approve whatever is found to work (an assumption not uncommon among Southern Baptists)?

6. *Institutionalism.* Much of the success of Southern Baptists has been related both to "charismatic" leadership and to Baptist astuteness

in the development of programs and institutions. For the future they will need to ask whether or how these two may continue to function together. The Southern Baptist Convention is not far from third century Christianity in letting the institutional supplant the charismatic. Witness:

● the growing creedalism within the SBC,

● the tendency to suppress charismatic churches or persons as a threat to the authority of the Bible,

● the replacement of "charismatic" with "executive" leaders,

● the whole complex process of decision-making, and

● the growing importance of institutions and a concomitant decrease of individual significance.

7. *Cultural Captivity.* Finally, there is always the cultural issue. Southern Baptists have been shaped in great part by their culture. Indeed, they excel in accommodating themselves to it. As the "old" south passes and the "new" comes into being, they will have to struggle, along with others, to develop and maintain a critical stance. They tend to favor "cheap" grace, but the Lord they claim to follow talked about "costly" grace. This may be the most critical issue in the end.

11

The Roman Catholic Church: Can It Transcend the Crisis?

There is no single formula for Catholic progress, to be sure. But if any human instrument stands above the rest, it is a reform of the process by which pastoral leaders are formed, selected and evaluated.

RICHARD P. McBRIEN

Not since 1605 has the papacy changed hands twice in the same year. The fact that this statistic was repeated in 1978 may not mean very much in itself (after all, neither Paul VI nor John Paul I was killed in battle, murdered or deposed), but surely it dramatizes the special character of the times in which we live.

The Catholic Church is by no realistic standard enjoying a period of normality, much less one of spiritual and institutional prosperity. On the contrary, there have been sharp declines in mass attendance, in the number and quality of vocations to the priesthood and religious life, and in the level of obedience to papal and episcopal teachings and directives.

Authority, Tradition, Priesthood

These trends are only symptomatic of problems lurking much deeper below the surface. One can better formulate them as questions: (1) How can the faith, spirituality and missionary impulse of large numbers of Catholics be reignited, or ignited for the first time in the case of the church's younger members? (2) How can the church more effec-

---

Father McBrien is a member of the faculty of Boston College's Institute of Religious Eduction and Pastoral Ministry.

tively proclaim the gospel of Jesus Christ in word, in sacrament and in its corporate witness? (3) How can highly qualified and intensely motivated Catholics, especially among the young, be attracted once again to the official service of the church as priests, as members of religious congregations, and as lay ministers in a wide variety of apostolates? (4) How can all of these ministries become more compelling, and therefore more effective, signs and instruments of the church's mission for the Kingdom of God? (5) How can the church's pastoral leaders construct and communicate teachings on complex and controversial issues of faith and morality in such a way that those teachings elicit respect, if not always agreement? (6) Indeed, how can the credibility of Catholic authority in general be restored, whether that authority be vested in particular offices, in the Bible, in traditions, in teachers, in parents, or in other embodiments and carriers of the Christian message and spirit?

The emphasis here is on authority, tradition and priesthood because these are part of the constellation of signs and values which have characterized Catholicism, if not also distinguished it from other corporate expressions of Christian faith. If the Catholic Church is successfully to transcend its present historical crisis, it will do so through recovery and reappropriation of its special ecclesial and theological identity.

No emphasis has been more characteristic of Catholicism over the centuries than the sacramental. Paul Tillich in his *Protestant Era* and, more recently, Langdon Gilkey in his *Catholicism Confronts Modernity* are among those outside observers who have not failed to note this point. Catholicism is committed to the principle of mediation: the created world mediates the presence of God (what was once called "natural revelation"); Jesus of Nazareth mediates the redemptive activity of God (Catholic theologian Edward Schillebeeckx refers to Christ as the "sacrament of encounter with God"); the church mediates Christ. The seven sacraments mediate the saving work of Christ in and through the church; priests and other ministers continue — even supervise and direct — the mediating action of God in Christ. The word of God is mediated through the preaching and doctrines of the church; and their reliability, in turn, is ensured by those who have been set apart (*cleros*) to oversee (*episcopos*) the whole Spirit-directed process. The love, mercy and justice of God and Christ are mediated through the love, mercy and justice of the church in mission.

Signs of Life

Contemporary Catholicism is marked by vitality, growth and even excitement at those points where it reaffirms its abiding commitment to the sacramental principle. Indeed, Catholicism since the Second Vatican Council has emphasized anew its conviction that the church is first and foremost the people of God and, as such, the sacrament of the Lord's presence among us *(Dogmatic Constitution on the Church, n. 1)*. The church is, before all else, a mystery—that is, "a reality imbued with the hidden presence of God" (Pope Paul VI).

1. Because the Catholic Church perceives itself primarily as a people rather than as a hierarchical organization (and the issue was sharply drawn at Vatican II in the debate over the ordering of chapters 2 and 3 of the *Dogmatic Constitution on the Church*; i.e., whether the chapter on the hierarchy would come before or after the chapter on the people of God), co-responsibility is now in process of becoming fully operative at every level of the church's ecclesiastical life and government. And the new pope, John Paul II, was already a champion of the collegial principle at the Second Vatican Council and in subsequent international synods of bishops. He remains so today, even if he might understand that principle differently from more progressive theologians and bishops.

2. The liturgical renewal, under way from the earliest decades of this century, has advanced at a truly extraordinary pace, so much so that Catholics take for granted that worship (the Eucharist, the new rites of baptism and of reconciliation, etc.) must be intelligible, meaningful, joyous and spiritually enriching—and at the same time engage the active participation of all for whom and by whom it is celebrated.

3. Ministry is seen less and less as a clerical preserve and increasingly as a service open in principle to every qualified member of the church, without regard for sex, marital status or ordination. The emergence of pastoral-ministry degree programs in Catholic colleges and universities is only one indication of this important trend. The prominence of laypersons in the religious education field, often as parish directors (DREs), is another.

Involvement in the Sociopolitical Order

4. The church's commitment to social justice, already mandated so forcefully in the great papal encyclicals from Pope Leo XIII to Pope Paul VI and in Vatican II's *Pastoral Constitution on the Church in the Modern World,* moves constantly into higher gear—whether through the lobbying activities of the United States Catholic Conference, the broadly based "Call to Action" conference in Detroit, the U.S. Bishops' Campaign for Human Development, or any number of other, less heralded social-action ventures at the diocesan and parish levels. Nor are the recent popularity and influence of liberation theology to be discounted, its several deficiencies notwithstanding.

Correlative with this renewed involvement in the sociopolitical order is the church's increasing sensitivity to the public impact of its style of life. A bishop's purchase of an expensive residence evokes strong protest. Congregations of religious women commit themselves to live simply, as a way of identifying with the poor. The urge to travel first class when economy or even standby will do is noticeably on the wane. Where it is not, such journalistic outlets as the *National Catholic Reporter* will see to it that excesses are properly reported and skewered in public view.

5. Theological renewal also reflects Catholicism's persistent effort to exploit its own best traditions. Scholars like Avery Dulles, David Tracy, Richard McCormick and Charles Curran continue to stand out in the United States, as Karl Rahner, Edward Schillebeeckx, Yves Congar and Hans Küng do on the European front. The sacramentality of Jesus Christ is underscored in recent efforts to construct a Christology "from below," focusing on the humanity of Christ ("man for others") as the mediating principle of divine grace. Revelation is understood no longer as simply a "deposit" of truths given once and for all and then given over to the proprietary care of the magisterium, but as a continuing process of divine self-disclosure and self-communication through the "signs of the times."

6. Because of the widening of its theological and educational horizons, Catholicism today is more deliberately and intentionally ecumenical in its ecclesial practice than ever before in its history. Dialogue has replaced polemics (the bilateral consultations are, of course, a principal

case in point); ecumenical collaboration in seminary training is the rule rather than the exception (the Boston Theological Institute is a good example); common prayer and sometimes intercommunion set a new tone for joint retreats, study days, workshops and social-action projects.

7. Whereas holiness and spirituality were once regarded as the private pursuits of priests and nuns, an increasing number of laity are engaged in the quest for a personal relationship with Jesus Christ, the nourishment offered by God's biblical word, and a life transformed and enriched by the Holy Spirit. And even priests and sisters have come to acknowledge a certain aridity in their own spiritual formation and routine. The Catholic Charismatic Renewal has provided an alternative style of Christian experience for many thousands of U.S. Catholics. Books once condescendingly categorized as "spiritual reading" shoot to the top of the religious best-seller lists. Interest in retreats and spiritual direction is heightened among the young as well as the middle-aged.

Playing by the Old Rules

But our report is necessarily mixed; otherwise, how explain the facts with which we began? For every impulse toward growth in U.S. Catholicism there seems to be a corresponding pull in the opposite direction:

1. Where parish councils exist, they are often without decision-making authority, are distracted by relatively trivial issues, and do not attract the most gifted and involved members of a local community. Few dioceses even have a pastoral council, and almost none of these works at or near its potential. Vatican bureaucracies try to play by the "old rules," whether in attempting to put over the revised Code of Canon Law or in correcting "abuses" or "distortions" in American Catholic pastoral practice. And no one needs to be told that autocratic styles of leadership still obtain in more dioceses, parishes and religious communities than many would care to dwell on. Bishops, meanwhile, are still selected by a process that is at once secret and restricted. Those who are appointed to the large, prestigious archdioceses are, for the most part, theologically "safe" and pastorally "prudent"—which means that they are often either firmly

conservative or personally colorless.

2. The liturgy of the church is too often corrupted by theological ignorance and aesthetic clumsiness. Some planners and celebrants haven't learned the difference between therapy or play on the one hand, and the worship of God refined and structured by the objective spirit of Roman liturgy on the other. On the other side, even such modest break-throughs as the use of altar girls at mass are still stubbornly resisted.

3. Ministry, newly broadened to appeal to lay as well as clerical and religious candidates, frequently attracts the hurt, the alienated, the naive and the intellectually weak. And in the case of the ordained ministry of priesthood, one senses a bull market in rigidity, fascination with clerical prerogatives, and psychic and intellectual flaccidity. Women, meanwhile, are still excluded from ordination, and so, too, are the married and those who would like the option to marry. The new pope, on this score at least, gives little promise of change. Indeed, he has been explicit in his opposition to the ordination of women.

Lost in a Fogbank of Denunciations

4. The commitment to social justice is sometimes embarrassing in its simplicity and romanticism, and offensive in its appalling selectivity of targets. South Africa is always a sure bet to bring out the marchers or elicit a convention resolution, but never the bloodbath drawn by the Khmer Rouge "liberators" of Cambodia or the panic and starvation induced by its subsequent Vietnamese "liberators." Catholicism's historic care for the clarification of moral principles and the responsible application thereof is lost in a fogbank of pop-Marxist, hate-America-first "prophetic" denunciations and exhortations. On the other side, conservative opposition to Catholic social activism is as vehement as ever, and occasionally the bishops yield to the pressure where it counts; i.e., in the writing of their budgets.

Meanwhile, the right-to-life zealotry escalates without a word of reproach or even the mildest of public criticisms from the church's leadership. How can any Catholic, committed to his or her church's rich social doctrine, be less than outraged by the senseless defeats in 1978 of Senator Dick Clark in Iowa and Congressman Donald Fraser in Minnesota because they failed to pass this one-issue test?

5. There is such stress at times on the humanity of Jesus that his

Lordship is all but lost. He becomes a model or an exemplar, but no more. And revelation is so "ongoing," so much in "process," that we risk losing all meaningful contact with our roots and our principal points of passage. At the other end of the spectrum, small groups continue to agitate for suppression of "heresy," generating a chilling effect on the invitation of competent theologians to lecture in certain dioceses or to serve as consultants to the body of bishops.

6. Ecumenism, if the truth be told, is almost dead in the water, at least at the officially approved levels. U.S. bishops regularly receive reports on the progress of bilateral consultations (most recently at their November 1978 meeting), and just as regularly ignore them in practice. We are no closer to intercommunion, even under canonically controlled circumstances, nor to the mutual recognition of ordained ministries, recommended by the most sophisticated of the dialogues—the Roman Catholic-Lutheran consultation.

7. The new surge of Catholic spirituality is not unmixed with biblical fundamentalism, authoritarianism and political conservatism. What began as an essentially progressive movement has developed too often into an anti-intellectual, Jesus-the-Spirit-and-I pietism. The charismatic movement might just as possibly be a sign of the sickness of contemporary Catholicism as of its vitality. Complete returns are not yet in.

Needed Reforms

How, then, are we to get from here to there? For the Roman Catholic, as for any Christian of a high-church tradition, the course requires renewed fidelity to one's own theological and pastoral identity and to the principle of quality in official leadership. The papacy, the episcopacy and the ordained priesthood are not simply ecclesiological problems to be explained away under the hot lights of ecumenical exchange. They are gifts to the church, without which the church lacks something constitutive to its being as the Body of Christ and to its mission as God's holy people.

There is no single formula for Catholic progress, to be sure. But if any human instrument stands above the rest, it is a reform of the process by which pastoral leaders are formed, selected and evaluated. Pope John XXIII showed the world what the papacy can be like and what it can accomplish in the name of Christ and for the sake of the

Kingdom of God when the right person occupies the chair of Peter—just as Gregory XVI in the 19th century showed us how disastrous such a pontificate can be when the bark of Peter has an unintelligent naysayer at the helm.

Closer to home, the same can be said of the Catholic Church's present episcopal, institutional and intellectual leadership. Place Notre Dame's Father Theodore Hesburgh as the cardinal-archbishop of a major U.S. diocese like New York or Chicago and then as president of the National Conference of Catholic Bishops, and see what new life the Spirit can breathe into the church. Adopt the Canadian model where bishops of smaller dioceses are effectively eligible for positions of national leadership, and a new course can be plotted for U.S. Catholic policies. Among the more promising of such U.S. bishops are James Malone (Youngstown, Ohio), Cletus O'Donnell (Madison, Wisconsin), John Cummins (Oakland), Frank Hurley (Anchorage, Alaska), Walter Sullivan (Richmond, Virginia), Rembert Weakland (Milwaukee), Frank Rodimer (Paterson, New Jersey), and Howard Hubbard (Albany).

And then let these be joined by the extraordinary leadership talent among the religious communities of women: Nadine Foley, Margaret Brennan, Kathleen Keating, Sara Butler, Sandra Schneiders and the like. For the Catholic Church is going to go nowhere from here without the active participation and support of its most capable and committed women. Indeed, it is almost an axiom of recent U.S. Catholic history that the sisters have been the one group consistently out in front in exploring new styles of Christian existence, new kinds of apostolates, new modes of decision-making, new ways of educating. It may be the success of the women's movement within the church and the emergence of leadership from that movement which will determine the forward course of Catholicism for the next several decades.

Pope John Paul II has the power to free that creative energy if he chooses. It may be still too early to tell which ecclesiological and pastoral instincts will eventually dominate his pontificate: his commitment to collegiality and to the dignity of every single person or his traditional attitudes toward teaching authority, women, and sexuality in general. Which of two predecessors will guide his ministry—John XXIII or Paul VI? If John, the renewal of the Catholic Church will be advanced;

if Paul, the tensions and conflicts of the past 15 years will intensify, and Catholicism will have to wait at least another generation (and another papacy) to emerge from its present trauma.

In the end, it is the new pope's sheer power of intellect and apparent depth of character which give one hope.

12

Presbyterian Prognosis: Guarded

The two chief groups of Presbyterians are the only mainline church folk who are still fighting the War Between the States.

JANET HARBISON PENFIELD

"The church is a mess."

"In the past year, I think, we have turned the corner and are coming back."

"Things look healthier on the surface, but we are still sick underneath—it is only a remission."

Those three remarks of the past several months came from a woman Presbyterian leader and from two different Presbyterian moderators (chief elected officers). Sleuths in the Presbyterian paddock may be able to figure out who said what. Although there are quite a few "Presbyterian" denominations in the United States—the newest being a couple of hundred breakaway congregations called the Presbyterian Church in America—there are just two Presbyterian denominations that signify. These are the Presbyterian Church in the United States (southern) and the United Presbyterian Church in the United States of America (mostly northern). This article will deal only with these two—and perhaps more with the northern than with the southern wing.

Split Presbyterians

Any discussion of the present state and future prospects of Presbyterianism in the United States is complicated by the fact that the two

---

Ms. Penfield is a free-lance writer and the editor of In Common, *a newsletter published by the Consultation on Church Union.*

chief groups of Presbyterians are the only mainline church folk still fighting the War Between the States. The UPCUSA is big—over 2.5 million members even with losses that have totaled about half a million in the past ten years. The PCUS has around 900,000 members. The northern church has quite a few outposts in the south. The two denominations have a number of union presbyteries (regional groupings of congregations) and are talking about the possibility of union synods (bigger groupings, made up of presbyteries). The two denominations have a seminary that is related to both.

But they are not one church, even though they have been discussing the possibility of reuniting ever since the Civil War broke them apart—and most recently, since 1969. A joint committee proposed one plan of reunion, and then, when the original plans drew criticism from all points of the compass, offered another, simpler scheme of union.

This plan is now ostensibly being studied by members of the two denominations. Meanwhile, there is a joint strategy committee, which is working to merge, or at least to harmonize, as much of the Presbyterian enterprise as possible. The two denominations have agreed to hold their national legislative meetings in the same place every other year from now on, starting in Kansas City in 1979.

Unlike other mainline Protestant churches, the Presbyterians hold a national legislative clambake every year. This General Assembly is made up of equal numbers of ministers of word and sacrament, and ordained ruling elders. The ruling elder is a hybrid animal who is ordained but still lay (to the puzzlement of members of other churches). Ruling elders, chosen from and by the congregation, make up what is called a "session," which governs a congregation and sends its ordained people—two by two, ministers and ruling elders, as if they were waltzing into the ark—to the monthly meetings of the next higher "court" or "judicatory," the presbytery. The presbytery can discuss such lofty subjects as the denomination's confession of faith and such mundane ones as the price of presbytery suppers. It ordains ministers. It generally has and spends quite a bit of money on projects it figures out or approves. It may consist of representatives from a handful of congregations or of a mob representing a hundred or more local flocks. The two main branches of Presbyterianism in the United States are identical in the way they organize to run their affairs. This commonality should make reunion easier.

Reunion? Not Now

There seem, however, to be other snags. Lest this article turn into an elementary seminar on Presbyterian polity, let us consider why most people don't think Presbyterian reunion is coming any time soon, so that Presbyterians, perhaps more than other American Protestants, are doomed to quite a few years more of navel-gazing.

The chief surface obstacle to reunion between the northern and southern Presbyterians is what is called the "three-fourths provision." In a fit of absentmindedness some 50 years ago, the PCUS voted that whenever a change in its constitution is at stake, three-fourths of the presbyteries must approve. Since there are about 60 presbyteries in the southern church, 45 have to OK a constitutional change. Such overwhelming enthusiasm for changing anything is hard to come by in any organization, even one of presumably like-minded Christians. The UPCUSA requires only two-thirds of its presbyteries to approve a constitutional change.

It is thus very tempting for northern Presbyterians to blame the failure to reunite on the southern wing. At a recent PCUS General Assembly, indeed, a wonderfully wrought (in the view of some) new confession of faith and the idea of a book of confessions of the church (the latter notion adopted ten years ago by the northern church) went down to defeat. Thirty-nine presbyteries were for it (not quite two-thirds), 21 against. The proposed new confession may be used in the churches and undoubtedly will be by many. And the vows a candidate for ordination to the ministry must take were brought up to date, making it possible for young would-be pastors to join their elders without affirming that they believe that the Westminster Confession (now over 300 years old) contains "the system of doctrine taught in the Holy Scriptures." Changing ordination vows does not require three-fourths approval.

But union would. Wily schemes for outwitting the three-fourths rule by weighting the presbyteries so as to make some more equal than others seem rather unrealistic to many. In any case, they could not take effect for some years. And whatever the rules, it is not at all clear that members of the southern church really want to be merged into the much larger northern one. The camaraderie, the good-ol'-boy atmosphere, the reflective conservatism, the high standards of giving of time and money which prevail in the PCUS might be diluted. And many in the northern church are no more eager. Black members of the UPCUSA in the southeastern states fear a loss of their local autonomy if they were merged into the overwhelmingly white PCUS presbyteries.

Women look darkly at the fact that there are still about a third of all the PCUS congregations that have no women deacons or elders. (There are a lot of northern churches that don't, either.) And the southern church recently ruled that if a man in his wisdom still finds himself conscientiously unable to participate in ordaining women, that belief should be no bar to his own ordination. He should simply make himself scarce when women are to be ordained.

The UPCUSA has been having its own hassle over the tender consciences of some of its male members. After the usual process of ratification by a majority of presbyteries, there has been written into the UPCUSA Book of Order Section 47.01, which requires that both men and women be elected to sessions of local churches. Women have been eligible to serve as elders in congregations since 1930, and many have served. But a number of congregations (as many as 1,300?) have never had a woman serving on their sessions. Some, at least, of these are dominated by men who believe that women are relegated by Scripture to the position of the ruled, and must never by numbered among the rulers.

Opposition to Section 47.01 has been organized by some of these men (and a few women)—this despite the clear intention and repeated statements of denominational leaders that they have no intention of casting into outer darkness those congregations that disagree with the majority, and will administer 47.01 in a pastoral spirit. To some, the fuss about ordaining women seems, to say the least, "antiquarian" (*Presbyterian Outlook*). The truth is that it is merely another manifestation of the congregationalism Presbyterians can't seem to shake. Men of the southern church, though, are probably reassured to see the northern church fighting this particular battle again. And women of both churches are more inclined to view reunion as a doubtful blessing.

Specific recommendations that the two denominations merge their vocation agencies, their publications and the like have met with a less-than-enthusiastic response from those who would be expected to merge. A proposal that the two main journals of the denominations be melded into one was characterized in the southern General Assembly as "the last thing we should do before we call the U-Haul," particularly as the editor of the southern journal said that nobody had consulted *him* about the proposal. Perhaps the definitive word about current prospects for reunion was spoken by the PCUS journal, which felicitously admitted that "eventual union of the churches seems to be definite eventually" *(Presbyterian Survey,* July 1977, p. 71).

Other Ecumenical Affairs

Presbyterians are traditionally middle-of-the-road Protestants in most ways, and inclined to be ecumenical in stance just so long as their openness doesn't seem too likely to lead to a confrontation with real merger possibilities. Thus both the main Presbyterian bodies are active in, and have taken a strong lead in, the Consultation on Church Union, the ten-denomination effort to bring about organic union of a large portion of American Protestantism. Only when it appeared that a real plan of union might be looming up for a vote did the U.S.A. Presbyterians briefly take themselves out of COCU. They came back the following year, since it is unthinkable that people should be talking about future ecumenical options and they not be there.

Both the National Council of Churches and the World Council of Churches receive the support of the Presbyterian denominations. Lately, the PCUS has not even made threats to dissolve its relations with ecumenical bodies. (General Assemblies of that denomination used to be characterized by hairbreadth escapes from withdrawal to a totally sectarian stance.) The southern branch of the Presbyterians not long ago distinguished itself by holding an epoch-making ecumenical conference and a series of local seminars on ecumenical questions, as well as by voting that a token number of members of other denominations may in future attend General Assemblies as regular members, with voice though without vote. Some observers feel that this may be the beginning of a real ecumenical breakthrough in which denominational assemblages will at least listen to the views of those whom they purport to esteem as Christians like themselves.

Restructure and Afterward

Both the reunion of Presbyterians and church union in general, however, are rather low on Presbyterians' worry lists. Looming very large until recently has been what some refer to as "destructure." Both main branches of Presbyterianism have been suffering from a shortage of money at the national level, even though members' giving to the church has risen quite dramatically over the past few years. The money has been going mostly to local congregations and to presbytery causes, as well as to other marginally church-related enterprises near at hand. Inflation has eaten up some of the money gains. But distrust of national staffs and national programs is what has given the *coup de grâce* to enterprises like the UPCUSA's *Trends* (it died after an issue on homosexuality), support for church-related colleges, inner-city experimentation—the list is nearly endless. The PCUS national staff is said to be half as large as it was ten years ago.

Structures were admittedly unwieldy and out of date. But without the crisis of confidence and the money crunch—interrelated but separate causes of shrinking national programs—the restructuring surely would not have been so devastating. In the northern church at least (the PCUS seems to have succeeded in thinking small without quite so much trauma) there was a long period of crisis—partaking of the nature of a grief reaction, as one observer noted. Enchantment with business-model forms of operating resulted in a new national church organization so complex and confusing hardly anyone could understand it. (Most of the Potemkin-village aspects of this part of restructure seem to have been quietly scrapped.) Since many of the "old hands" were not rehired, or departed in disgust; since in hiring, as somebody said, "mediocrity went out looking for mediocrity and found it"; since for quite a while people didn't know exactly what their jobs were, and most of the secretaries who ultimately answered the phones seemed to have come on the job the day before yesterday—for all these reasons, local confidence in the national machinery, already at a low ebb, declined still further.

If the Presbyterian, lay or clergy, thinks much about the national or world church, it is, alas, apparently still with a lot of suspicion. The *Presbyterian Layman*, an unofficial publication which always has been "agin" the government, says it is now the largest Presbyterian journal in point of circulation. It very probably is. Anybody can afford to read it, since it comes for nothing. In its pages distrust of the whole national Presbyterian establishment, the newly-shined-up and refurbished one just as much as the old, is expressed in dozens of ways, some truer to the facts than others.

National Presbyterian leaders sometimes wish people would think about them more than they do, and above all RSM—Remember Send Money. Those close to the national scene are increasingly impressed with the high quality of present staff members, and increasingly depressed by the continuing congregationalism that manifests itself particularly in the determination of local churches and presbyteries to spend their money on projects close to home.

Enter, the Women—with Banners

The role of women in the church is something Presbyterians are increasingly obliged to think about. The church seems to be making a valiant effort to include women. The southern branch chose a woman, Patricia McClurg, as the staff head of one of its main national divisions. A good sprinkling of women can be found on most of the national Presbyterian staff lists. There are even a couple of presbytery executives in the UPCUSA who are women. Task forces on women's concerns multiply. Women seminary students, and a few women seminary professors, have changed the looks if not the attitudes of seminary campuses in the past few years. Considerable numbers of women seminary graduates are looking for jobs, and sometimes finding them, though the number of women who are senior pastors in charge of staffs of "big-budget" churches is not overwhelming. In fact, I have yet to hear of the first one.

On the other hand, the UPCUSA has had two women moderators of the General Assembly, both very able people—the second, Thelma Adair, having the added qualification of being black. An ordained woman minister of word and sacrament has been vice-moderator of the UPCUSA General Assembly.

Women tend to maintain that while originally, in the first restructure of the UPCUSA, they were given quite a few professional national staff jobs, when the re-restructure came about following a continuing falling-off in funds, many of these recently hired women were "terminated," in the polite phrase.

The situation of blacks and other minority group members is perhaps somewhat better, at least in proportion to their numbers in the denomination. But white maledom, generally speaking, remains triumphant in the Presbyterian churches. United Presbyterian Women, the official national group of the UPCUSA (the PCUS doesn't seem to have one), is generally disregarded by the male brass. (In some areas, and notably in money-raising, UPW seems to have more creative ideas than the rest of the church put together.)

Congregational pastor-seeking committees remain reluctant to consider calling ordained women to their pulpits, although they make the proper gestures. It is particularly difficult for a woman to move from her first job into a second one. Many women are discovering that specialized ministries—chaplaincies, ecumenically funded short-term projects, ministries to single people and older people—are a lot easier for them to enter than ordinary parishes. There have been no male revolts against the increasing numbers of women in Presbyterian power posts to compare with the clashes the Episcopal Church is witnessing. Fewer and fewer Presbyterians find anything unseemly in the sight of a woman in the pulpit. Future prospects for significant influence of women in the real decision-making of the church look good. But the women will have to keep the pressure on. The men liked things better the way they were 20 years ago than the way they may be 20 years hence. For evidence, see discussion of reunion prospects in preceding paragraphs.

Too Many Seminaries?

There are not only many more women students in Presbyterian seminaries nowadays; there are many more students, period. Not all of these are Presbyterians. But then a large percentage—the exact number is unclear—of Presbyterian candidates for the ministry are in non-Presbyterian schools. Some of these are conservative nondenominational seminaries—and some are traditionally more liberal schools like Union (New York), Yale and Harvard.

Despite the universal admission that there is a tight job situation in the Presbyterian church, and despite the fact that the draft (which some people thought drove Vietnam-avoiders into the ministry) is no more, the number of theological students grows and grows. "Twenty per cent more in our seminary than last year," says one seminary official. "If we don't let qualified candidates in here, they'll find somewhere else to go," remarks another.

The UPCUSA Council of Theological Seminaries has no real control over the seminaries related to the denomination. Each is an independent entity with its own board of trustees and faculty. Even though the faculties have to be approved by the General Assembly, and the seminaries receive a (sadly small) fraction of their operating budgets from the General Assembly, the church at large does not run its theological schools. The existence of the Presbyteries Cooperative Examinations, which candidates must take prior to ordination, is a mild form of quality control over seminary education. But the ultimate responsibility for ordination remains with the presbyteries. And their standards, according to report, are quite variable.

Though everyone agrees that there are too many Presbyterian seminaries, there is scant agreement as to which ones should be phased out—even if this course of action were a possibility. And while everyone agrees that a good theological education can be obtained in any one of the present Presbyterian-related seminaries (and in many others), most sideline commentators can see room for improvement, too. The changes they suggest often point in diametrically opposed directions:

"Why don't they teach preaching any more?"

"Students don't get enough grounding in biblical languages . . . in pastoral care . . . in practical details of running a congregation."

"Some of the students graduate without ever conducting, or even witnessing, a funeral . . . they have no idea how to conduct a session meeting . . . church history began for them with the freedom rides in the 1960s."

Things, in short, were better in the good old days.

Theories on what to do about the shortage of jobs for ordained ministers are also varied. Some local committees that must pass on candidates' qualifications seem to be tightening up their standards. Other observers feel that, "Until the church starts to grow in numbers again, things can only get worse," or, contrariwise, "There's no real job shortage—just timid congregations," or, "The development of more specialized ministries is the only answer."

Ordain Avowed Homosexuals?

Apparently much less seemly in the eyes of many than a woman in a pulpit is the presence of an avowed homosexual there. Everyone agrees that there are undoubtedly already ordained ministers of word and sacrament in the Presbyterian church (and ruling elders, too) who are homosexual in tendency if not in practice. "If they just wouldn't come out of the closet," moaned one minister, glooming over the fact that the Presbyterians have had the issue of the ordination of homosexual people put before them in a way that can't be ignored.

"A little hypocrisy is sometimes a good thing," suggested one sage of the church. And a little hypocrisy is what the Presbyterians seem to have settled for on the homosexual issue, at least for now. Neither the PCUS nor the UPCUSA is willing to ordain an avowed, practicing homosexual. Both maintain that the Bible forbids it.

The northern church confronted the issue directly at a recent General Assembly. In spite of the irenic majority report of a special study committee that had looked into all aspects of the homosexuality question—a report that would in effect have given presbyteries the option of deciding to ordain or not ordain homosexual people according to whatever light the Holy Spirit happened to have given them at a particular time—the General Assembly came out firmly against ordination of homosexuals to any office in the church. Avowed, practicing homosexuals may be members of the church, the report that was adopted maintains. They are people and the objects of God's love. They should be loved by Christians, too, and their civil rights should be protected. Their right to hold jobs in secular society should be upheld, also. But they should not be ordained.

Many Presbyterians, including some avowed, practicing homosexuals, see the adoption of this stance as at least an improvement over the total ignoring of homosexuality that obtained in the past. Thorough study of the topic took place all across the northern church before the homosexuality decision was made, and this is a gain in itself. Sex is a topic Presbyterians (and other Protestants, too) have always had trouble with. The very existence of homosexuals sets up conflicts in Presbyterians between their clear understanding that Jesus Christ came in order to save sinners (which is all of us) and a visceral revulsion "straights" often feel toward "gays." In the course of the recent discussions, quite a few Presbyterians who claimed they had never met any homosexuals did meet some, and heard them speak, and saw that they were really quite nice people.

And a Few More Problems

There does not seem to be a group of towering leaders of the Presbyterian church today as there was, say, 20 years ago. Perhaps the tall men of those days merely looked like giants because they loomed so far above us. But today's thinkers seem to be hidden away in seminaries or off in the wilds writing books. The likes of John Mackay and Eugene Carson Blake (Hermann Morse, Charles Leber, Paul Calvin Payne, too) are not moving and shaking the UPCUSA today. James McCord, president of Princeton Seminary, and William P. Thompson, stated clerk (chief executive officer) of the northern church, sometimes seem to be Mr. Poo and Mr. Bah as they pass back and forth top posts in the National Council of Churches, the World Council of Churches, and the World Alliance of Reformed Churches. But McCord really majors in running his seminary, and Thompson (besides having the built-in handicap of not being an ordained minister, and therefore of not quite being a member of the club) has his hands full running the affairs of the denomination—and not infrequently, over the past several years, carrying two problem-filled jobs at once.

For Presbyterians, perhaps because they feel so strongly that God is Lord of all of life, not just of Sunday churchgoing, seem to get themselves into situations that evoke conflict. Grants of the Fund for the Self-Development of People have caused a number of flaps in the church; so have those of the Legal Defense Fund. Angela Davis is still a fighting name in the United Presbyterian Church.

Differences of theological viewpoint between those who believe the church must speak Christ's reconciling word by doing as well as preaching and those who concentrate heavily on personal piety and wish the church would stay out of the world continue to torment Presbyterians. Differences also divide those who believe in "the inerrancy of Scripture," whatever meaning they attach to the phrase, and those who feel that recent biblical scholarship has cast new light on old texts. (Some of the former, but not all, are as devoted to social action as some of the latter.) The splits are not simple. To reconcile these two points of view within the church may be the chief unfinished business of Presbyterians. Whether it can be done may be in the next few years their chief test. Many of the younger Presbyterian leaders whose voices are beginning to be heard combine in themselves vigorous Bible-based personal faith and a fierce drive to make the church count for more in struggles toward justice in the world.

Sprouts of Hope

Presbyterians of this stamp see at least a few sprouts of hope in the church. For instance:

● A broad program to educate Presbyterians about hunger in the world, to seek solutions to the conditions that bring about world hunger, and to try to transform the life styles of Americans is gaining momentum through the UPCUSA. If the ink and paper expended so far in this effort were edible, they would go far to ease the world's hunger pangs. But more than talk is going on: the Hunger Fund has appropriated millions of dollars to various projects in the U.S. and around the world.

● The "six great ends of the church"—the Six Big Ones, in the phrase of a Presbyterian phrase-maker—are on the study list of the whole UPCUSA. That this study is considered important may signal an end to the "theological amnesia" that has caused "a profound lack of identity and lack of purpose and direction" among Presbyterians of late, according to one of the denomination's chief thinkers. (The six great ends, in case you had forgotten, are proclamation of the gospel; shelter, nurture and spiritual fellowship of the children of God; maintenance of divine worship; preservation of truth; promotion of social righteousness; the exhibition of the kingdom of heaven to the world.)

● A high-powered conference on mission that set forth directions for the mission of the church both in the U.S. and abroad for the foreseeable future was recently held by the PCUS.

● Though the Presbyterians are still losing members (the PCUS far less than its northern cousin, but then the PCUS is smaller to start with), the rate of decline has slowed. And the denominations are now living within vastly reduced budgets—not happily, perhaps, and wishing they had more money, but "making it."

● National structures, after their shaky start, are beginning to look as if they might stand. The denominations have fought off efforts to tinker around some more, and have settled in to give the present arrangements a chance to prove themselves. According to one expert, it takes about five years for structures to shake down after an upheaval. The point to making the changes in the first place—at least part of the point—is to dehorn the creative thinkers and leaders who are getting too far ahead of the troops. This was accomplished in the late, dismal reorganizations to the point that nobody could decide much of anything. At times, indeed, at least from the UPCUSA point of view, it looked as if Somebody Up There—or wherever—was really trying to frustrate the national church; disasters and catastrophes overtook key leaders to an extent that scarcely seemed normal.

● Presbyterians are once more concentrating on evangelism and new-church development—growth, in short. A presbytery conference on evangelism drew three times as many people as had been expected. Since studies indicate that churches grow where leadership is strong, particularly the leadership of a pastor, there is less tendency to downgrade the importance of theologically able, personally well-equipped ministers. The oversupply of candidates for jobs and the cumbersome Presbyterian system of pastor-seeking and pastor-placement (much emphasis on church profile forms and other *paperasse*) mean that some churches are staying pastorless for perhaps inordinately long times. But quite a few instances of happy unions of pastor and congregation are reported, too.

Although some within the denomination say they see an increase in the creeping congregationalism among Presbyterians—that disease which either causes or accompanies loss of confidence in a connectional system—there is evidence that Presbyterians are still much as they always were, if one but scratch the surface.

A recent sociological survey attempts to isolate characteristics that particularly distinguish members of various religious groups. Those marking Reformed believers in general include: a conviction that the ministry belongs to the whole people of God; a concomitant belief in representative government; an emphasis on the sovereignty of God; an expectation that learning, especially biblical and theological learning, will mark the leadership of the church; a concern to understand the historical and confessional roots of the church; a broad concern for social issues. On this last point, there is a divergence between ordained ministers and members, the latter placing more emphasis on individual salvation, and the former on healing the ills of society. This split is really nothing new; it has caused the Presbyterian churches many a headache over the years.

Presbyterians (according to this survey) expect worship to include instruction. They are not narrowly denomination-minded but tend to accept all other Christians in a nonjudgmental way. Presbyterians emphasize the sinfulness of all humankind, including themselves.

Perhaps, indeed, the Presbyterian tendency to see the world through dark glasses makes it hard for Presbyterians to recognize signs of hope when they appear. Renewed health and excitement are reported from many congregations. Ministries to single people, older people, people in trouble, the sick and the dying increasingly interest both pastors and laypeople. The UPCUSA has embarked on a Major Mission Fund that is expected to raise at least $10 million more than the $60 million originally planned.

The Doubts Still Nag

But despite these apparent signs that the Presbyterian church is no longer so sick that it can scarcely hold its head up, and may indeed be getting better, it is hard to mark anything more optimistic on its chart than "condition: guarded." Nobody is really sure what will be the effect of the homosexuality decision. New dissension over the degree of involvement the church should assume in society is always a likelihood. Disagreements about the style mission should take are endemic and in some quarters worsening. Many feel that the church won't really be taking the gospel to the whole world until it begins to send out Americans as missionaries in the old-fashioned way and in the old-fashioned numbers. Others are quite certain that the younger churches don't want the old-style mission and won't stand for it. Although the equality of women before Christ was theoretically settled in the northern church more than 40 years ago, women's status may yet send some congregations—or lots of women—out of the denomination.

Sensing the fragmented temper of the church, the panjandrums who set up the UPCUSA Major Mission Fund have provided for national projects, synod-sponsored projects, and presbytery-initiated ones. With all that local option, there should be something for everyone.

Quite a few observers see the success of the Major Mission Fund as a sort of test of the strength of the northern church. "The Major Mission Fund shows we're on our way," runs a frequently held opinion. "But if we get into more internal dissension, we may blow it all."

13

The Disciples and
the Churches of Christ:
Common Roots, Divergent Paths

The churches' seemingly separate futures will in
no small measure depend on evaluations of the
vitality and limitations of their diverse legacies.

W. CLARK GILPIN

Despite common ancestry in an American religious movement which knew itself as the "Reformation of the 19th century," the Churches of Christ and the Christian Church (Disciples of Christ) today exhibit only faint family resemblances. For a century the congregations of the Christian Church have moved steadily, if at times hesitantly, toward life as one of the "mainstream" Protestant denominations. From the Federal Council of Churches to the Consultation on Church Union (COCU), they have involved themselves in ecumenical relationships; with a restructure of polity during the past decade, they have amplified the connectional dimension of a traditionally congregational ecclesiology.

Meanwhile, *the* Churches of Christ (the article is important) have fiercely resisted identification as yet another denomination. Within a diverse and loosely associated "brotherhood" they have borne witness to their local congregations as whole and autonomous manifestations of the church. In the present decade, while the Christian Church has slowly declined to 1.2 million members, the Churches of Christ have

---

Dr. Gilpin, an assistant professor of church history at the Graduate Seminary of Phillips University, Enid, Oklahoma, is an ordained minister of the Christian Church (Disciples of Christ).

achieved a membership of approximately 2.5 million; the two wings of the "Reformation" seem classic examples of the contrasting religious patterns assessed by Dean Kelley in *Why Conservative Churches Are Growing* (Harper & Row, 1972).

Shared History

This disparate development has insulated the groups from each other. For the person in the pew, commerce between the two communions, whether intellectual, religious or social, is rare. Yet members of both churches have maintained an abiding—some might say excessive—interest in their shared early history. The 41 volumes of founder Alexander Campbell's religious periodical, *The Millennial Harbinger*, remain in print ($350.00 the set) more than a century after original publication ceased. Such pride of ancestry, if exercised critically, may prove singularly beneficial. The churches' seemingly separate futures will in no small measure depend on evaluations of the vitality and limitations of their diverse legacies.

This concern for tradition is itself a matter worth noting, for the founders of the Disciples of Christ had slender regard for matters traditional. When, in the first decade of the 19th century, Thomas and Alexander Campbell immigrated from the north of Ireland to western Pennsylvania, the division and disarray within their own Presbyterian tradition as well as in the other Protestant churches of the frontier profoundly disturbed them. They were soon fired with zeal—not to begin another church but to propagate a movement of purification and reunion within the existing churches. They called on church people from the denominations

> to *begin anew*—to begin at the *beginning;* to ascend at once to the pure fountain of truth, and to neglect and disregard, as though they had never been, the decrees of Popes, Councils, Synods, and Assemblies, and all the traditions and corruptions of an apostate Church. By coming at once to the primitive model and rejecting all human inventions, the Church was to be at once released from controversies of eighteen centuries, and the primitive gospel of salvation was to be disentangled and disembarrassed from all those corruptions and perversions which had heretofore delayed or arrested its progress [*Memoirs of Alexander Campbell*, by Robert Richardson (Lippincott, 1868–70), Vol. I, pp. 257-258].

The Campbells' effort to unite Christians on the foundation of what they perceived to be the New Testament pattern of preaching and discipline thus included an iconoclastic attack on the historic traditions of the churches. The search for the "ancient order" was simultaneously a severe judgment on the present order.

The Campbellite Formula

The document that articulated this program was the *Declaration and Address* written by Thomas Campbell in 1809. Pleading for Christian union through a return to New Testament Christianity, Campbell celebrated the freedom and ability of the individual Christian to interpret Scripture untrammeled by the authority of creed or clergy. An honest look at the Bible, unbiased by preconceived theological notions or denominational ax-grinding, so Campbell argued, would lead the individual to the conclusion that it spoke clearly and with a single voice and that its pattern could be duplicated in the present day. "Where the Scriptures speak, we speak," Campbell announced; "where the Scriptures are silent, we are silent." This formula, so he and his son Alexander believed, could achieve public unity for the church while allowing liberty to the private opinions of its members.

The *Declaration and Address* was published, it should be observed, not as the constitution of a church but as the manifesto of a voluntary society of reformers, the Christian Association of Washington County. And although the society quickly evolved into a congregation and affiliated with the Baptists, the reformers continued to consider themselves a movement. They joined the Baptists not with the idea of being "merely" Baptist but rather on the assumption that they were the leaven by which the Baptist loaf would rise to true Christianity. Strife ensued and, taking a host of Baptist converts, the Disciples of Christ struck out on their own. By the early 1830s, through the persuasive evangelism of Walter Scott and through union with Barton Stone's Christian movement, what had begun as a voluntary society became a rapidly expanding association of churches. Twenty years later the Disciples of Christ were the seventh largest religious group in America.

The remarkable growth of the churches was prompted by the clarity of their message and the ambiguity of their identity. They were not a denomination, it was regularly insisted; they were a movement, a brotherhood. In those optimistic early days, to join a Disciples congregation was to mesh one's personal commitment with the new destiny of the Christian faith. The Campbellite formula was the hallmark of the fellowship: the restoration of primitive Christianity, freedom in Christ, and union among Christians.

But within this church of reformers that formula was asked to do double service. It was at once a challenge to American Protestantism and, increasingly, a platform for Disciples churchmanship. Despite its documented effectiveness in the former capacity, it was to prove increasingly unstable in the latter.

Division and Controversy

Rejection of churchly traditions in favor of Scripture, "the living oracles," had quickly established the distinctive features of Disciples worship and polity: weekly communion, believer's baptism by immersion, and a prominent role for the laity within a congregationalist polity. But when further issues of organization and discipline arose, factions within the church tended to argue their cases by elevating to pre-eminence a particular element of the formula: restoration, freedom or union.

By the end of the 19th century the brotherhood, finding the issues irresolvable, had split. The Churches of Christ, maintaining doctrinal conservatism and emphasizing the element of restoration, proclaimed the organization of missionary societies and the use of instrumental music in worship to be abominations utterly lacking in scriptural warrant. The Christian Church, keeping cautiously open to the currents of critical biblical scholarship, adopted the element of unity as the distinctive Disciples contribution to the faith and proceeded to develop missionary societies and to listen to organ music with an easy conscience.

Controversy was not laid to rest by division, however. Disagreement about the relation between baptism and church membership, about the relation between biblical criticism and biblical restorationism, and about the administration of missionary work split the Christian Church again in the 20th century. The Churches of Christ, too, seemed perennially rocked by controversies, ranging from matters of millenarian theology to the financial support of radio and television ministries. Today the Campbell-Scott-Stone tradition exists in three wings: the Churches of Christ, the Christian Church (Disciples of Christ), and the nondenominational fellowship of Christian Churches and Churches of Christ.

An Unfinished Task

The inability of the traditional Disciples formula to address emerging ecclesiastical and social issues has continued to vex the churches. In 1963 Christian Church historian Ronald E. Osborn evaluated the situation for the Christian Century series "What's Ahead for the Churches?" and found that "though various attempts have been made to combine the elements in differing proportions (RF_9U_4, RF_4U_7) or to concentrate on one or two of the elements, washing the others out, discomfiture has been the recent lot of Disciples as the tradition simmered in uneasy flux" ("Formula in Flux: Reformation for the Disciples of Christ," The Christian Century, September 25, 1963, p. 1163).

Earlier Disciples have thus presented both the Churches of Christ and the Christian Church with an ironic heritage—a movement to restore the church, but one whose self-understanding has inhibited sustained theological reflection about the church's nature and mission. The effort to frame the Disciples message within a comprehensive doctrine of the church still stands before these diverse communions as an unfinished task. Since the two have appropriated their history differently, the common problems will likely receive two quite different sets of answers. But events of the past decade seem to have placed each denomination further along the road toward a richer ecclesiology.

A Movement with a Message

One problem to be confronted could be characterized as the long-term effect of originating from a voluntary society. The Disciples have cherished the image of being a movement with a distinctive message to promulgate. But this message-centered understanding of the fellowship has all too often had as its corollary a contractual understanding of the church. The result has been that withholding funds and withdrawing from "the movement" have been used as tactics for voicing opposition to policies or trends of thinking.

One important reason for decline in Christian Church membership since the late '60s, for example, has been the withdrawal of congregations that objected to the restructure of the denomination's polity. The hallowed designation "brotherhood" can be somewhat misleading, therefore, implying as it does that "the ties that bind" run deep in the blood and transcend issue-related disagreements. In fact, it is precisely this dimension of "brotherhood" which is most at stake for the churches in the immediate future.

The issues here are perhaps most apparent in the Churches of Christ, where emphasis on restoration of New Testament Christianity has placed ideological purity at a premium. The temptation has been to make loyalty to the message and uniform understanding of it tests of fellowship. The sense of being what Churches of Christ historian David E. Harrell has called "a peculiar people" has often lapsed into intolerant exclusivism. Reuel Lemmons, editor of the widely circulated journal *Firm Foundation,* shares the opinion of many church leaders when he laments "the disfellowshipping mania" which regularly threatens to erupt in the congregations. This excessive regard for uniformity, Lemmons declares, has made the churches more interested in "guarding the ramparts and ferreting out the heretics" than in mission. Concern by laypersons and ministers for doctrinal "fidelity" has often been directed toward the faculties of leading church-related colleges, such as California's Pepperdine and Abilene Christian in Texas. Over the past decade these institutions have pursued a delicate course between the expectations of the supporting churches and the canons of modern scholarship.

In the past, the churches' apprehensions about individual thinking occasioned the departure of many talented and well-educated members. In 1966 a group of such exiles published *Voices of Concern* as a public expression of regret that the Churches of Christ had not fostered an "atmosphere in which independent minds may feel at home." The editor, Robert Meyers, expressed hope that new currents of open-mindedness in the churches betokened "a more charitable tomorrow. Thousands are restless and dissatisfied with the aridity of exclusivism and authoritarianism. Bright young minds are refusing to be put off with answers that have no more to commend them than the hoary beard of antiquity" *(Voices of Concern: Critical Studies in Church of Christism* [Mission Messenger, 1966] pp. 2-3).

Has that "more charitable tomorrow" arrived? To a surprising degree the answer is Yes. The Churches of Christ are tolerating a significantly wider spectrum of theological opinion within the fellowship than would have been expected even a decade ago. It remains to be seen whether that tolerance for diversity will extend beyond strictly doctrinal issues to the points at which religious concerns clearly interact with social attitudes. Discussion of the place of women in the ministry, for example, has not yet fully developed in the churches. But, as made clear in a 1971 series by Leroy Garrett in the *Restoration Review*, "the Restoration mind" is concerned with more than whether or not to use a plurality of communion cups during the Lord's Supper; it is also doing its homework on such matters as social justice and race relations. Whatever the exact outcome, those ministers and editors calling for "unity in diversity" may be expected to play an increasingly influential role in the Churches of Christ.

Beyond the Local Church

A second ecclesiological problem being confronted is the status of the churches' mission beyond the local congregation. On this issue the most dramatic recent changes have been within the Christian Church (Disciples of Christ).

Nineteenth century Disciples feared hierarchical authority to such degree that any organization beyond the local congregation was regarded with suspicion. The Churches of Christ have insisted on leaving missionary work to the initiative of the local church, and any joint efforts are typically coordinated by the elders of a large or particularly active congregation. Even for the "cooperative" Christian Church, missionary and benevolent societies were organized and maintained strictly as adjuncts to the actual church—that is, the local congregations. Society officers were given such secular titles as general secretary or president, and annual conventions of the denominations were mass meetings, not representative deliberative gatherings.

During the late '50s, perspectives began to change in the Christian Church. A panel of scholars was commissioned to reassess the church's heritage, and its three-volume report, published in 1963, gave theological impetus to the rethinking of polity. In 1968 the churches accepted a new "provisional design" for the denomination, which in a moderately revised form was approved as "the design" by the 1977 General Assembly. The restructured polity incorporates the old denominational boards and agencies into a more inclusive concept of the church existing in three basic manifestations: local, regional and general. Changes in names reflect the changes in thinking. The International Convention of Christian *Churches* is now the General Assembly of the Christian *Church*. The chief executive officer of the denomination, Kenneth L. Teegarden, is now the general minister, and the state secretaries are now regional ministers.

The broad effects of these significant revisions cannot yet be assessed, but one important feature is surely the expanded responsibility placed at the church's regional level (corresponding roughly to states or clusters of states). Particularly notable is the region's role in care for seminary students and in the oversight of ordination—responsibilities formerly left to the local congregation. The regional ministers are playing a larger part in the denomination's financial deliberations and as advisers in ministerial placement, and one of their number, James A. Moak of Kentucky, recently completed service as moderator of the church's General Assembly. For a denomination not infrequently beleaguered by the distinction between local congregation and general agency, this mediating structure would seem an important addition to the church's life.

Ecumenical Dialogue

A final ecclesiological problem confronting the Churches of Christ and the Christian Church concerns relations with those whom Alexander Campbell liked to refer to as "the parties"—that is, denominations of American Christianity. For a tradition which had Christian union as one of its founding principles, this at first seems an odd problem. But in fact the iconoclastic dimension of the Disciples message made it difficult for this movement-become-a-church to appreciate traditions lacking a "thus saith the Lord" from Scripture. Some of the earliest Disciples missionaries, for example, were sent to Europe to "restore" Christianity on the Continent.

This restorationist repudiation of denominational Christianity has served for decades to isolate the Churches of Christ from the concerns of many American Christians and, equally, has made their concerns nearly incomprehensible to the outsider. Here again, new perspectives are developing. Such scholarly journals as the *Restoration Quarterly* are publishing a number of articles whose historical and theological concerns extend far beyond the old rubrics of biblical exegesis and the history of the restoration movement. Similarly, *Mission*, which began publication in 1967, has received praise from such analysts of the current religious scene as Edwin Gaustad and Martin E. Marty for the skill with which it addresses broad concerns of the Christian faith from a restorationist prespective. Although the old exclusivism dies hard, it is clear that many members of the Churches of Christ are diligent in the effort to bring the tradition into clear dialogue with current issues in theology and ethics.

For the Christian Church, in which the restoration theme has long been deeply submerged, ecumenical discussion and studies of merger have been an increasingly prominent feature of the communion's life throughout the 20th century. In 1977, for example, the Christian Church and the Roman Catholic Church established a five-year International Commission for Dialogue on the general theme of the visible unity of the church. Thus far, representatives have met for study conferences in Indianapolis, Indiana, and in Rome. Also in 1977, the Christian Church began discussions toward possible union with the United Church of Christ. In the fall of 1979 these conversations entered a second phase in which the two churches covenanted to engage in six years of work and study together on three broad topics:

1. the theology and practice of Baptism and the Lord's Supper, giving particular attention to the meaning of the sacraments in our time and their significance for worship and witness;
2. the nature, task, and equipping of ministry, both ordained and lay;
3. the identifying of and responding to the continually emerging new forms and tasks of God's mission, with special attention to the constant need for the church to reform itself.

These joint study tasks are intended to help the two churches discern whether and how their lives and witness would be enhanced by union. The relationship is being pursued in ways compatible with the membership of both in the Consultation on Church Union, and it will be occurring at all levels of the lives of the two churches.

In sum, internal diversity of thinking, more positive relations with the broad Christian tradition, and revisions of polity have set a demanding yet potentially fruitful theological agenda that addresses the whole spectrum of the Disciples of Christ tradition. The movement's founders had hoped that their message would allow them "to ascend at once to the pure fountain of truth"; for their descendants in the Churches of Christ and the Christian Church the goal remains the same, but the route is more arduous.

14

Judaism Today: Survival and Authenticity

The quiet, unanticipated Jewish revival generally takes the form of deed, as befits the pursuit of Jewish authenticity.

EUGENE B. BOROWITZ

The major changes in American Jewish attitudes in the past decades were powered by the general community's shift from confidence in liberal democracy to the assertion of ethnic self-interest. From 1967 to 1973, we gained a self-conscious ethnic realism, and from 1973 to the Camp David agreements we lived in a time of emergency.

The earlier period was given special intensity by our finally confronting the Holocaust and by our intense identification with the State of Israel resulting from the Six-Day War. The Holocaust still pains us on three levels. First, and with incomparable trauma, because of the murder of 6 million of our people. Second, because Allied leaders knew of the butchery and did nothing. Third, because our Jewish leaders then silently accepted that decision not to act. Moved by the general social mistrust of the late 1960s, we Jews have felt that we had special reason to be wary, and we have therefore insisted that our leaders err now only on the side of overasserting our ethnic self-interest.

By 1967, Israel's accomplishments had become a major component of world Jewry's pride and self-respect. The Israelis had saved Jewish lives, reclaimed our ancestral soil, built an economy, fashioned a cul-

Rabbi Borowitz, professor of education and Jewish religious thought at Hebrew Union College–Jewish Institute of Religion in New York City, is founder and editor of the Jewish ethical journal Sh'ma.

ture, created a welfare state and, despite almost unbearable pressures, remained a democracy. There are not many governments founded since World War II of which that can be said. The threat to Jewish existence dramatically exemplified by the Six-Day War brought home to world Jewry how precious Israel's survival and vitality are to all Jews everywhere. The State of Israel symbolizes the Jewish will to live despite the Holocaust. Its continued existence is therefore a human and Jewish testimony of metaphysical import. So in succeeding years, to see the Israelis cruelly isolated in international affairs, to see gun-toting terrorists welcomed to the rostrum of the United Nations while the barely healed survivors of the Holocaust were termed racists, brought most Jews to insist that nothing should take precedence over our devotion to Jewish survival and thus to the State of Israel. Our activism on behalf of Soviet Jews derives from this concern.

The 1973 war showed that one substantial Israeli blunder might lead to destruction. Until Camp David, our community lived with a constant sense of threat. Previous American pressures on the Israelis to settle with the Egyptians as the United States thought proper brought most of our leadership and many of our people to the brink of panic. We discovered zealots among us. Though a minority, they have occasionally been able to carry our majority along with them. How much influence they still have after the Camp David accords, which have been warmly received by most Jews, is difficult to assess. More important, a functioning Israeli-Egyptian peace treaty will end the emergency mentality that has energized our community for over a decade. Nothing going on among us has similar power to arouse our Jewish loyalties. Our maturity will be tested, then, by our having to face the long-range questions about Jewish existence.

But for the moment everything significant about contemporary Jewish life is based on our passionate ethnicity, with its focus on the State of Israel.

Survival Issues

There have always been other serious threats to Jewish survival. Most Jews are far from being learned, observant or pious. About 40 per cent of the marriages involving a Jew are with a non-Jewish partner. Our lovers of the State of Israel do not learn Hebrew, and our appreciators of eastern European culture do not speak Yiddish much. Jewish religiosity also seems a veneer, rarely going beyond a few rituals and an occasional synagogue visit. Inflation and aging are hurting our expensively budgeted, child-centered synagogues.

The problem of the place of women in Jewish life now seems largely confined to Conservative Judaism. After a bit of hesitation, Reform Jews, taking a step consistent with their faith, ordained women as rabbis and invested them as cantors. By contrast, despite an occasional Orthodox voice calling for some liberation of women under Jewish law, our traditional authorities and the masses of Orthodox women seem content with the current assignment of special roles and responsibilities. Conservative Jews have long argued that the processes of traditional Jewish law might be used to authorize such change as modern Jewish life demands. Sanction has recently been given for counting women in the *minyan*, the quorum for services. Yet Conservatism's dominant institution, the Jewish Theological Seminary, does not yet accept women students for the rabbinate. A commission of Conservative Judaism's Rabbinical Assembly has recommended that "qualified women" be admitted to ordination as rabbis. If the commission's report is approved by the faculty, then women could begin entering the seminary to train for the rabbinate. Not ordaining might defend the Conservatives' legal authenticity, which the Orthodox challenge. But finally to ordain women might only stamp the Conservatives as slow Reform Jews.

Some of us, myself included, are troubled by the radically lessened interest and involvement of organized American Jewry in general social problems. Since Lyndon Johnson told American Jewish leaders that the Israelis would get no Phantom jets until American Jews stopped pressuring the United States to get out of the Vietnam war, we have been increasingly docile on the ethical questions facing our nation and world. The common liberal concerns—détente with Russia, reduced armaments, a tough attitude toward nuclear power—were contraindicated by the State of Israel's political interests and thus seemed antithetical to Jewish survival.

Civil rights for all minorities once moved us passionately, but the American Civil Liberties Union's defense of native Nazis' right to demonstrate in Skokie lost that organization about 25 per cent of its

Illinois members and caused much Jewish disaffection nationwide. How far our shift to conservatism has gone is unclear. In the 1976 Carter election, as against that of Nixon in 1972, Jews voted roughly as liberally as they had in the past. With the Camp David agreements instantly restoring Jimmy Carter's tarnished popularity in the Jewish community, the continuing drift of Jews to the Republican Party is now problematic.

The Israeli situation similarly determines the future of Jewish-Christian relations. The lack of institutional Christian support for the State of Israel immediately prior to and during the Six-Day War of 1967 seemed a betrayal of the ecumenical mood of the 1960s. Since then, Jews have made strenuous efforts to clarify that, as a religion, we Jews are structured not as a church but as an ethnic group. Mainline Christian denominations, once our natural allies in liberal activities, still find it difficult to connect the survival of the State of Israel with an appreciation of Jewish faith. The evangelicals, once feared because of their missionizing bent, are now friends because, for biblical reasons, they are ardent supporters of the Israelis.

Federation and Synagogue

The inner dynamics of our community have recently been well described by Daniel Elazar in *Community and Polity*. Thirty years ago, with the movement of Jews to the suburbs, the synagogue became the central institution of American Jewry. Today it must, at the least, share power with our unified fund-raising and allocating local community agency, the Federation. It is the instrumentality through which our relation to the State of Israel is most directly expressed, its chief beneficiary being the United Jewish Appeal. There is also a loose American federation of Federations. Through it, Jews of means and influence meet their peers. Thus it is primarily in the Federations, not synagogues, that what normally passes for power is structured.

The Israelocentricity of the Federations' fund-raising has had an interesting effect. A generation or so back, their focus was largely local and national charities, and their leadership was regularly accused of "not being very Jewish." The classic charge was that they gave millions for Jewish hospitals which sometimes had no kosher kitchens for observant Jews, while giving little to Jewish education.

In the past decade Federations have "Judaized." Practically, if they do not assure Jewish survival, they will have no donors. Idealistically, the issue of Jewish survival has gotten them involved in the intensification of Jewish life, including the funding of Jewish day schools, once considered an "un-American activity." As successive Israeli emergencies have brought American Jews to give more, local Jewish activities have benefited in the process. While synagogues have been tight for funds, Federations have, relatively speaking, had money for Jewish programming.

But once Federations move on from fund-raising to sponsoring Jewish activities, they easily run into conflict with synagogues, which are not without considerable power. In the past few years American Jewish religious life has recovered from the numerical and financial low period of the early 1970s. Despite our continuing zero population growth and our relative suburban stability, there has been some growth in synagogue formation. A threatened oversupply of rabbis has not developed. This growth has occurred in the face of a small but steady stream of synagogue mergers in small towns and changing neighborhoods, a process aided by the disappearance of practical differences between most Jews regardless of denominational labels. Only a minority among us takes ideologies seriously. Mostly we divide between those who prefer more tradition in their lives and those who prefer less—but almost all of us are determined to make up our own minds as to just what we propose to do as Jews. This vulgarization of the Reform principle of personal autonomy is the standard by which most American Jews, in fact, conduct their Jewish lives.

The potential for conflict between the Federation and the synagogue currently seems unlikely to lead to major difficulty. Neither institution can easily do without the other; the leaders of neither group seem interested in a power grab or a fight. Until now, the Israeli peril made it necessary for both sides to subordinate their immediate interests to the general good. Now the likely lessening of tensions in the Middle East will probably result in a falling-off in gifts to Federations, thus cramping their expansionism.

Leadership Roles

In small communities at least, the Federation's leaders are also the synagogue's leaders. Perhaps that fact explains our version of the passing of "the age of the giants," the days of a Stephen S. Wise or an Abba Hillel Silver. Today, only people who are directly involved with the prime minister or one or two other officials of the State of Israel have pre-eminent status among American Jews. Perhaps technology is also to blame. We are inundated with information by the media. Only a major national organization or a major issue (quickly co-opted by organizations) can hope to claim media attention. Since our national Jewish organizations are democratic, our leaders have fixed terms. They arise, are publicized and then are succeeded by new two- to four-year-term heroes.

The case of Arthur Hertzberg is instructive. He is perhaps the only congregational rabbi who has managed to become a national Jewish figure. Yet for all his intellectuality and charisma, he has been projected into the attention of most Jews by heading a relatively marginal organization, the American Jewish Congress. Now that his term of office is over and he has not been able to move on to any other national or international position of significance, it is not clear how he will be able to exercise any significant leadership role.

Despite all of this—perhaps in confirmation of it—one exceptional leader has recently emerged: Alexander Schindler. Characteristically, Schindler is known not by his office as president of the Union of American Hebrew Congregations, the Reform synagogal group. Rather, he came to national prominence by his astute response to the surprise election of Begin and his masterful displays of indignation without disloyalty during the Israeli-Carter crunch. Schindler got his opportunity for leadership by being chairman of the Conference of Presidents of Major Jewish Organizations—the long-term, if informal, instrumentality through which many American Jewish organizations coordinate their pro-Israel activities. Previous chairmen have seemed more the creature of the office than leaders on their own. Schindler did so outstanding a job that, though every Jewish organizational politician was panting to succeed him when his term in office was up, he was given an unprecedented six-month extension.

Elie Wiesel is in a class by himself. He leads no organization; he has only the power that comes from his being. But as man and writer, as survivor of Auschwitz and determined Jew, he personally symbolizes our will to survive. These days no one but him and a few Israelis—Begin, Eban, perhaps Rabin and Peres—are guaranteed to fill an auditorium. But we listen to Wiesel with a unique respect.

As our situation has given us few leaders, so our emergency mentality has tended to stifle debate. Invective and propaganda have made it impossible to discuss our Jewish responsibility to Palestinians, the security of the State of Israel being accepted as axiomatic. From a long-range perspective, no one has been willing to think about the effects on the American Jewish community if the State of Israel finds peace or if, without catastrophe, it gradually becomes unviable. Paradoxically, American Jewish life has benefited so from the Israeli peril that many cannot imagine, and some fear the fate of, an American Jewish community without a commanding overseas cause.

This macrosociology needs to be balanced by a micro view which reveals some extraordinarily positive phenomena. Books on Jewish topics are published with such frequency that the Jewish Welfare Board's book council has given up hope of reviewing them all in its publication. Hebrew is taught in dozens of American universities; Yiddish is no rarity. Chairs of Jewish studies are a commonplace. The quality of students coming into the rabbinate is exceptional. Academic work in Judaica exceeds in quantity and quality anything dreamed of 20 years ago—an accomplishment led and epitomized by the groundbreaking scholarship of Jacob Neusner of Boston University.

The Limits of Unbelief

Our religious evolution has also been utterly unexpected. As recently as ten years ago we were at the height of the death-of-God debate, and the only question seemed to be the form of nonbelief Judaism would soon take. But we reckoned without the collapse of confidence in general culture and the insight gained from our ensuing confrontation with nihilism. The agnosticism which was endemic in the Jewish community had always assumed that the university and high culture would generate the values our tradition grounded in God. It was therefore easy for us to accept the death of a God who would do nothing about the Holocaust.

But with general culture unworthy of ultimate confidence, a universe empty of God was also empty of any standard of value. In such a situation one has as much right to be a Nazi as a Jew—a blasphemy even Jewish "disbelief" will not tolerate. Jews saw in the crumbling American society and the general decline of Western civilization what true belief in nothing implied. With nihilism a living option and a social reality, Jews began to discover the limits of their unbelief. Some panicked into Orthodoxy; the law is their defense against anarchy—Herman Wouk's defense of Captain Queeg. Even fewer sought refuge in Asian or Christian sects. A large group, yet still a minority, slowly pressed through to the recognition that, though they believed little, they did not believe nothing. And from the acknowledgments of some Jews that they do believe something have come the sparks of a tiny Jewish spiritual renewal.

One may detect this renewal in the shift of tone in our theological discussions. We still inquire where God was in the Holocaust, but we have run out of fresh ways to ask the question or to explore possible answers to it. The topic is more a duty than a living challenge—something we know we must keep ever present but that we have not yet been able to make a part of our ritual. The pressing questions now come from wondering how, as individuals or a community, we can survive this age of pervasive uncertainty.

One sign of this development may be found in the emergence among us of a small but vigorous modern Orthodoxy. It holds faithful observance of the Torah to be the necessary antidote to the pathology of modern civilization yet is secure enough in its Jewishness to accept whatever in our culture seems beneficial and does not conflict with the content or the tone of tradition.

A somewhat larger and non-Orthodox group is determined to honor the tradition more than previous Jewish liberals did. They too turn to their Jewish roots, for they have realized that they cannot make contemporary culture their ultimate concern. Yet they remain sufficiently influenced by its notions of personal autonomy and universal ethics to break with Jewish forms when these seem in need of better statements; e.g., on women's rights. In both cases the search is communal as well as individual. The non-Orthodox are particularly interested in creating small communities, *havurot,* where person-to-person encounter is as much a part of Jewish spirituality as is prayer and ritual. They are against hierarchy, preferring not to live in dependency upon profession-al clergy but to do Jewish acts on their own. One gauge of the extent of this attitude is provided by the phenomenal success of the first *Jewish Catalog*, which sold about 200,000 copies.

Some, Orthodox and non-Orthodox alike, have moved beyond the old Jewish rationalism to the study and practice of Jewish mysticism. Our two most accessible guides in this realm are Zalman Schachter of Temple University and Arthur Green of the University of Penn-sylvania. If this is more than a fad, there may yet be a flowering of Jewish mysticism in America. By contrast, the current attractiveness of the Lubavitcher Hasidim seems of limited lasting effectiveness. Their refusal to compromise with modernity is appealing to Jews conflicted by how modern and un-Jewish they have become. But while some are drawn by the Lubavitcher to commandments they had forgotten, few become Hasidim. For all our sentiment and guilt, we are not willing to surrender to an absolutist way of life, largely shaped by mystical doc-trine and, some would add, late medieval superstition.

The Theological Agenda

This quiet, unanticipated Jewish revival generally takes the form of deed, as befits the pursuit of Jewish authenticity. As an intellectual matter, it mainly is expressed as historical or literary study about Juda-ism. The most lively field of creative Jewish thought at the moment is bioethics. Such writers as J. David Bleich, David Feldman, Fred Ros-ner, Seymour Siegel and Moshe Tendler regularly utilize the rich re-sources of Jewish tradition to respond to modern problems.

A generation's struggle has now largely concluded with theology proper reasonably well established as an academic Jewish discipline. There are thinkers one needs to know, issues which shape the current agenda, and specific options which have already been worked through or which demand further exploration. Here too the focus is on Jewish survival. Our theologians seek an intellectual structure which expli-cates our belief that being faithful Jews is of cosmic and not merely ethnic significance while yet indicating what Jews share with all hu-manity in our common creation in God's image.

For some little while now, Jewish theologians have been out of step with their Christian colleagues. We Jews secularized and universalized our faith long ago when we were emancipated. Being fully of the world, we are no less believing that God wants us to be Jews, that we should not give up our particular faith and tradition so as to blend into the general stream of humankind. Insofar as our Christian colleagues are still shocked by discovering how great a non-Christian world there is and are unable or unwilling to assert some form of Christian particularism, we find their work of only occasional interest.

For many of us now, the once-fashionable philosophy of Mordecai Kaplan has become increasingly unsatisfactory. Kaplan believes all religious truth is universal; we then express it, quite naturally, in an ethnic way. Hence the Jews should do Jewish things because that is their people's way of doing them. The merit of this suggestion is clear. Our ethnicity does have some power upon us, particularly in a time when the melting-pot theory of America is in high disrepute. But ethnicity is hardly commanding. What our folk mandates in its actual living is more likely to be vulgar and self-serving than the high idealism we connect with Judaism or the deep self-discipline Jewish survival requires. Equally troublesome too is Kaplan's pre-Holocaust optimistic trust in science and human nature.

An increasing number find Martin Buber's thought far more acceptable. Buber teaches that persons are fulfilled in relationship to a God who stands over against us. He then moves to a theory of nonorthodox revelation and a keen appreciation of Zionism and Jewish ethnicity. If that could somehow be linked to his colleague Franz Rosenzweig's affirmation of the totality of Jewish law, at least in principle, the central problem of liberal Jewish theology would be solved. Abraham Heschel's work now seems so intimately linked to his corruscating style and his charismatic person that it finds only admirers, not disciples who can extend and amplify it.

Contemporary Statements

By now, the existentialist generation which revolted against the dominant rationalism of World War II Jewry has itself become the theological establishment. The various papers of Jakob Petuchowski, Lou Silberman and Arnold Wolf among the Reform Jews, and Arthur Cohen, Herschel Matt, Fritz Rothschild and Seymour Siegel among the Conservatives, made possible the development of a new Jewish theological consciousness. Yet the hopes for a full-scale working-out of the existentialist position remain slim. Emil Fackenheim has now turned away from his early insistence on God's revelation as the basis of modern Judaism. He considers the central certainty of post-Holocaust Jewish theology to be the command to preserve the people of Israel, particularly in the State of Israel, and enhance its existence. (So his *Encounters Between Judaism and Modern Philosophy,* and his recent collection of papers, *The Jewish Return into History.)* He is currently at work on a systematic exposition of his theology, and its appearance will be a major Jewish intellectual event.

My own theological efforts to clarify the inner dialectic of classic Jewish belief and to respond to it in personal faith and freedom have recently reached a new phase. In a comprehensive paper, "Liberal Jewish Theology in a Time of Uncertainty" (in the *CCAR Yearbook* for 1977), I have outlined my systematic Jewish theology, its levels of discourse, the linguistic modes appropriate to them, the living options confronting us on each of these levels, and the decisions I must make as a result of utilizing a rigorously comparative theological method.

In direct contrast to these two positions, Steven Schwarzschild of Washington University still believes that it might be possible to integrate the ethical rationalism of Herman Cohen with an untendentious reading of Jewish tradition—an ambitious project indeed. No major work in the process or phenomenological style seems likely to appear soon. Hopes for some major statement of contemporary Orthodox theology are equally limited. Irving Greenberg, Marvin Fox and Michael Wyschogrod limit themselves to occasional essays. Joseph Baer Soloveitchik, the dean of the modern Orthodox rabbinate, continues to dazzle his hearers with his *halachic* and cultural erudition, but what little he publishes is mostly exposition rather than demonstration. Eliezer Berkovits, who recently settled in Jerusalem, seems the sole Orthodox thinker with the knowledge and daring to try to explain in contemporary intellectual terms the nature of traditional Jewish belief today.

This is not much for a community proud of its intellectuality. Even worse, we cannot point to many young thinkers critical of the errors of their elders and eager to find better intellectual paths. Perhaps that too is a function of having lived through a decade of constant emergency. But if Camp David has put that behind us, I do not see that we can long go on doing things that we have not thought about very profoundly. The theological task remains critical for long-range Jewish survival.

15

Canada's Churches: Living in a Cosmopolitan Culture

The churches of Canada have new moral issues to confront and must find some way to heal their internal rifts without homogenizing themselves.

TOM SINCLAIR-FAULKNER

The task of "listing" where the Spirit bloweth is rarely an easy one, particularly when such a catalogue must cover Canada—a country that is larger in geographical area than the United States, and one whose population numbers more than 23 million people, speaking two official languages. What makes the list manageable is that most of the population lives within a narrow belt of land along the U.S. border (a fact reflected in the heavy American influence on Canadian culture) and that three-quarters of the people claim to belong to three major denominations: the Catholic, the United and the Anglican churches.

In his introduction to this book, Martin Marty refers to the "competitive business model" that defines American church life. But in the Canadian economy, divine and otherwise, the rule has been public enterprise, not free enterprise, with a healthy dose of what Herschel Hardin has called a "redistribution culture" (*A Nation Unaware*, 1974). Faced with the task of taming the less gentle half of the continent, Canadians found it more natural to consolidate than to compete, to enlist the state as a backer, and to create coast-to-coast institutions that reflect regional realities but are capable of shifting some resources from

Dr. Sinclair-Faulkner is a layman of the United Church of Canada and a historian in the department of religion at Dalhousie University in Halifax, Nova Scotia.

the "haves" to the "have-nots." Put these tendencies together with an absence of the Enlightenment deism that helped to build a wall between church and state in the United States, and one has a country in which there is only public Christianity and no "civil religion."

But during the 1960s Canadian Christendom started to come apart. Previously a "Christian country," Canada became, by act of Parliament, merely a country "founded upon principles that acknowledge the supremacy of God." Public schools whose charters called for the formation of "Christian citizens" dropped religious instruction and replaced it with teaching "about" religions, with "values education" or with nothing at all. Departments of religious studies appeared on university campuses, and departments of theology dwindled. The queen still spoke to her subjects on Christmas Day, but the prime minister shifted his annual fireside chat to New Year's Day and began to show a certain public coolness to delegations of church leaders ready to proffer advice.

The Santa Claus parade (Toronto's most significant liturgical event) was switched from Saturday to Sunday over the protests of church leaders but with the full support of pewsitters, and Jacques Cartier's huge electric cross occasionally had to share Montreal's Mount Royal with Lord Krishna's Juggernaut. Church sanctuaries have been broken into with increasing regularity lately, and in 1974 English Canada elected its first Catholic priest to the House of Commons—both signs that the Canadian public holds the Christian churches in less awe than it once did.

The most dramatic structural changes have occurred in the wake of the "quiet revolution" in Catholic Quebec: public education, health and welfare, previously run by the church, have been taken over by an increasingly laicized state. In Alberta some politicians have suggested that it is improper for clergy to act as agents of the state in performing marriages, and aldermanic candidates everywhere are sometimes heard to mutter about ending tax exemptions on church properties. Sales of lottery tickets, condemned by many churches, are now being handled by those other Canadian temples, the nationally chartered banks.

According to the 1971 Canadian census, there were almost ten times as many Canadians who did not believe in God as there had been in 1961. (In Quebec there were 12 times as many.) Changes in the way the census is administered probably exaggerated this swing, but even so, the 1971 figure is lower than that of the 1976 Gallup poll, which listed 7 per cent of the Canadian population as agnostic or atheist—more than twice the proportion that showed up in the United States (*Reader's Digest*, October 1976).

Growth and Decline

Nevertheless, Christendom is not coterminous with Christianity. Even as Canada began to lose its officially Christian character, the Canadian churches were caught up in the effervescent spirit of the 1960s. The president of the University of Toronto called Harvey Cox's *Secular City* the best book he had read in 1966, and the CBC television network gave birth to a new religious show called *Man Alive*. Sixty United Church writers were called together to produce a New Curriculum for Sunday schools, aiming to bring together the best insights of biblical theology and educational psychology. They successfully enlisted 40 local congregations in the testing-and-refinement phase of the program.

Meanwhile, in Quebec the French speaking Catholic Church, inspired by Vatican II, developed an equally exciting catechetical program called *Viens vers le Père*. It was soon translated into English (Come to the Father) and began to be widely used by Anglophone Catholics as well. In this heady atmosphere ecumenical ventures of all kinds thrived. The Anglican and United churches moved toward organic union, and all the major churches of Canada came together for the first time to sponsor a Christian Pavilion at the World's Fair in Montreal in 1967.

Despite these encouraging initiatives, the churches were visibly faltering. The New Curriculum was largely abandoned after only two years of a projected six years of use, and church union (Anglican and United) was formally laid aside in 1976. *Come to the Father* has been subjected to heavy criticism, but there is still no replacement in sight. Evangelical Christians declined to cooperate in the stark Christian Pavilion at Expo 67, preferring to support Moody's cheerful "Sermons from Science" instead. Many pewsitting members of the major churches echoed the evangelical sentiments after being blitzed by the Christian Pavilion's Good Friday message.

Because of heavy immigration from Europe, the proportion of the population claiming to be Catholic had reached 46 per cent by 1971 and bids fair to become a Canadian majority by 1981. But Gallup surveys show that the proportion of Catholics attending weekly mass has decreased sharply, from 83 per cent in 1965 to 55 per cent in 1976, and the numbers in religious orders have dropped even more significantly—primarily because fewer and fewer young people are coming forward to be priests and nuns, but partly because many religious are asking to be laicized.

The government census takers say that the number of those claiming membership in the major Protestant churches continues to grow, but my sampling of the membership rolls shows a steady decline in absolute terms since the mid-'60s. The United Church is the most centralized of all the Protestant churches of Canada and therefore provides the most complete statistics, but it is also much less urban than most of the other churches and therefore less prey to the acids of modernity that seem to be eating at all of them. The number of declared candidates for the United Church ministry went into a steep decline, from 718 in 1963 to a low of 94 in 1968; by 1976 it had climbed back to 502, largely because of an influx of female candidates (roughly 25-30 per cent of the total). United Church giving did not keep pace with the cost of living between 1970 and 1978, and the church had to close down one of its newspapers and sell its only publishing house.

Evangelical churches claim to be growing swiftly, but they may be in the same boat as the major churches. One careful study in a western Canadian city showed that 72 per cent of the new members in 20 evangelical congregations had previously belonged to similar congregations; 18 per cent were born into the congregations studied, and only 9 per cent were converts from "the world."

Worldly Influences

The world, on the other hand, seems to be gathering strength. The role of government in Canadian lives is expanding, often at the expense of the churches. Young people who used to dream of going overseas as missionaries tend now to dream of going with CUSO, a kind of Canadian Peace Corps. Folk who used to tithe see an unprecedented chunk of their income channeled back to the community through taxes. Labor leaders in Quebec (previously a mainstay of the Catholic Church) are certifiably the most agnostic of any group in the province, and many of them locate their ultimate concern in the drive to establish an independent, socialist Quebec. One can almost hear them asking, What has Jerusalem to do with Athens?

The churches are in no position to claim a monopoly on transcendence in Canada today. Popular singers like Bruce Cockburn, Buffy Sainte-Marie and Gilles Vigneault offer a variety of religious visions, while the claims made on behalf of ice hockey by high priests like Bob Pulford are infinite. ("A Canadian kid who can play this game well is the luckiest kid in the world; I mean it. There is no limit to how far he can go.") The characters of novelist Robertson Davies strive to see the marvelous ". . . without wearing either the pink spectacles of faith or the green spectacles of science," and Margaret Atwood offers an interior shaman to her readers in *Surfacing*. Medical staff members, many of whom are not found in church on Sunday, flock to hear Elisabeth Kübler-Ross offer a non-Christian vision of life after death, while more traditional folk deliberately substitute a radio or television "hymn sing" for Sunday worship.

Nor has the world been hesitant to challenge the churches directly. The most widely read Canadian book on religion during the past generation was *The Comfortable Pew* (1965), a critique of church life written by agnostic Pierre Berton at the request (or perhaps the expense) of the Anglican Church. In 1977 the best new play being performed in Montreal was *Dernier recours de Baptiste à Catherine*, a devastating portrait of the role of the church in 19th century Quebec written by Michelè Lalonde, who plays ironically on the theme of resurrection.

Changes in the Churches

If this is where the churches of Canada have been, where are they now going?

Liturgies in the Protestant churches are little changed from those of past decades, but a few good hymns are being added to congregational repertoires: for instance, "Lord of the Dance" (text by Sydney Carter) and "From the Slave Pens of the Delta" (from the gifted pen of Anglican Dean Herbert O'Driscoll). One good old hymn has undergone a radical and still controversial change among Anglicans and United

Church folk: "Jesus Loves Me! this I know, *And* [not "for"] the Bible tells me so." There have been ecumenical crossovers: "The Huron Carol" of Jesuit Jean de Brébeuf is regularly sung by Protestants, and "A Mighty Fortress" has popped up in Catholic monthly missals.

The Vatican II changes in liturgy have plainly delighted many Catholics, but there is an untabulated minority that detests the abandonment of the Tridentine mass. It is not uncommon to see angry parishioners writing to *La Presse* to complain about papal dictatorship; and in English Canada, Newfoundlander Anne Roche observes, "University masses are wild and foolish. They would embarrass a card-carrying atheist." Perhaps the most compelling plea made by the "traditionalists" is for the right to practice the mode of worship most acceptable to them, letting the others go their own way. Given the fluid, highly mobile character of today's society, it is a constant source of surprise to me to see how bent both Protestant and Catholic congregations are on attaining orthodox homogeneity in liturgies, rather than encouraging particular congregations to develop distinctive styles of worship.

It may be that the need for diversity is being met through extraparish institutions like the various training and retreat centers that have matured in recent years (e.g., Naramata in the Rockies, Maison Thomas d'Aquin outside Quebec City, ACTC on the Atlantic coast) or by the interesting festivals of faith that have been sponsored in recent months by the United Church. Municipal prayer breakfasts, Full Gospel Business Men's Fellowship gatherings, and Women Aglow groups seem to meet a need for warm, pietistic experiences not usually available in the major churches. But parishes do not always find it easy to live with extraparish institutions—witness the tension between Montreal parishes and the shrine of St. Joseph.

Although the parish ministry has been reaffirmed everywhere, there are some interesting parallel developments taking place. The most successful is clearly the emergence of Clinical Pastoral Education (CPE) programs, now open to parish clergy but originally intended to train hospital chaplains. It is characteristic of modern society that several autonomous "worlds" apparently have emerged: for example, the business world, the school world, the sports world, etc. Parish ministries seem to relate primarily to the home and rarely succeed in having any impact on these other worlds (see Thomas Luckmann's *The Invisi-*

ble Religion). The CPE programs have launched clergy into the hospital world, where they manage to stay faithfully on their feet among the fierce baals of medicine. CPE's relevance to the parish is still a point of controversy.

The United Church in particular has begun to find room for husband-and-wife team ministries, but there are still congregations that see clergy couples as offering an opportunity for the church to get two for the price of one, or that treat the new team as a variation of the old minister-and-wife team. The Anglican Church has moved painfully to ordain women to the priesthood. I see no indication that many Anglicans welcome this development, but it is clear that all organized opposition to the move has collapsed.

There is a decided growth in speculation about lay ministry in Canada. After Action Catholique collapsed in Quebec during the 1960s, the church appointed a study commission on the laity which attempted to give substance to the notion that laypeople have a divine calling in the world. The commission's lay chairman, Fernand Dumont, is probably the most important Catholic theologian reflecting actively on the Quebec scene today. Still, one is not quite certain what "lay ministry" means. The United Church has produced two major studies on ministry in general, one in 1968 and another in 1977, both affirming lay ministry and both causing considerable anxiety among the ordained members of the church. On key points the reports have been distressingly vague: for instance, the latest report encourages laypeople to conduct celebrations of the Lord's Supper on special occasions, but is coyly silent on the matter of baptisms. I take this inconsistency to mean that, despite heroic efforts, the ordained clergy in Canada have not been able to achieve a consensus on the meaning of ordination itself.

Perhaps the most intriguing development in the Catholic Church is the growth of the charismatic movement. Its impact on parts of the English-speaking church is remarkable, but in Quebec the changes have been dazzling. Even in the 1960s, would one have expected to see two cardinals publicly kneel before a 15-year-old girl, asking her to pray for them? Or 45,000 Catholics at the Olympic Stadium being led by a laywoman in singing "I have come for Life"? Still, the last word is not yet spoken with respect to the charismatic movement. Some have held that it is too individualistic, too emotional. Last fall the Quebec bishops issued a countervailing letter encouraging a "pastorale de l'intelligence."

Addressing Moral Issues

Setting aside the charismatic movement, I see no evidence that the churches have succeeded recently in bringing a vision of the "holy"—Otto's "awesome, marvellous mystery"—before the Canadian public in any dramatic way. But there have been determined efforts to bring an effective Christian witness to bear upon important moral issues. In each case the churches have done their homework well, but division has accompanied their efforts.

Ecumenical task forces like GATT-Fly and Project North have become adept at analyzing economic structures and fingering their "demonic" side at shareholders' meetings and in the secular media. These task forces have roused the ire of some segments of the business community, including those which recently constituted themselves as the Confederation of Church and Business in order to present their grievances. In 1977 the Anglican Church produced a brief but searching reflection on issues of death and dying which have stymied both the Canadian Bar Association and the Canadian Medical Association. But when a badly written *Globe and Mail* article "broke" the story, the emotional reaction frustrated efforts to give the report a satisfactory hearing at General Synod.

One issue has been more divisive than any other: the abortion question. The major Protestant churches have given cautious approval to abortion under certain circumstances, while the Catholic Church has opposed it. Catholic Charities have pulled out of Toronto's United Appeal over the issue of Planned Parenthood. Yet some members of the hierarchy do not seem to be as committed to the Right to Life movement as its lay leaders would like them to be. Further, one begins to hear more and more of Catholic women who seek legal abortions upon learning that the fetus they are carrying will probably be born with brain damage.

And finally, despite increasingly frantic efforts on the part of federal political leaders to mobilize Canadian sentiment against Quebec's separation, the churches in English Canada have so far restricted themselves to sober statements which recognize Quebec's right to self-determination, express regret for past injustices, and urge mutual understanding. Unfortunately there are few Protestant church folk able to read French, let alone speak the language, but some Protestant congregations are now establishing youth exchange programs with Francophone parishes. The only vigorous Protestant call for national unity is a catchy new evangelical song called "United We Stand." I for one hope that the Québécois never find out that the author is a French Canadian who now pronounces his name English-fashion.

The Catholic Church in Quebec, after decades of identifying Catholicism too closely with French Canadianism, has firmly declared its intention to stay with Quebec no matter what the decision on independence, provided it be taken without violence. It has required several years for English-speaking Catholics to grasp that the Francophone hierarchy is serious about its newfound neutrality, and it remains to be seen whether these two limbs of the Body of Christ will be able to pass through the next difficult years without serious mutual recriminations.

In the end, what comes about will depend in large measure on the vision of the churches themselves. Will there be an effort to restore Christendom, to seek a Nehemiah who will rebuild the city and its walls? I hope not: neither Darius nor Artaxerxes seems interested in supporting this sort of urban renewal today. Paul's vision for the Corinthians is a better vision. The churches of Canada live in a largely pagan, cosmopolitan city of relatively recent foundation. They have new moral issues to confront and must find some way to heal their internal rifts without homogenizing themselves. They need to practice communion, to learn a new song of divine love, and to speak in the end of the central importance of resurrection.

16

The UCC: Can Freedom and Order Live Happily Ever After?

The present reality of the United Church of Christ is shaped by the tension between autonomy and covenantal relationships.

ROBERT G. KEMPER

The basic unit of the life and organization of the United Church of Christ is the local church [Article IV, the Constitution of the United Church of Christ].

Polity is to the United Church of Christ what water is to fish. It is the environment in which our denomination lives. Our limitations are limitations of polity; polity molds our function and shapes our destiny. Our heritage is encapsulated in 3 Fs: faith, freedom and fellowship. Those three combine and intertwine—and sometimes snag—to create the free-church polity of the United Church of Christ. That polity is the milieu of the UCC's contemporary shape and future prospects.

Autonomy and Covenant

At 45 I have only adolescent memories of the furor of the '50s over what was called "the merger"—the proposed union of the Congregational Christian Churches and the Evangelical and Reformed Church. The merger was consummated in 1957, but the way was strewn with

---

Mr. Kemper is the senior minister of the First Congregational Church (UCC) of Western Springs, Illinois.

family fights, ecclesiastical battles and civil lawsuits. A generation of church leaders gave their energies to the formulation and establishment of a "united and uniting church." The trauma of birth centered in a phrase rarely heard these days in ecclesiastical parlance—"local autonomy." A volatile, vocal minority from the CC side was persuaded that the proposed Basis of Union would erode the heritage of congregational self-rule. As is often the case in history, the minority lost the battle (and went on to form the National Association of Congregational Christian Churches) but substantially affected the final shape of the merged church. Writ large upon the forms of the new denomination was autonomy, specified and underlined so that deviation was almost impossible.

Not only was the autonomy of local churches established; so also was that of associations, conferences, national and international mission boards. So widespread is autonomy that there is some question whether the United Church of Christ is indeed a denomination. Certainly it is not if uniformity and cohesiveness of ecclesiastical machinery are the standards. It would not be a denomination if autonomy ran wild and free through all the layers and levels of the church. But such is not the case. There is a corrective restraint. The free and autonomous bodies bind themselves into organizational patterns through covenants. These exist among members in local churches, between churches and other churches in regional and national groupings, and among individuals, churches and God. Through these multiple and multilayered covenants, freely established, faith and fellowship are realized in the United Church of Christ.

Upon closer examination, the water in which the fish swim is really a compound in which hydrogen and oxygen are held in tension. Similarly, the polity of the United Church of Christ, the shaper of all the particulars about the church, reflects a tension between autonomy and covenantal relationships. Failure to account for and to struggle with the conflict, the negotiations and the beauty of that tension assures the observer a misreading of the data about contemporary life in this diverse denomination. Brothers and sisters in other denominational traditions who hunger for church union might learn from the United Church of Christ that the compromises each church accepts may become the essence of the new body that is created.

Thumbnail Sketch of a Congregation

It is appropriate to assemble the data about contemporary currents in this denomination by looking at a particular congregation. We have no *typical* congregations. We are black, yellow, red, brown, but mostly white. We are found in 49 states, but mostly in eastern and northern states. We have 223 churches of more than 1,000 members, but most of our churches have fewer than 200 members. We are rich and poor, but mostly middle class. In aggregate, we have about 1.75 million members in about 6,850 local churches. United Church of Christ congregations are bananas, not onions: the skin on the outside does not necessarily disclose what lurks beneath its visible outer layer.

Let me tell you a little about the one local church of the United Church of Christ that I know best. I will not tell you *all* about it but only about those aspects that reflect the reality of the aggregate. I am the pastor of the First Congregational Church of Western Springs, Illinois, a suburb of Chicago. The very name of the church suggests something of the tension between autonomy and covenant. The church is a member in good standing with the Chicago Metropolitan Association and the Illinois Conference, and it supports the total denomination with benevolence dollars. But its name is First Congregational Church. Why? Because the local congregation has the right to select the name under which it will incorporate and operate. Twenty years have passed since the creation of the United Church of Christ, and we have not yet seen fit to alter our name, nor have we been pressured to do so. We should, of course, change the name, but without a coercive authority to make us do so, we tarry.

We are losing members. We have had a 20 per cent decline in the past ten years. That loss *could* be due to ineffective pastoral leadership, or to disenchantment with social issues, or to rampant secularism. All three are possible reasons, but geography, changing cultural mixes and time make a more realistic (but more insidious and less dramatic) explanation. We are an older congregation—no demographic pyramid here. Our demographics form an inverted bell. Most of our members are between 50 and 70; few are under 30.

We are still recovering from the rancor of the '60s. A church that champions independent judgment and freedom of conscience is not well equipped to take congregational stands on divisive issues of public policy. In the '60s we mostly argued with each other and changed neither ourselves nor the situations we confronted. We still have militant, activist types, and we have reactionary obstructionists. We have flare-ups over homosexuality, multinational corporations, and challenges to free-enterprise economics; but these are never of the scope and passion of the controversies of the '60s. I have not heard the term "communist front" in years.

Our self-image is that of a friendly, family-oriented, neighborhood church. Isn't that how most churches perceive themselves? Of course, 20 per cent of our members are single (mostly widows and widowers), our church school and youth program have about half the numbers they had in the '50s, and most of our members drive to church.

Very few of my parishioners were born and reared Congregationalists. We are an amalgam of all sorts, and that may explain why the name of the church has not been changed. We have no strong sense of denominational identity. Local church governance is far higher on our priorities than denominational issues.

The faith of this particular congregation is harder to characterize, but even in that difficulty it is probably representative of most of the churches in the denomination. We have disciplined and conscientious disciples, and we have agnostics who like good church music. We have varieties of worship forms—not the contemporary and traditional Sunday morning cafeteria offerings we used to have—but there are Sundays when a surplice is appropriate and Sundays when no vestments are used. Despite the absence of uniform expressions of faith and liturgy, this congregation probably does have a uniformity of desire for each of its members to know and live his or her faith.

We use the Statement of Faith of the United Church of Christ in liturgy, confirmation and new-member instruction. But *how* we use it is illustrative. It is never presented as a test for orthodoxy; rather it is offered as a summary of the heritage (biblical, historical and theological) we have received; each is encouraged to know and to live as the Spirit leads within the rubric of this statement. Not surprisingly, we have never had a heresy trial; we've had some lively arguments, but never an excommunication.

That thumbnail sketch of a particular congregation may sound like a maddening, vexing potpourri of syncretism and laissez-faire religion, but it illustrates many current elements in the denomination and incarnates the tension of freedom and order.

Compulsive Pulse-Takers

Our local demographics are typical. The United Church of Christ is losing members; it now has fewer members than when the two predecessor denominations combined 25 years ago. But the geographical explanation is also typical. The UCC has many members (40 per cent) in Pennsylvania, Ohio, Illinois, Massachusetts and Connecticut—all states which have lost population (only 9 per cent of our members reside in the south and southwest).

Concern for social justice characterized our predecessor bodies, and it is likewise very much a part of the contemporary denomination; but how to achieve a measure of justice, what is required, and what are the consequences of that mandate are still debatable issues on any particular subject. A recent General Synod wrestled with an incredible 92 issues, including South Africa, civil rights for homosexuals, unemployment and abortion. Despite a lengthy list of decisions to be made or positions to be taken, some participants thought it was an "issueless" Synod. It was, compared with those of earlier days with their many special-interest and caucus groups. The real test is not what the Synod decides, but how autonomous churches and boards respond to those decisions.

Another example of stance is the UCC's struggle with evangelism. Ever since Key '73 and Dean Kelley's book *Why Conservative Churches Are Growing*, there has been churchwide concern for evangelism. The decline in membership, though not necessarily germane, has also fired the talk about evangelism within the UCC. Certainly the slick, authoritarian, acculturated evangelism of the day does not fit our style or tradition. The problem is this: How does one win allegiance to a body of belief when that body is so disordered? Evangelism in the United Church of Christ is something like a presidential primary; we know the party we support, but which candidate we will choose is uncertain.

As for the faith of the denomination, I can only point to a curious phenomenon of our history. For a noncreedal church, we have probably produced more platforms, compacts, statements and affirmations than any other mainline denomination. There is mounting pressure for a revision of the 1957 Statement of Faith to ensure more inclusive (less sexist) language. What I take that phenomenon to mean is that we really are a pilgrim people; as we walk through time, we reflect upon what our faith means in the given context of this moment of history. In short, we are compulsive pulse-takers. We want to say where we believe the Spirit is leading us *now*. We do not divorce ourselves from a historic and inherited faith; rather, we try to express that heritage in the context of the contemporary.

Leadership Styles

Leadership in a denomination of such heritage and concept does not come easy. Autocracy is out; we are the least likely of the denominations to have a *putsch*. But judging from the recent flap over "the process" at the last General Synod, there is a growing restlessness with participatory democracy in the form of management by objectives. We have had "prophets" like Truman Douglass, but they have attracted more prophets rather than disciples. Special-interest groups (caucuses) have made their influence felt, but their ad hoc nature makes them short-lived—or we institutionalize them into the machinery.

The absence of a hierarchical structure militates against a "star system." It is much harder for individual personalities to be shakers and movers in a pliable ecclesiastical milieu. Nevertheless, in the public sector, many UCC constituents point with pride to former U.N. Ambassador Andrew Young as one of our clergy. Avery Post, the recently elected president of the church, brings a distinguished record of leadership as a pastor and as minister of the Massachusetts Conference. Walter Brueggemann of Eden Theological Seminary in St. Louis, Missouri, combines erudite biblical scholarship with a passion for the vitality of the church at its many levels, and he makes an ever-widening impact on ministerial students, local church leaders and the denomination. In free-church polity, communicators play a crucial gatekeeper role in the flow of information and shaping of opinion. The consistently high-quality writing of Davie Napier and Browne Barr receives appreciative audiences. Everett Parker of the Office of Communication and J. Martin Bailey, editor of *A.D.* magazine, are imaginative and effective communicators. James Glasse, president of Lancaster (Pennsylvania) Theological Seminary, is a substantial force in the renewal of UCC clergy.

There are three areas in the contemporary church in which we are struggling to find an appropriate style of leadership for *this* denomination. They are the local church pastorate, women's concerns and bureaucratic missions and ministry. All three have been squeezed and buffeted by the tension of autonomy and covenantal relationships.

In free-church polity, each autonomous congregation calls its own minister, who serves in a covenantal relationship with it. Associations ordain clergy on request of local churches, but there is no clear strategy or even connection between the seminary which educates for ministry, the association which ordains, the local church which calls, and the denomination which has the machinery for career development and placement. It is all a crazy patchwork quilt. Statistically, we do not have a clergy surplus; we may even have more churches than pastors. But in the parlance of the day, many of those churches in need of clergy are not "economically viable." The crunch comes not at the beginning level, but at the second or third pastorate. At that level there are far more pastors than churches available. This pattern has important implications for women clergy, those over 55, and almost any pastor "seeking call." We have what we call a "placement system," but it is not much more than a central file. The momentum of the process often depends on whom you know—and luck. Such attendant matters as recruitment, standards, continuing education and, of course, the whole question of effectiveness are a muddle of options and opinions.

We do not have—and never have had—a "mother church" complex. Many of our clergy are émigrés from such systems. We do have a good vested pension program, but we have only guidelines for its formula and for all other forms of compensation. Most clergy accept that disorder as the price of autonomy, but a pastor in trouble with the local congregation is a pastor in trouble indeed.

Appeals to higher authority fall on deaf ears when the congregation is the highest authority. With such exigencies of pastoral life, the local church pastor may be thrust into a political role vis-à-vis the congregation. He or she is often frustrated trying to meet the varied and sometimes conflicting role expectations inherent in autonomous churches.

New Role Models for Women

"Women's concerns" attract considerable attention at the moment. The ordination of women is not much of a stumbling block; we were ahead of our time on that issue. But placement is another matter. Local-church autonomy can mean local prejudice from which there is little recourse. It is likely that most of the women clergy in the UCC will gravitate to specialized ministries because denominationwide rules cannot be forced on local churches. On the other hand, women clergy who have established competency in a whole range of clergy skills have ready acceptance. As with novelists, everyone wants your work after you have proven competency. The problem is in getting that competency established.

Laywomen in the churches represent an enormous force that is underutilized for lack of leadership. What that leadership will come to look like is hard to say because there are so many levels of awareness among laywomen. Most local churches are not surprised by the sight of women moderators or trustees or ushers. At its inception the denomination made a conscious decision about women that was ahead of its time. We decided not to have national or regional staff services for women's organizations in the churches, though our predecessor organizations had had formidable structures for women's work (as we used to call it). The decision probably cost the church millions of dollars in benevolence monies, but it was made before other churches began to have denominational agencies on the laity rather than men's and women's fellowships. Because of our openness, strident voices are heard most, but a moderate voice, that of Barbara Brown Zikmund of Chicago Theological Seminary, electrified the General Synod with a call to end the "we"/"they" divisions of the past.

The secular implications of women's issues are more awesome. As a local church pastor I have not found much merit in the strident feminists seeking a greater role for women in the life of the local church. Most of my working hours are spent with women in the ministry of the church. My deeper suspicion is that the secular force of the feminist revolution may substantially alter the nature of voluntary organizations. Women have supplied the primary energy of local churches; those women who choose to alter their former patterns leave a void in the structure of organizations which had depended upon their energies. Just try recruiting a year's complement of female church school teachers if you think there are no changing patterns here!

A new role model of the Christian woman is needed. Maybe we no longer accept the old models of piety followed by the woman who served many a dinner, led devotions and taught the sixth grade Sunday school class. That woman may be gone, liberated. But who is she now? And where is she? Who are her models?

Where Does the Buck Stop?

The third leadership problem is in bureaucratic ministries. Leading a mission agency, judicatory or missionary institution for the United Church of Christ is like chaperoning a teen-age dance: you have your ideas about what is right and necessary, but does anyone else want to listen to you? In the passion for autonomous churches, our forebears also created autonomous mission boards, seminaries, colleges, associations and conferences. As a result we have autonomy sprouting everywhere. The United Church of Christ would have driven Harry Truman crazy: he couldn't have figured out where the buck stopped. In truth, the benevolence buck passes through an incredibly complex, layered structure. We encourage a combined mission appeal but at the same time allow some directed giving to particular institutions. In my first months in Western Springs, I was visited by representatives of the nearby seminary, college, retirement home and city mission society. It was not my winsome personality that brought them but the crazy patchwork quilt!

The heroes of the United Church of Christ may be its bureaucrats. In a sense they have no constituency at all. In another sense, they have too many constituencies. Most agencies have their own boards of directors which set policies. They have the persons served who have claims upon the agency. Funding comes from local church and denomination. And the agencies have their own integrity. Further, the local churches have a built-in antibureaucratic mentality. "Who works for whom?" is a favorite war cry when bureaucratic salaries are disclosed—or, sometimes, not disclosed. It is a wonder that anything at all gets done by the denomination!

Forecasting the Future

Assuming that we will continue to muddle through that morass of leadership problems as we have in the past, I think the United Church of Christ has a bright and vital future. At the risk of engaging in spiritual thumbsucking, let me state the case for optimism.

A free church rooted in the Christian tradition may become more attractive in the future. Where are all those evangelical young people going to go when they grow up spiritually? I have a hunch that their religious conceptions may seek fresh air; a liberal church which invites them to join a continuing pilgrimage in faith, with no pat answers but with abiding affirmations, may be an attractive possibility.

The congregation as an extended family offers hope to changing patterns of nuclear family life. In most communities the church is an integrator, mixing sexes, ages and sometimes races and economic groups. A church self-consciously egalitarian may rise, not decline, in influential ministries if a culture increases its desire for inclusiveness.

Yet I fret about geography and demographics; we need churches in the Sunbelt! But I am not as sure as I once was that increasing numbers represent an unequivocal good. It is true that there are undercurrents of resentment about the ever-encroaching bigness of the institutions of organized society. The bureaucratization of life may force people to seek smaller, more manageable enclaves where their thoughts, needs and faith are shared with others—another way of defining fellowship in the United Church of Christ.

I also expect our churches to be favorably affected by the "young-old" (persons in their 60s and 70s). Demographically this population group is growing, and its members are in our churches. Negative stereotypes abound about this group. It is supposed that they are poor, ill-fed, uncared for and conservative. Bernice Neugarten of the University of Chicago convincingly debunks those stereotypes and predicts that the "young-old" have enormous potential for social utilization, particularly in the voluntary organizations. Our church has unwittingly discriminated against this group. But if we will loosen the biases and take off the blinders, we may be surprised that a major element in church renewal is not just the next generation but a new generation created by longevity, affluence and social policy.

And, finally, the United Church of Christ has an ecumenical future. In that, we are experienced—maybe so experienced as to be cautious, or maybe just experienced enough to know that boundaries and barriers can be overcome when the Spirit seeks such. We have begun to talk in earnest with the Christian Church (Disciples of Christ). No one knows where those talks will lead, but even that we would talk of church union with sister churches must suggest that despite all the travail of church union, we believe in it and are willing to seek it in ever-widening dimensions.

The future is not all sanguine. I brood about the precariousness of the balance I have described here. I am not worried about the loss of autonomy. We have institutionalized it. On the contrary, I fret over the other force, the covenant relationship. That we cannot institutionalize. The covenant lives on in men and women of goodwill who will listen to the hurts and hopes of others, who will hear the faith stories of others, who will find in the Lordship of Christ a common allegiance which tempers their petty pretenses of building empires and spheres of influence, who will seek in pious meditation and vigorous action a greater good than they alone can achieve. Without that corrective balance, autonomy degenerates into a self-serving libertarianism. If we are becoming a free people under God, then we are free to live in sustained relationships with all God's people.

In a Yazoo City, Mississippi, press conference President Carter was asked how his southern heritage was shaping his presidency. The southern experience of the United Church of Christ is very limited, but the president's answer was a parallel to our recent past. The president pointed to his religious environment, his preference for local approaches to problems, and the chastening experiences of the civil rights movement. To a member of the United Church of Christ, all that sounded very familiar.

17

The Reformed Churches: Enlarging Their Witness

The great thing that has happened in the Reformed churches recently is a new awareness of themselves and of their responsibilities and their possibilities.

HOWARD G. HAGEMAN

The churches that bear the name "Reformed" are only a fraction of the churches in this country that represent the Reformed tradition. It is one of the curiosities of that tradition in the U.S. that, while Baptists are always called Baptists and Methodists are always called Methodists, many Reformed Christians are called Presbyterians! The difference, of course, goes back to the place of origin. Though both groupings belong to the Reformed family, the Presbyterian churches look to Great Britain for their beginnings, while the churches that are called Reformed had their origin in a variety of countries on the continent of Europe.

Two denominations in the U.S. include "Reformed" in their titles today—the Reformed Church in America and the Christian Reformed Church. Both look to the Netherlands as the country of their origin, though in different ways. The Reformed Church in America, which celebrated its 350th anniversary in 1978, goes back to the earliest colonial times when New York was New Amsterdam; in addition, it has been enriched and enlarged by many immigrants from the Netherlands in the 19th century. The Christian Reformed Church was made up almost totally of 19th and 20th century immigrants from the Netherlands

Dr. Hageman is president of New Brunswick (New Jersey) Theological Seminary.

who represented a division that took place in the Reformed Church there in 1834.

By American standards, both churches are small. The total membership of the Reformed Church in America is 360,000, and that of the Christian Reformed Church is 288,000—far less than 1 million in total. Over 25 per cent of the CRC's membership is in Canada, where that church has ministered extensively to Dutch immigrants since World War II. While there are a few RCA congregations in Canada, they represent only a tiny fraction of the denomination's total membership.

Ecumenical Considerations

Perhaps the best way to begin discussing the future of these churches is to consider their relationships with each other. Though closely related historically and theologically, they have had very different ecumenical histories. As one of the oldest American denominations (and one of the strongest in two of the original 13 colonies), the Reformed Church in America has always had an ecumenical posture, dating back to the early United Missionary Societies. It was an original member of the Federal Council of Churches, and of the National and World councils.

Despite this history of ecumenical openness, however, the RCA has had a consistent record of refusing to combine with other denominations in organic union, beginning with the old northern Presbyterian Church in 1876, followed by the then Reformed Church in the United States (now part of the United Church of Christ) in 1889, the former United Presbyterian Church in 1949 and, most recently, the Presbyterian Church in the United States in 1969. From this record it should be abundantly clear that while it in no way rejects a posture of ecumenical cooperation, the Reformed Church in America is nonetheless unwilling to surrender its denominational identity.

The Christian Reformed Church, on the other hand, has followed a much more isolationist course from its beginnings in this country in 1857. Though it has from time to time looked favorably on some conservative alliances, it has eschewed joining either the National or the World Council of Churches, seeking fellowship rather with groups like the Orthodox Presbyterian Church or, more recently, with the new Presbyterian Church in America.

Within this decade, however, the two Reformed churches have begun conversations with each other. Not surprisingly, these talks have been disconcerting to the liberal wing of the RCA, which sees in them the threat of a church locked into Reformed confessional orthodoxy. The conversations have been equally distressing to the conservative wing of the CRC, which sees any cooperation with the RCA as leading to all the evils of participation in mainstream American Protestantism. But a strong middle group in each denomination has insisted that the two churches must address themselves seriously to the schism that has marred the lives of both for more than a century.

It would be impossible to predict where these conversations may lead. Probably no organic merger will take place within the next decade; many stubborn problems still must be resolved. But there is no doubt that talks will continue with greater seriousness. Instead of seeking ways in which they can react to each other—the pattern of the past—the two denominations should in the coming decade seek increasing areas of cooperation. It would be foolish to predict exactly what areas those may turn out to be, but it would be equally unwise not to point out a growing pattern of walking together for the future of the two churches.

Growth, Decline and Stagnation

During the past few years neither denomination has grown; both have stagnated. At an earlier period the Christian Reformed Church enjoyed a pattern of growth, but it seems to have been the result of heavy Dutch immigration to Canada; the rise leveled off when the immigration ceased. Despite protests to the contrary, neither church has yet discovered how to break out of its ghetto. In the case of the CRC and the midwestern section of the RCA, church growth has been largely a matter of remaining within areas where the denominations have had historic roots.

In the RCA there have been some recent exceptions to this traditional pattern. One is the development of a sizable number of Hispanic (and, to a lesser degree, black) congregations in northeastern urban areas like Brooklyn, the Bronx, Newark and Hudson County, New Jersey, which once were centers of traditional Reformed Church strength. The usual pattern of church flight from these areas seems to have been arrested as the RCA has begun to minister to the groups that have moved in. The fact that a denomination which had no record of previous work in Hispanic countries has had some success in meeting the needs of Hispanic immigrants to northeastern cities may mean that, on this front at least, the RCA has been able to break out of its ghetto.

The other obvious exception is the enormous success of Robert Schuller in Garden Grove, California. While all kinds of questions have been raised about Schuller from within the Reformed Church—some arising from petty jealousy and some based on serious concerns of theological integrity—the fact remains that the Schuller pattern has worked in Orange County, California, at a time when the rest of the church has been in stagnation or decline. The question for which no one seems to have the answer is how much of the Garden Grove Community Church's success is the result of its leader's charisma (at least several attempts at imitation elsewhere have been disastrous failures) and how much is the result of principles applicable elsewhere in the country.

The RCA's top leadership has obviously decided to bet on the thesis that at least some principles of Schuller's successful church are transferable. The denomination has recently raised a $5 million church growth fund, part of which is to be used in developing new congregations in the Sunbelt, particularly in Texas, where up to this point the Reformed Church in America has been totally unrepresented. Realizing that congregations, like individuals, do not do well in isolation, and that isolated congregations of the RCA have not been successful in the past, church leaders plan to develop clusters of congregations, rather than lone outposts, in these new locations.

At this point, therefore, the RCA is on the threshold of expanding into a rapidly growing area of the country where it has not previously had congregations. It should be pointed out that expansion of this kind seems necessary, since demographically the church is locked into areas like the northeast (where population is declining) and the midwest (where it is at least stagnant). Assuming that the move works, a decade hence there may be a growing number of healthy Reformed churches at various places in the Sunbelt.

If this happens, given the churches which already exist in southern California, Arizona and Florida (to say nothing of the growing number of Hispanic congregations back in the northeast), then at least two predictions of trends for the next decade would seem to be in order. The first would be a shifting of the power centers away from New York and Grand Rapids to some unspecified location where the growth of the church will be taking place.

Theological Positions

The more important prediction, however, has to do with what this shift could mean to the theological character of the Reformed Church in America. That character in recent years has been a middle-of-the-road ecumenical Protestant stance, hotly challenged but never dominated by a much more conservative evangelicalism in certain parts of the midwest. Given the overwhelming evangelical ambience of the Sunbelt, however, and the safe assumption that the RCA must reflect that attitude in order to succeed in the area, it is not difficult to predict that what has been the dominant theological position of the church may very well in the next ten years become a minority one as the conservative evangelicalism of the new Sunbelt churches joins forces with the existing strength of that position in the midwest.

The Christian Reformed Church presently contemplates no such massive invasion of new territory, but population movements have already involved it in areas where there has hitherto been no Reformed witness. The usual pattern has been for a new church to be formed with a nucleus of Christian Reformed people whom industry has transferred to an area in which there is no existing CRC congregation. The nucleus is hardly enough to sustain congregational life unless other people in the community can be attracted. It is here that the enterprise has met with serious problems, for the CRC has always insisted on a life style different from that of its Reformed sister—the maintenance of Christian schools, opposition to secret societies, two worship services (morning and evening) on each Lord's Day, etc. By and large, the American Protestant world has not been sympathetic to these demands, and CRC growth in new areas has therefore been small.

It is safe to assume that the next decade will see questions being raised in the CRC about the essential character of many of these traditional demands for the life of the church. To what extent are they holdovers from situations in the Netherlands in which they were meaningful, and to what extent are they applicable in the U.S. in the last quarter of the 20th century?

Though the Christian Reformed Church is geographically limited and has usually chosen to live outside the mainstream of American Protestantism, it ought not to be cast in its traditional stereotype of hopeless Dutch conservatism. While there are undoubtedly those in that church who would like nothing better than to perpetuate the pattern of the past, there are a growing number of people in the CRC who believe that their inheritance has something significant to offer to the U.S. Already the holistic approach of Abraham Kuyper to theology and society has enabled the Christian Reformed Church to undertake some significant ministries in urban areas. It will be interesting to see how this group will seek to enlarge the future ministry of the denomination in other areas of this country.

Women and Ordination

In the recent past the attention of both Reformed denominations has been taken up with the role of women in the ministry. In 1972 the Reformed Church in America repealed its ancient prohibition against women serving as elders and deacons in consistory (both ordained lay offices) but retained the prohibition against their serving as ministers of the word. After 1972 repeated attempts to do away with that prohibition fell just short of the two-thirds of the classes (presbyteries) necessary to make the change. Since the language of the denomination's *Book of Church Order* already reads "persons" and not "males" in its rules governing ordination to the ministry, what is at stake here is really the repeal of a 400-year-old interpretation rather than of a specific law. Because of that fact, after it was announced to the 1978 General Synod that the proposed change had again failed to win a two-thirds majority, several classes proceeded to ordain women on their own. One classis had in fact already ordained a woman in 1973, but in compliance with a strong request from General Synod, no other ordinations of women took place between 1973 and 1978.

Once the question had become a judicial rather than a legislative one, however, that kind of action soon followed. Several complaints against the classes which had ordained women were filed with the General Synod, but the Judicial Commission to which the complaints had been referred reported that it could find nothing in Scripture or in the *Book of Church Order* to sustain such complaints. By a vote of 150 to 120 the Synod voted to accept the report of the Judicial Commission, with the result that the matter was permanently settled, though not without numerous complaints that it had been done by "back-door method." Since at the 1977 General Synod a women elder did well in the race for the vice-presidency (in the RCA the vice-president of General Synod is heir presumptive for the presidency the next year), it seems well within the realm of possibility that during the coming decade a woman (elder or minister) will be elected president of the General Synod, the highest office the church can bestow.

In the Christian Reformed Church the debate is at a much earlier stage; it may be longer and more heated, but advances have already been made. At its 1978 Synod the denomination voted to open the office of deacon to women. Whether the CRC will proceed to admit women also to the offices of both elder and minister remains to be seen. It is as deacons that conservatives can most easily envision women serving. The CRC may adopt the gradualist pattern of the RCA, or it may be forced to follow the more authentically Reformed tradition of viewing the three offices as a unity that cannot be broken.

Liturgical Change

Theologically speaking, the RCA is now more at peace with itself than it has been for many years. While there is still a very vocal and active right wing, a broad centrist evangelicalism across the church gives a more unifying position than has previously been the case.

Attracting much discussion is the recent proposal of the RCA's theological commission that baptized children be allowed to receive the Lord's Supper. While the report of the commission was turned down by the Synod of 1979 by a relatively narrow margin, it is hard to believe that that will be the end of the matter. In a church that has a strong commitment to covenant theology, that practice would seem to be the logical outgrowth of the theological premises, but the measure is being strongly opposed by those who feel that it would represent a serious lowering of the solemnity of the sacramental occasion. Paul's admonition that "everyone should examine himself first and then eat the bread and drink the cup" is usually cited by the opposition. But since no change in the *Book of Church Order* is required, it seems likely that the new practice, which has already begun in some congregations, will be taken up by many others, though the whole question of Christian initiation will continue to be an unresolved problem in both churches—as it is in Western Christendom generally.

Liturgically speaking, both churches have come a long way in the past decade, and attention to liturgical integrity and significance seems to be a sure characteristic for both in the future. Gone are the days when liturgical concern could be dismissed as the hobby of a few aesthetes. The CRC has at least one congregation which realizes Calvin's ideal of the celebration of Word and Sacrament every Sunday. While no such congregation exists in the RCA, a growing number of churches have forsaken the traditional pattern of a quarterly and very penitential observance for a more frequent and joyous form of celebration. The number of congregations which celebrate the Supper monthly or on the great festival days is a growing one.

In times past, committees have been appointed to "revise the liturgy"; their task was to alter the punctuation and modernize the language of the 16th and 17th century liturgical forms. Those forms are still printed for congregations that wish to use them, but the number is a decreasing one, even in parts of the church where a few years ago the traditional forms were virtual "sacred cows." The traditional revision committee has been replaced by a permanent worship committee which is to continue to suggest meaningful liturgical forms for congregational use.

Worship and Preaching

The charismatic movement has undoubtedly played a part in freeing up the liturgical life of both churches. Though it has had almost no strength in the CRC and only a small representation in the RCA, it has had a much larger effect on the worship of both churches than its numbers would seem to indicate. Worship had been almost uniformly stiff and formal and largely dominated by the *domine* (the traditional Dutch term for minister) to the extent that in many congregations he read the Apostles' Creed and the Lord's Prayer as a solo; in recent years the liturgy has become more varied and relaxed, with a great deal more participation by the people.

While there are still some congregations in which the traditional patterns are maintained, the number is increasing in which the old Calvinist liturgical framework (preparation, proclamation, response) is being restored; the fleshing out of this liturgical skeleton is done in a variety of ways, depending on the situation of the individual congregation. It is not difficult to imagine that within the next few years this pattern will become almost universal in Reformed churches, together with an even wider observance of the Christian Year than is now the case (and the present practice is far more extensive than it was a decade ago).

Preaching continues to be central in the life of both denominations, and there is no indication that this focus will shift. It may well be that sermons will continue to grow shorter (they have already shrunk from 45 minutes to 20 within living memory), but that trend will persist because of increasing congregational liturgical and sacramental life and not because of any lack of emphasis on preaching. A move toward de-emphasis of preaching did appear in the '60s, but it has now been completely reversed; there is every indication from this generation of Reformed seminary students that good biblical preaching will be a continuing interest for some years to come. While Reformed churches have not recently produced any great preachers in the traditional sense (what denomination has?), both the RCA and the CRC have more than a fair share of competent preachers who take their task seriously. One likes to think that the next ten years will see that number increase.

The Future of Missions

The Reformed Church in America became involved in the world missionary movement much earlier than did the Christian Reformed Church. The RCA has therefore had to face, in a way that the CRC has not, some of the problems which that movement today involves. Specifically these are a shrinking financial base at home and the rise of the indigenous churches of the Third World. Numbers of Reformed Church members have decried what has happened to the world missionary movement as a result of these factors and have urged a return to "old-fashioned" missionary work in a hitherto untried territory.

Partly in response to these pressures and partly in connection with its church growth movement, in 1977 the RCA decided to launch a new venture in Venezuela; it already has one missionary in the field. It would not be accurate to call this an "old-fashioned missionary effort among the heathen," since there are Pentecostal groups in the area with which, it is hoped, close cooperation will be possible. In that sense, the new program is more in line with the mission philosophy of those who advocate working in concert with an indigenous church. The fact remains, however, that the project in Venezuela represents the first new missionary move in a long time in the Reformed Church in America and may well be a harbinger of things to come in a reinvolvement with the world mission of the church in the next decade.

Since reference has already been made to the charismatic movement in connection with liturgical life, something more ought to be said about the future of that movement in the Reformed churches. In a real sense, it depends on the future of the charismatic movement in Christianity generally. Is it a wave of the future, or will it, having done its work, subside and become lost in the general life of the church? Because of a traditional Dutch rationalism (which can be conservative as well as liberal), it has never made the headway in the Reformed churches that it has in some others, though there are some RCA congregations in which the charismatic movement has proved to be divisive.

My own hunch is that, so far as the Reformed churches are concerned, charismatics may continue as a small minority for some time to come, but the movement's principal effect on these churches has already been felt. Especially in the RCA, where for more than two centuries a theology based on experience has been a lively tradition, it has been able to reinforce that tradition and enlarge its sphere of influence. In both liberal and conservative wings of the RCA there is less rationalism and more piety than was the case 20 years ago. That fact may well account for the apparent growing theological consensus, but it would seem to be the lasting effect of the charismatic movement in the Reformed churches and one that probably will not change in the future.

Five or six years ago, when enrollments in the three seminaries of these two denominations began to show a marked increase, there were dire warnings about the placement problems that were being created for the future with an increasing number of ministers for a shrinking number of congregations. There can be no question that the situation has been tight, though it has never reached the proportions that were predicted. But given the quality of the large number of men and women who have been preparing for the ministry, it would almost seem that the Lord of the church knew more about the future than the church did!

Certainly the great thing that has happened in the Reformed churches recently—something which one hopes can be continued into the foreseeable future—is a new awareness of themselves and of their responsibilities and their possibilities. For the moment at least, they have put behind them any thought of looking to another denomination for their future—unless it be that more of their future lies with one another. They have realized that while their smallness is something that can be a hindrance in many fields of endeavor, it can also be a virtue enabling them to do at least some things which cannot be undertaken by many larger denominations.

As for the immediate future of the Christian Reformed Church and the Reformed Church in America, many problems lie ahead: many tensions that will have to be resolved and at least some tendencies that make me personally uneasy. But I am also aware of a spirit and sense of excitement that may well ensure for these churches a better future than their recent past would indicate.

AFTERWORD

MARTIN E. MARTY

It is no secret that the introduction to this book was a magazine article written about the other chapters before any of them had been produced. For that reason it is natural for me to want to have a last word after reading them, to see how well the anticipation and the fulfillments matched. This closing comment is designed not to let me parade my presciences or blush over my missed points of expectation, but to promote further thought and inquiry on the part of readers. Several features stand out in the chapters.

First, with few exceptions, the authors stress "order" more than "faith." I wonder whether this is not in many ways an American or at least an Anglo-American trait. Roman Catholicism and Eastern Orthodoxy have the matter of ordering church life down so cold that they do not find it necessary to heat it up. Roman Catholics are arguing, of course, about papal infallibility and collegiality, about priests' councils and senates and the power of the laity. But as important as adjustments on those fronts are, it seems that their bigger questions are these: How well does the pope function? How well do other ranks of clergy and laity fulfill their roles? And Catholics also seem more ready, given their relative agreement on the magisterium or official teaching of the church, to face the crisis of faith that marks our age. Orthodoxy has even less of a dispute going over order, but lives in the face of Islam and communism, where it must ask questions of faith all the time.

In the World Council of Churches, it has been continental Protestants who have made the crisis of faith an urgent question. Alongside French Catholics in particular, they have stared into the face of practical and metaphysical atheism and have seen what modernity has done to the meaning of faith itself. Meanwhile, the Anglo-American world has for several centuries been busy with ordering the church: episcopal, presbyterian, "presbygational," synodical, congregational and anarchic forms of order have vied. More recently, bureaucratization,

marked by what Max Weber called *Rationalität,* an all-embracing
spirit of rationality, has undercut all the orders and produced a kind of
stamp which both moves and bothers the authors of these chapters.

Well and good. But reading these together, I am struck that those
church bodies which are least self-preoccupied about headquarters
seem to be more free to touch the vital faith and practice of their members. Naturally, at church conventions and at headquarters there have
to be obsessions with who owns the property and who runs the pen-
sions and where the locus of power lies. But as one who goes to and fro
among the congregations of congregationalism and their counterparts,
it occurs to me that the real crisis has less to do with order than the
ordering people think. Have you ever pictured a teen-ager drifting
away from Presbyterian churches because they have too much or too
little centralized power? The young people drift because they are
bored, or unchallenged, or too challenged by issues of basic belief and
impinging practice. Do you picture the evangelistic pitch of the evangelistic churches to be, "Come with us to the proper polity"? More
likely they are doing what evangelists are said to do, telling hungry
people where to find bread or, better, giving it to them. We may not all
and always like the flavor and shape of the bread, but we had better
know what is going on.

Concern for headquarters, staff lines, and congregational powers is
legitimate, but it has its limits. The churches are not held together by
confessions as much as confessionalists might like to think, nor are
they gatherings of people who share cognitive dimensions of belief and
that is that. They are marvelously complex batches of people who in-
herit common histories, stumble onto certain premises, get drawn into
specific loyalties, share or refuse to share table fellowship with others,
snoop on each other or do not care about snooping, or whatever. Far
down the list of priorities are the questions about constitutionalism and
bureaucracy, except when these show up negatively.

Another way to put it: if tomorrow, by some divine fiat or swoop,
all the ordering questions of the churches were solved, would faith and
practice be much different? Could it be that we become expert at polity
because tinkering is easy when it comes to something so visible? We
invest millions in reordering, and not one thing changes in the fortunes
of the churches or their impacts on the world. We have committees to

simplify, and we support them well, and they generate more committees but do not simplify.

If the obsession with order surprised me, the concern over division
did not, and most essays showed it. The churches do their fighting *with*
themselves, not *between* themselves, for reasons that go deep into the
human psyche and confirm the doctrine of original sin. Someone may
argue that these result from the occasions when churches do take matters of cognition, creed and confession seriously, since so many battles
seem to have to do with matters of faith. But I wonder whether they
have not for the most part grown up on the sparse soil of modernity,
and are noxious growths to fill the void where vegetation should be.

The churches have not learned how to make conflict creative. The
new spirit is one of kill, not convince; of hound out, not win over. The
more fundamentalist wing of each body seems marked by a fanaticism
which C. J. Jung would measure and mark as "overcompensated
doubt." The more moderate wing fumbles, being busy showing that it
is not as guilty of faithlessness as the right portrays it, without finding
ways to show that a civil and mannered faith may be born of deep
conviction and not mere compromise. One might hope that the current
fashion would die out soon, but at the moment it seems to be spreading
into one of the bodies that seemed insulated against it, the giant Southern Baptist Convention. Our authors take such disputes seriously.

Other matters seem to me to be in proper perspective. I had not
remembered to make the issue of the role of women as urgent as many
of these authors do. One who spends many hours a week in the company of women divinity students, seminarians, ministers and lay leaders probably presumes that his consciousness has been raised so much
that the battle must be over. Of course, it is not, out in the trenches.
Pope John Paul II has made it live more than anyone could have fore-
seen when this series was chartered. But even the churches that thought
they had moved far on issues like ordination of women still have much
homework to do. Alongside the "women" issue is the concern over the
meaning of homosexuality, and several articles reflect what it has done
in the life of the denominations. I surmise that there it is a polity issue,
whereas in the local congregations it is a personal and thus much different one.

I am glad to see that the analysts of the churches that prospered in the decade past have also seen that their prosperity does not result simply from turning of backs against the *Zeitgeist,* the spirit of the times. Ours are times that seek experience and authority, and the churches that best fill the needs to which those two words point have prospered at the expense of others.

But our authors have also noted that the people who did the seeking come equipped with bodies, loves and interests: among these are embraces of the materialist world as it is, the goods and goodies of life, the power of one's own nation and caste and class. And these churches have offered a sort of package deal which includes, along with the idea of joining them, the notion that "all these things" of the world will be added thereto. And not all these things match the message of the churches that are doing the winning. Mere worldliness, in short, or the loss of one's soul while winning the world, is a concern in these churches.

For all the pains and aches of these bodies in question, it should be clear to the readers that both the authors and the members in almost every instance see good reasons to fight over the existence and mission of their groups. Denominations share more than their share of the fallibilities of all structures which seek to house, channel or receive the Spirit. But they are also warmly regarded as vehicles of the Spirit. They are not going to disappear so much as they are going to keep changing forms. The current collection of observations will mark an important stage of their response to modernity and, at their best, will suggest some initiatives by the denominations. Today they are dependent upon the health of their local units more than ever before, and while we keep our eye on the collections of congregations called denominations, we shall also have to observe the crisis and triumphs of faith and hope and love in the local churches—and in the whole *oikoumene,* the whole inhabited world in which synagogues and churches have their being.